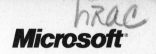

Effective Time Management

Using Microsoft® Outlook® to Organize Your Work and Personal Life

LOTHAR SEIWERT

HOLGER WOELTJE

Published with the authorization of Microsoft Corporation by:
O'Reilly Media, Inc.
1005 Gravenstein Highway North
Sebastopol, California 95472

ISBN: 978-0-7356-6004-5

2 3 4 5 6 7 8 9 10 M 7 6 5 4 3 2

Printed and bound in the United States of America.

Microsoft Press books are available through booksellers and distributors worldwide. If you need support related to this book, email Microsoft Press Book Support at *mspinput@ microsoft.com*. Please tell us what you think of this book at *http://www.microsoft.com/ learning/booksurvey*.

Acquisitions and Developmental Editor: Kenyon Brown
Production Editor: Teresa Elsey
Editorial Production: Online Training Solutions, Inc.
Technical Reviewer: Vincent Averello
Indexer: Fred Brown
Cover Design: Twist Creative • Seattle
Cover Composition: Karen Montgomery

[2012-01-06]

Contents

Foreword   ix

Acknowledgments   xi

Introduction   xiii

Chapter 1   **How Not to Drown in the Email Flood**   **1**

■ It's Not the Email Messages, It's How We Handle Them   4
    Don't Let Yourself Get Distracted   4
    Break Your Response Pattern   8

■ Keep Your Inbox in Order   11
    Process Your Email Block with the DANF System   12
    File Email Messages Accordingly   13

■ Create and Use Your Own Folder Structure   19

■ Flag the Messages You Still Need to Work On   22
    Don't Force Alarms on Yourself: The Reminder
    Functions of Outlook 2007 and Outlook 2010   24
    Keep All Items That Are Flagged for Processing
    in a Single View   27

■ Let Outlook Presort Your Inbox for You   28

■ Think Before You Communicate   31
    Make Your Text Easier to Understand: Always
    Adjust It to the Recipients   31
    Keep Your Phrasing Short, Precise, and Crystal Clear 31
    Use Well-Written Subject Lines to Make
    Everyone's Life Easier   32

■ You Try It   33

Chapter 2   **How to Work More Effectively with Tasks and Priorities**   **35**

- How to Run a Country Like the United States in the 24 Hours a Day Has to Offer—Set Priorities!   37
  - Focus on What Matters Most (the Pareto Principle)   38
  - Decide What's Most Important—Use the Eisenhower Matrix to Set Rough Priorities   39
  - Write Down Your Plans   42
- Use Task Lists to Plan Flexibly and Effectively   43
  - Tasks vs. Appointments   44
  - Tasks in Outlook   44
  - The Text Editor in Outlook 2010/Outlook 2007   48
- Define Your Own Views (Outlook 2003, Outlook 2007, and Outlook 2010)   52
  - Use Filters to Clean Up Your Views   53
  - Fine-Tune Your Priorities with the 25,000 $ Method   55
  - The To-Do List—View Tasks from Multiple Folders and Email Messages at the Same Time   60
- You Try It   61

Chapter 3   **How to Gain More Time for What's Essential with an Effective Week Planner**   **63**

- What Really Matters—and Why Does It Continue to Remain Undone?   64
- Take Advantage of Categories to Combine Tasks   66
  - Gain Perspective with Categories   66
  - Keep Track of Your Most Important Categories by Using Colors   71
  - Filter and Group by Category   82

■ The Kiesel Principle—Gain More Time for What Matters
Most Each Week   90

    Keep Your Life in Balance   90

    Plan Your Professional Life and Private Life Together   91

    Regularly Take Time for What Really Counts   95

■ How to Plan Your Week with Outlook   97

    Prepare Your Task List for the Week   97

    Plan Tasks and Appointments Together in Balance   100

    Plan Appointments with Yourself to Concentrate on
    the Essential Tasks   102

■ You Try It   107

Chapter 4   **How to Make Your Daily Planning Work in Real Life** **109**

■ The Basics of Successful Day Planning   112

    Combine Similar Tasks into Task Blocks   112

    For Advanced Users: Take Advantage of the Journal
    for Semi-Automatic Time Protocols   115

    Take Your Performance Curve and Your Disruption
    Curve into Consideration   118

    Focus on Your Important Tasks Without
    Interruptions During Productivity Hours   119

■ Order Must Prevail   121

    Hide the Tasks Intended for Block Building in the
    Week/Day Views   122

    Mark Tasks That Are Due Today and Tomorrow in Color   123

■ Gain a Better Overview by Using Appointment Lists   126

■ Fine-Tune Your Daily Planning   130

    Plan Pending Tasks with the 25,000 $ Method   130

◼ More Steps for Successful Daily Planning   133

   Make Further Appointments with Yourself   134

   Keep an Eye on Buffer Times   134

   Use the To-Do Bar to Keep Upcoming
   Appointments and Tasks in View   135

   How to Customize the To-Do Bar   136

◼ You Try It   137

**Chapter 5   How to Schedule Meetings So They Are
               Convenient, Effective, and Fun   139**

◼ The Problem: Way Too Many Inconvenient Meeting
   Requests and Insufficient Preparation   141

◼ Meeting Requests with Outlook—Basic Rules and Tips   142

   Find Free Times and Evaluate Replies   143

◼ Stay on Top of It: Calendar Overlay   149

   Use Meeting Requests Sparingly   155

   Optimize Your Calendar to Make Meeting Requests Easy   161

◼ Prepare Meetings Effectively   166

   Improve Efficiency by Preparing and Running
   Your Meeting Wisely   167

   Use Meeting Workspaces to Prepare Meetings   169

◼ You Try It   173

**Chapter 6   How to Use OneNote for Writing Goals,
               Jotting Down Ideas, and Keeping Notes   175**

◼ Why Do Important Documents and Notes Always Get Lost?   177

◼ Finally, a Place and a System for All Your Notes   178

   Use a Structured System When Planning   178

   Do You Still Use Paper Even Though You Have a Laptop?   180

   Discover the Advantages of OneNote   181

■ Basics for Notes in OneNote   182

    Take Advantage of the Digital Notebook Structure   183

    Work with Sections, Notebooks, and Pages   185

    How to Fill Your Pages   187

    Use Pens, Text Markers, and Colors   189

■ Meeting Minutes in OneNote   194

    Use Outlining for Preparation   194

    Keep Follow-Up Activities and Important
    Information in View   198

    Link Your Information: Use Outlook and
    OneNote as a Team   202

    Create Page Templates and Checklists   207

■ Always Keep Your Ideas and Goals in Sight   208

    "Printing"—Export Data from Any Program   209

    Read Between the Lines—OCR for Pictures   211

    Set Goals for Yourself—Not Just for Your Revenue   212

    Create Your Master Plan   216

■ You Try It   218

Chapter 7   **How to Truly Benefit from This Book**   **219**

■ How to Get a Handle on Your Time   221

    The Next Steps   223

    Test the Current Version of Office for Free   224

■ Take Responsibility—Do It Now!   224

    Time Management Is Self-Discipline   226

    Create Your Own Personal Action Plan   226

    Find a Buddy   227

    Start Immediately and Keep at It!   228

Appendix A   Recommended Reading **229**

Index *231*

About the Authors *247*

What do you think of this book? We want to hear from you!

Microsoft is interested in hearing your feedback so we can continually improve our books and learning resources for you. To participate in a brief online survey, please visit:

microsoft.com/learning/booksurvey

Foreword

MOST PRODUCTIVITY ENTHUSIASTS in the United States have never heard of Lothar Seiwert and Holger Woeltje. That's about to change. They are rock stars in Europe, and this book will rock in the U.S.

I met Lothar through my role as the 2011–2012 U.S. President of the National Speakers Association (NSA), through which he received the Certified Speaking Professional (CSP) designation. He invited me to speak at the German Speakers Association (GSA), where I witnessed his celebrity status. He's a member of the German Speakers Hall of Fame and received the Lifetime Achievement Award from the German Training and Development Federation. His books have sold over four million copies, and his co-author, Holger, has authored seven best-selling books. Rest assured they are well qualified as authors of this new Outlook productivity guide.

Under my moniker, The Productivity Pro®, I've been presenting keynotes and seminars on increasing output and saving time at work since 1992. As a Microsoft Certified Application Specialist in Outlook (MCAS), I've provided Outlook training to corporate clients (including Microsoft!) since the 1990s. Bottom line: There is simply no better tool out there for managing and integrating your email, tasks, notes, contacts, journal, and calendar. But many people simply don't know how to get the most out of Outlook. I'd estimate most people use about 15–25% of its capabilities. Most training consists of "here's your inbox; have fun!" Seiwert and Woeltje take the mystery out of all those settings, filters, checkboxes, and menu options, and give you a customized Outlook experience for the way you manage your time and work.

Outlook actually *is* your work, as all those messages represent something you need to do. But many people are paralyzed by the sheer volume of messages or don't have a systematic way of pulling action from email. So most people leave messages in their inboxes to languish and get buried by the onslaught of new incoming emails.

A single email could actually require you to:

1. Think about the end result of what you'd like to accomplish with the task. Who needs to be involved? Who should own it? What steps are required?

2. Reply to the email or send an acknowledgment with a promised deadline.

3. Convert the email into a task or appointment.

4. Do the required task offline.

5. Respond with the requested information.

6. Set follow-up reminders for pending action or promised deliverables.

7. Store the supporting information.

So many pieces involved in one little email! This book shows you, with many practical case studies, screenshots, step-by-step instructions, and relevant examples, how to complete these processes very quickly—although the offline work will still take some time. You'll discover a brand-new system for organizing your time and to-do's in a more productive, effective way.

How many hours do you spend in your email inbox each day? This book will show you how Outlook can help you to become more productive, so get ready for that figure to go down! If you let yourself be chained down by your email instead of letting it help you manage your life, you're never likely to get much done. Seiwert and Woeltje are about to set you free!

Laura Stack, MBA, CSP
Productivity expert, speaker, trainer
Author, What to Do When There's Too Much to Do:
Reduce Tasks, Increase Results, and
Save 90 Minutes a Day *(Berrett-Koehler, 2012)*
President, The Productivity Pro®, Inc.
President, National Speakers Association
Laura@TheProductivityPro.com
www.TheProductivityPro.com

Acknowledgments

WE HAVE TO THANK so many people for this book that we know it is impossible to write a complete list. That said, there are people we need to cite personally here because of their particular contributions.

We have to start with **Christian Obermayr**, former Product Manager for Microsoft Office: eight years ago he started the project for the German edition of this book, provided some cool additional tips and tricks, and carefully reviewed and tweaked every German edition ever since.

Special thanks to **Laura Stack**, CSP, America's Premier Expert in Productivity, CEO of The Productivity Pro, and President of the National Speakers Association (NSA), for her wonderful foreword. We offer sincere thanks to **Dan Poynter**, CSP, Para Publishing, for his support and encouragement.

Thanks also to **Achim Berg** and **Juergen Gallmann**, former CEOs of Microsoft Germany, who provided the forewords for the various German editions.

We offer sincere thanks to **Thomas Pohlmann**, former Editorial Manager of Microsoft Press Germany, who got the first German edition launched seven years ago; **Thomas Braun-Wiesholler**, Editorial Manager at O'Reilly Media, and **Claudia Petersen**, Sales Manager at Microsoft Press, who managed the eighth German edition of this book and played a huge part in getting it finally translated into English; and especially to **Kenyon Brown,** Senior Editor at O'Reilly Media, Microsoft Press Division, who did a tremendous job in keeping everyone involved moving forward as a team as well as managing this project. A particular mention goes to **Kathy Krause**, Editorial Specialist at Online Training Solutions, Inc. (OTSI): she has been our copy editor, carefully reviewing and correcting everything, and tweaking the language. We are not native English speakers, and she deserves all the credit if you can read this book well and fluently. Thanks also to **Teresa Elsey** and **Dan Fauxsmith**, Production Managers at O'Reilly Media, for managing the production side and keeping everything on track there. It has been a pleasure to work with all of you!

Thanks to **Nespresso** for providing the awesome coffee that kept us going through some tough writing and editing sessions, to all the people from **Lufthansa** and **Deutsche Bahn** who make our traveling easier and more enjoyable, and to everyone at **Apple**, **Amazon**, **Lenovo**, **Microsoft**, and **Research in Motion (RIM)**, who build the great technology, software, and cool gadgets that help us to be productive on the road and always keep connected to our families, friends, clients, and business partners, no matter where we are around the world.

A very big thanks goes to all of the **participants** from our keynotes, workshops, and seminars who implemented what we taught them. Whom we have the honor to support on their journeys to reaching their goals, overcoming challenges, and making their workdays easier. Who help us with their questions to adjust our methods and teaching to the ever-changing business and technology world. Who give us back so much with their feedback and sharing their personal success stories a few months or even years later. Hearing or reading about and sometimes even seeing in person how they've been able to improve their work results, achieve a balanced life again, and gain more time for their families and friends is the most precious reward for us we can imagine.

And, finally, thanks a lot to you, dear **reader**, for helping us to make this book a success. We hope you'll enjoy it and gain a lot from the tips, tricks, and strategies you'll find on the following pages. Now it's your turn to read this content, really think deeply about it, apply it to your work and personal life, and implement the techniques one at a time to harvest some big results!

—**Lothar Seiwert** and **Holger Woeltje**, September 2011

Introduction

ARE TOO MANY EMAIL messages, urgent deadlines, and stressful meetings driving you nuts? Is time running out on you? Do you sometimes feel like you didn't get anything important done at the end of the day, because all the urgent, small stuff kept you so busy you didn't even start the things that really matter in the long run?

It doesn't have to be that way. In today's modern world, characterized by complexity, information overload, and way too many distractions, Microsoft Outlook can help you to focus and prioritize, to separate the wheat from the chaff. But if no one ever showed you how to use Outlook in a really productive way, it can cause even more trouble: Reminders that pop up on your screen and distract you while you're in the middle of something else, desktop alerts for new email messages that keep constantly nagging you, and a task list with 357 overdue red entries—no wonder Outlook puts you in a bad mood as soon as you look at it! It's finally time to change that! You'll learn a proven time management system tweaked for use with Outlook. It'll help you to focus on what matters most and gain more time for important things while only requiring you to invest a little time each day for planning.

The authors of this book are two highly experienced time management experts from Germany, the largest national economy in Europe. They help executives all over the world to become more successful and will show you how to systemize and organize your complex everyday life, too. How to turn from being Re-active into Pro-active using rigorous task planning and weekly planning. And how to create daily plans that still work even when the unexpected occurs.

This book will show you, very concretely and with many practical examples, how Outlook perfectly supports you in implementing an effective time management system of this kind. Outlook offers many practical functions that help you keep things in perspective and save a lot of time during your hectic workday—as long as you use these functions wisely and set the right priorities. It's up to you to make use of this now—just invest half an hour each day in reading, understanding, and applying this knowledge for the next few weeks, and you'll greatly benefit from it sooner than you could have imagined!

Who This Book Is For

This book is for all Outlook users who want to improve their time management skills and want to use Outlook in an easier, faster, more productive way to organize their email, tasks, and appointments. It won't show you every available Outlook function, just the ones you need to achieve this goal as quickly and as easily as possible.

It'll still require some work to get there, but we'll skip things such as managing contact entries or changing your email signature. We'll also skip geeky stuff like the developer ribbon, the Forms Designer for customized Outlook forms, and configuring Microsoft Exchange servers—complex things that software developers and IT administrators use, but most Outlook users will never need at all. We'll still cover advanced functions such as customizing your Outlook views, filtering entries, and even adding custom fields, but these functions will be easy to learn and will help you a lot in focusing on certain projects and tasks you need to take care of today.

Assumptions

To understand and use this book, you already should know Microsoft Outlook on a basic level. Having used it for a few weeks is enough. You should also be familiar with your computer's operating system (such as Windows XP, Windows Vista, or Windows 7) on a basic level, and know how to click a menu, close a dialog box by clicking OK or Cancel, and recognize clickable buttons. If you are totally new to computers, Windows, or Outlook, and have never used it before, we recommend getting an additional book for beginners first, to take your first steps.

But if you have already used Outlook for a few weeks; know how to enter an appointment in your calendar; and can write, send, and reply to an email message, we'll guide you from there. Because many Outlook users have never used tasks before or stopped using them because they had no working system for using them, we'll even cover using Outlook tasks from the beginning.

Also, if you are a very experienced Outlook user or professional developer who has used Outlook for years and knows every single button and command by heart, you'll still benefit from this book because it shows you a system for organizing your work in a more effective way. You might also discover some new ways to use the Outlook functions you already know for implementing this system.

Again, this is *not* a technical Outlook manual explaining every function available, *but* a time management guide for everyone with basic Outlook knowledge. It'll show you the best and proven time management strategies and tactics to better organize your work and private life, focus on your goals and most important tasks to achieve what matters most to you, and use Outlook for your weekly and daily planning.

Half of this book is about time management, and half of it is about using Microsoft Office Outlook 2003, Outlook 2007, or Outlook 2010 to implement what you've just learned. So it's not an Outlook manual, but you'll still learn some very handy technical tips and tricks along the way, such as turning off distracting email alerts; coloring appointments in your calendar; filtering views to quickly switch between all tasks due today, all tasks for a specific project due anytime during the next three months, or all appointments grouped by location.

How This Book Is Organized

In Chapter 1, "How Not to Drown in the Email Flood," you'll discover how to stop being distracted by new email messages, how to improve your email writing style, how to keep your inbox clean and process messages much more efficiently, and how to file them, get the important ones done in time, and also keep track of things you can't do right away but will have to take care of in a few weeks or months.

In Chapter 2, "How to Work More Effectively with Tasks and Priorities," we show you how to set priorities, figure out what's most important, and use the Outlook task list in a genuinely effective way to keep track of everything you have to do. We'll also show you how to set filters to focus on specific things you want to see, such as all 14 tasks for today instead of all 921 for the next few months.

In Chapter 3, "How to Gain More Time for What's Essential with an Effective Week Planner," you'll find a system that helps you balance the different areas of your life better, regularly reserving some time for your family, yourself, your health, strategic decisions, and your most valuable projects, even when lots of urgent things are getting in your way. You'll learn how to use Outlook categories, group your task view by topic, and use weekly planning in Outlook to gain more time for what's most important after you've figured out what that is (for which you will need to read Chapter 2 first).

Chapter 4, "How to Make Your Daily Planning Work in Real Life," helps you to plan your day with Outlook and implement your weekly planning as well as your priorities from Chapters 2 and 3. You'll also discover how to display your appointments by city instead of by date (for example, to find out when you'll be in Miami or Los Angeles next time), how to automatically highlight tasks that meet certain criteria with a different color, and how to prepare your daily plans so they still work even when the unexpected occurs.

Chapter 5, "How to Schedule Meetings So They Are Convenient, Effective, and Fun," takes care of improving your meeting culture: how to organize meetings more efficiently, how to prepare a good meeting, how to find the right times with Outlook and prepare your calendar to help others find suitable times more easily, and how Microsoft SharePoint can help you avoid duplicate or outdated documents for meetings and quickly find the right ones.

Chapter 6, "How to Use OneNote for Writing Goals, Jotting Down Ideas, and Keeping Notes," introduces you to Microsoft OneNote, a great companion to complement Outlook for notes, meeting minutes, goals, small projects, and big ideas. You'll discover how to use OneNote, keep track of your notes, set goals, link the steps for achieving a goal to Outlook tasks, and file email messages or meeting agendas from Outlook to OneNote to take additional, more detailed notes there.

Chapter 7, "How to Truly Benefit from This Book," shows you how to successfully implement everything you've learned in the other chapters, and how to set up an action plan to take a few minutes each day or half an hour a few days a week to achieve your first results very soon and realize big improvements after two to five months.

We recommend that you approach this book chronologically, chapter by chapter. When you have the whole picture and understand how the system explained in this book works, you can always use the index at the end of the book to quickly refer to any special function or concept if you need to look it up again. You could also start with Chapter 2, Chapter 5, or Chapter 6 instead of Chapter 1. You can always switch the order and go back later, as long as you read Chapters 2, 3, and 4 in a row and read Chapter 7 only after you've read everything else first. Still, we recommend starting with Chapter 1, going chronologically chapter by chapter, and finishing with Chapter 7.

Additional Video Lessons Online

You'll find a complimentary video course online:

- Get a comprehensive overview of what you've learned in this book.

- Discover additional tips and tricks.

- See how to implement the system from this book in full-color Outlook screen-capture videos.

These video lessons are free for all readers of this book. They'll show you how to better organize your task list, your calendar, and your inbox and how to use the system from this book in Outlook. They also include some additional tips and tricks.

To claim your complimentary video course now, just go to

> *www.technoproductivity.com/outlook-2007* (videos for Outlook 2007; most of the things shown also work with Outlook 2003)

or

> *www.technoproductivity.com/outlook-2010* (videos for Outlook 2010)

How to Get Support & Provide Feedback

The following sections provide information on errata, book support, feedback, and contact information.

Errata & Book Support

We've made every effort to ensure the accuracy of this book and its companion content. Any errors that have been reported since this book was published are listed on our Microsoft Press site at oreilly.com:

http://go.microsoft.com/FWLink/?Linkid=227512

If you find an error that is not already listed, you can report it to us through the same page.

If you need additional support, email Microsoft Press Book Support at *mspinput@microsoft.com*.

Please note that product support for Microsoft software is not offered through the addresses above.

We Want to Hear from You

At Microsoft Press, your satisfaction is our top priority and your feedback our most valuable asset. Please tell us what you think of this book at

http://www.microsoft.com/learning/booksurvey

The survey is short, and we read every one of your comments and ideas. Thanks in advance for your input!

Stay in Touch

Let's keep the conversation going! We're on Twitter:

http://twitter.com/MicrosoftPress

CHAPTER 1

How Not to Drown in the Email Flood

IN THIS CHAPTER, YOU WILL

- Disable new email notification.

- Create an appointment or a task from an email message.

- Create a new contact entry for the sender of an email message.

- Create tasks and appointments from individual parts of a longer email message.

- Insert multiple email messages into existing tasks and appointments.

- Set up new folders.

- Create your own search folders.

"You've Got Junk...!"

THESE DAYS, office workers spend an average of two hours per day processing email. Despite the enormous advantages this type of communication provides, many of us consider it a monster that leads to distraction, misunderstanding, stress, and even more problems down the road. You will spend much of your time in Microsoft Outlook working with email, which is enough of a reason to devote the first chapter to tactics and methods for solving mail problems. You will learn how Outlook supports you, and we will share tips and tricks to help you efficiently handle electronic mail.

ROBIN'S EVERYDAY FRUSTRATIONS DURING THE PROCESSING OF EMAIL

Actually, Robin Wood wanted to be done with his monthly report for his manager an hour ago, but... well, the little desktop alert window keeps popping up to announce a new message again and again. Each time he thinks, "This might be important!" but so far it hasn't been, not today, not yet. "Hmm, now that I've got the message open anyway, I might as well answer really quick." No sooner thought than done. Fifteen minutes later, he finds himself back in front of his report. "Wait a minute...where was I?" It takes him a moment to get the hang of those numbers again...

A little while later, a new message is announced. "Not again!" Robin grumbles. Yesterday an especially favorable offer for a smartphone that could also be used privately was sent to all employees. Since then, this is the 18th message in which somebody has sent order information or an inquiry not just to the originator of the offer but also to all other recipients of the original message by inadvertently hitting Reply All, thus adding to the other senseless junk in their inboxes. "Well, at least it's kind of interesting to see who's ordering the phone, and what questions they are asking, even though I've already owned it for three weeks now and don't really have to decide whether to get it or not..." So he reads the entire message before deleting it.

Just before lunch, he is finally done with the report. Before heading off to the cafeteria, he quickly goes through his latest messages. His team leader is politely reminding him that she had asked him to revise a document concerning the trade show preparation and to send it back to her two weeks ago. Time is running short. "Ooops, drat!" He had totally forgotten about that. He scrolls about 310 messages down, and there it is: the request for a review two weeks ago, which he hadn't been able to work on right away—after all, back then he still had 10 days to do it. And then, unfortunately, he had completely overlooked it sitting there in his crowded inbox. He'll take care of it right after lunch, even if there are other pressing issues....

The most ubiquitous and worst problems with email have the following causes:

- **Constant interruptions** You frequently want to respond right away when noticing a new message. Maybe out of curiosity, or maybe because it represents a welcome distraction from such boring tasks as crunching endless columns of numbers. Or maybe you just feel like you have to do right by everyone and answer immediately.

- **Sending junk to others** How often do you get messages that are only slightly relevant to your work or have nothing to do with it at all and don't require any kind of answer or response from you? How often do you put an additional three people on the recipient line just in case they might be interested? Once in a while, this triggers a veritable "answer marathon."

- **Unclear formulation** Certain issues might be as clear as day to the sender, but they may not be as obvious to the recipient and don't become clear in the message body either. For example: "Would be nice if we could still integrate Feature XY—but maybe that's too complex." Is that an idea, a question about whether something is possible, an indirect comment that the person responsible isn't qualified to do it, a suggestion that it should be left out, or a kind plea to integrate the feature?

- **The emotional factor** In comparison to other forms of communication, email seems to be virtually preprogrammed for misunderstandings. It's hard to get an undertone or tongue-in-cheek meaning across, you can't see the facial expressions or gestures of your counterpart, and you are delivering a relatively long monologue without the option of immediately inquiring about or responding to ambiguities or other problems. Have you ever spent two hours writing an angry answer to an email message that resulted in an escalation of the discussion? Or decided to discard an angry answer instead of sending it after spending an hour writing it?

- **Answering without thinking first** Sometimes we switch to response mode, because it just seems so much quicker that way. But we end up investigating issues or triggering discussions that are actually irrelevant. Or we provoke multiple inquiries or superfluous (re)work, because in our rush to answer we forget to include certain information.

- **Insufficient order leading to the data graveyard** Did you ever forget to answer an important message or at the crucial moment discover that you were unable to locate essential information? Some people have more than 500 or even thousands of messages in their inbox. Even though the search function or a good memory ("Didn't Lisa Miller send a request concerning project XY a couple of weeks ago?") can help in 90 percent of the cases, the remaining 10 percent of open questions and pending issues are buried under a mountain of junk.

Let's Get Started and Change This!

The following steps will help you manage your daily email flood:

- Don't allow yourself to get distracted. Answer consciously, and think about your answers first instead of responding immediately to each message.

- Send the message only to recipients who really need it.

- Write in a recipient-oriented fashion. Make sure your communication is clear and unambiguous.

- Create a system for processing incoming email. Keep track of follow-up activities so they are available when required. Know where to find saved information quickly and reliably. With a bit of practice and a few weeks of getting used to the system, pretty soon you won't forget things any longer.

- Use a system to keep your inbox in order. Keep no more than 30 messages in your inbox—and you will always keep track.

In this chapter, you will find time-tested tips and methods to do this and learn how Outlook can support you perfectly.

It's Not the Email Messages, It's How We Handle Them

Now that we've named the problems that prevent us from working effectively, let's find their causes. What is our part in the problems? Are we causing them or making them worse? If we can't prevent or eliminate them, we must accept them and change our way of handling them.

Don't Let Yourself Get Distracted

Let's start with the distractions: Do you really need to check email constantly and answer right away without finishing other tasks in peace? Or could it just be a bad or debilitating habit? Or maybe it's a subconscious attempt to dodge the task at hand? What would be the worst thing that could happen if you simply ignored the inbox for the next two hours? Usually the answer is "Nothing." On the contrary: you might just be able to finally finish that monthly report—and you would no longer have that queasy feeling in your stomach.

But what if your manager needs an answer right away and now she's going to get it two hours late? Well, if you don't always answer every message within 3 minutes (and who can do that on a continuous basis?), your manager should realize that the issue can either wait or that she has to call you on the phone to get an answer.

"Educate" Pushy Senders

In urgent cases, a phone call is the better choice anyway: an immediate dialogue that allows both of you to answer directly, instead of a series of alternating email monologues with wait times in between. Unless your job is to respond quickly to inquiries via live chat or email as part of a support or customer service team, it's absurd to expect immediate answers to email messages. Therefore, if somebody is pushy or complains, ask him or her politely to just give you a call next time, if it's urgent. You could use the argument that a phone call would also let the inquirer find out whether you are even available at that time.

> **NOTE** Your company might have specific policies as to the time frame in which to answer email messages, or you can set that time frame yourself and let your email contacts know what it is, such as 48 hours at most. But make sure to adhere to this time frame. Take note of the following:
>
> - Turn on your out-of-office notification if you are taking a few days off or won't be able to answer messages within the promised time frame.
>
> - Think of all eventualities. It's best to grant a representative (a colleague or assistant, for example) access to your inbox, in case you suddenly get sick. Make sure to let certain contacts know this, if you are expecting confidential email messages.

Disable New Email Notification

Turn off the notification for newly arrived messages. It will only distract you; worst case, it might motivate you to interrupt and postpone an important but unpleasant task yet again. Even if you only take two to four minutes to answer a message "in between," it will enormously slow down tasks that require your full concentration over an extended period. For each interruption of more than a few seconds, you will have to invest a few minutes more to reach full concentration again and get back to working at the same speed as before.

If you are expecting an urgent and important message that is of the highest priority because you require it to continue your work, you might want to ask the sender to follow up after the time-sensitive message has been sent, for example with a phone call or text message (called *SMS* in some parts of Europe). This is a better option than letting yourself get interrupted by every newsletter or junk mail message for the next five hours, or checking every two minutes to see whether the message has come in yet, because you will always find another subject in your inbox that will distract you. You could also agree with the sender on a time when the message should arrive. This way you will not need to check beforehand.

How to disable the visual and/or acoustic new email notification

1. Microsoft Outlook 2010: Click **Options** on the **File** tab to display the **Outlook Options** dialog box, as shown in Figure 1-1.

    Microsoft Office Outlook 2007/Microsoft Office Outlook 2003: On the **Tools** menu, select **Options**.

2. Outlook 2010: In the left pane of the **Outlook Options** dialog box, click **Mail**.

    Outlook 2007/Outlook 2003: On the **Settings** tab, click **Email Options**.

3. Outlook 2010: Clear all check boxes in the **Message Arrival** pane.

    Outlook 2007/Outlook 2003: In the **Email Options** dialog box, click **Advanced Email Options**. Clear all check boxes in the **Upon arrival of new items in the Inbox** pane (or at least clear **Show Desktop Notifications** and **Play a Sound**).

4. Close all dialog boxes by clicking **OK**.

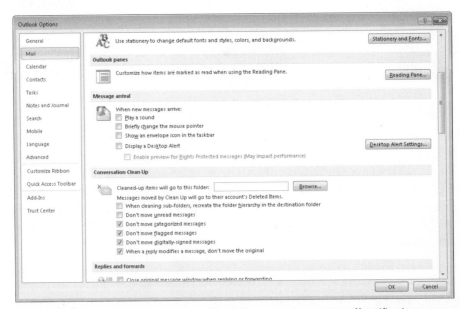

FIGURE 1-1 Don't let yourself get distracted by each new message—turn off notifications.

How to disable the automatic downloading of new messages

If you want to finally work through all the existing messages in your inbox without receiving new ones, as long as you are not explicitly calling them up via Send/Receive All Folders or Send/Receive, you can avoid receiving new messages altogether.

- In Outlook 2010, click **Send/Receive Groups** in the **Send & Receive** group on the **Send/Receive** tab, and then select **Disable Scheduled Send/Receive**.

In Outlook 2007/Outlook 2003, do the following:

1. On the **Tools** menu, click **Options**.

2. On the **Mail Setup** or **Email Setup** tab, click the **Send/Receive** button, and in the **Transfer Groups** dialog box, under **Settings for group "All Accounts"** and under **In Offline Mode**, clear the **Automatic Transfer Every x Minutes** check box. If you have set up several groups, you need to perform this step for each group.

3. Close all dialog boxes by clicking **Close** or **OK**.

Process Email Messages in Blocks

Think about how often you really need to check your inbox for new messages. Most people intuitively check it much too often. Wouldn't it be enough to devote one hour twice a day, 40 minutes three times a day, or 30 minutes four times a day to handling email? (You will find more information about the advantages of organizing blocks of tasks for processing in Chapter 4, "How to Make Your Daily Planning Work in Real Life.")

WHAT IS A BLOCK?

In the context of time management, a *block* is a specific amount of time you set aside to bundle together a lot of small tasks for processing all at once— for example, you could schedule yourself to take care of all of your email and return calls from 1 P.M. until 2 P.M. By doing so, you won't be constantly interrupted while doing larger tasks, taking a small break and then making a call, then another one.... More importantly, you'll be able to focus on the big and important tasks instead of always thinking "Oh, I've got to squeeze in nine calls somewhere"—you'll have a whole hour from 1 P.M. until 2 P.M. to take care of that.

The creation of blocks is especially helpful when processing email messages. Unimportant messages can be answered faster or deleted immediately. "Ten more messages after this one. Yikes, I still have other things on my plate, but this one isn't even important. So I'll keep it short and hurry up." (You'll learn more about the DANF System for processing email messages in the section "Keep Your Inbox in Order" later in this chapter.)

Sometimes hours of waiting time until your next email block starts, added to your normal response time, can even lead to fewer incoming messages, because your colleagues may find it quicker to research certain information by themselves, instead of sending a message to you.

Break Your Response Pattern

This next tip may initially take a bit of time, but you will recover the invested time elsewhere. Before answering an email, pause for three seconds and listen to yourself. Evaluate your emotional state to determine whether you can answer neutrally. If you are angry, irritated, scared, very nervous, or a little confused, wait a while before you answer, if at all possible. Ask yourself: "Why is this inquiry in my inbox, who sent it, what happens if I send a short reply now; is email truly the right answer medium?"

Most of the time, you will reply in a similar way as before—just a little more deliberately. Once in a while, however, you will discover that these questions lead to a noticeable improvement. Sometimes even a mail marathon, which could drag on for hours and over several email messages, can be prevented with a two-minute phone conversation.

If you want to call the sender (or a recipient) of an email, but he or she has not added a signature with a phone number, you don't need to switch to your contacts to retrieve the required information. Simply right-click the person's address in the preview window (or in the open message) in the From, To, Cc, or Bcc field. If your *Contacts* folder contains phone numbers for this person, they will be displayed in the shortcut menu, as shown in Figure 1-2. (Depending on your Outlook version and system settings, you may need to click Business Card or Look Up Outlook Contact first.)

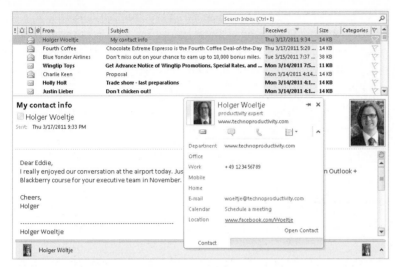

FIGURE 1-2 In the shortcut menu, you can select the business card or the phone number or open all saved contact data for the contact.

View Current Sender Information with a Mouse-Click: The Outlook 2010 Social Connector

Outlook 2010 shows you current information about the sender and the recipients of the active message directly below the message in the so-called Social Connector (see Figure 1-3), so you don't have to do a search. In Outlook 2003 and Outlook 2007, this personal contact area is not available out of the box, but Microsoft provides it as a free download called the Outlook Social Connector for upgrading those earlier versions of Outlook.

If you are looking at an email message in the reading pane or (by double-clicking it) in its own window, Outlook displays a miniature photo of the sender in the lower-left corner of the reading pane, assuming that such a photo exists in your data (otherwise an empty silhouette is displayed), and the sender name next to it (see Figure 1-2 shown earlier). On the right border, the photos/silhouettes of all the other mail recipients are displayed, and to the right of them you'll see a small upward-pointing arrow. If you point to one of these photos without clicking it, Outlook shows the name of that person and (if it exists in your contacts) his or her job title and company name. You can click the arrow head or a photo to view an enlarged version of the Social Connector.

After you have clicked a person's picture or name, you can select that person's available data to the right of his or her photo. For example, Outlook can find the contact's upcoming meetings, email messages you have received from the contact, or only email attachments from that contact. Clicking the respective item opens it directly.

FIGURE 1-3 Current information is always at hand with the Social Connector in Outlook 2010.

You can also view RSS feeds and status updates from the social networks of this person and add this person to your own social networks by using the Add command below the person's photo. For example, you may find a new client via his email address at LinkedIn, add him to your LinkedIn contacts, and from there import his company, mailing address, and phone number into Outlook. If your business partners are using the status entries on social networks, you can also see who has become a new parent, or who is on vacation or a business trip in a different time zone and can therefore only be reached in the evening. Of course, this only works if all parties involved are revealing this kind of (personal) information publicly and are continuing to maintain their social network pages. Make sure to set an information limit for yourself that makes sense. What do you want to know about which person? Otherwise you won't get any work done due to all the Facebook and Twitter updates you are receiving, and you may not be able to pull yourself away from the computer during your time off, either...

AVOID UNNECESSARY MESSAGES WITH THE TEAM FUNCTIONS OF OUTLOOK AND SHAREPOINT

Instead of conducting all communication via email, it can be helpful to save defined reports (such as project status reports, agendas, and meeting logs) at central locations at predetermined times. You can do this by using a Microsoft SharePoint site on your organization's intranet.

You can find out more about the team functions of Outlook and SharePoint in Chapter 5, "How to Schedule Meetings So They Are Convenient, Effective, and Fun."

When a colleague sends you an email message requesting the telephone number of a contact, the simplest and quickest thing would seem to be to answer him right away with the requested number. However, this is not necessarily the best solution.

If you frequently find yourself in this kind of situation, you should ask yourself why. Maybe there is no central address management. If you create and maintain a public contacts folder or address list on a SharePoint site with data about your contacts for the team, you will save time and get interrupted less often, because the people who would normally send you email messages can just look for the answer themselves and find it quickly.

Keep Your Inbox in Order

The first step on the way to an empty—or at least orderly—inbox is to build blocks of email messages, which allows you to work more productively already. The second step is the consequent and disciplined use of a system to process the messages in the block.

The minimum number of remaining messages you end up with in your inbox at the end of an email block or work day will vary. Depending on the type of business you are in, your way of working, and your position and corporate culture, 20 messages might already be a great result. Other users in certain working environments may get down to five or even no remaining messages. As long as you have no more than 20 to 30 messages in your inbox, you can retain an overview and quickly find what you need. And, last but not least, it will just make you feel calmer, which is much better than the stress of having a "mountain of data" with 2584 messages, giving you a guilty conscience because it's so hard to find things in there.

Process Your Email Block with the DANF System

Maybe you remember the old saying about how to reduce the amount of papers on your desk: "Pick up each piece of paper only once." This is also a good guideline regarding email. Many messages can be processed when you read them for the first time; others may require two or three steps. Therefore, when you start with your email block, go through all messages one after the other and evaluate them according to the following aspects and questions (Delete, Act Now, File – or the *DANF System*, for short):

- **Delete it** Being able to delete incoming messages saves the most time. Delete as many as possible as quickly as possible. The first question you should ask yourself is: Can I delete this mail without hesitation? Frequently, a quick look at the sender and the subject line is enough to make this decision.

- **Act Now** Work on important and urgent messages immediately when you start working your email block. Do the same for small issues that only take three to four minutes to process. If you leave these messages for later, they may pile up endlessly and it'll take more than an hour to catch up after two days. Planning a future deadline, creating a task for taking care of small issues, or looking at them multiple times in a list of "small stuff still pending" will end up costing you more time and energy than taking care of them immediately. After all, you don't need to interrupt a different task, because your current task is taking care of your email block. Therefore, hurry up and get rid of them—doing so will take you one step closer to an (almost) empty inbox.

- **File for later** If it looks like processing the message will take more than five minutes, and it doesn't require immediate attention, file it into your folder structure. But make sure you save it in such a way that you can take care of it the next time you click it—and that you will find it again when you need it. (You can learn more about folder structures in "Create and Use Your Own Folder Structure" later in this chapter.)

> **IMPORTANT** When you are effectively dealing with the message flood, the Delete key is your best friend and most important ally! It's also there to assist you on your BlackBerry.

You can also use the four priority levels of the Eisenhower diagram (see Chapter 2, "How to Work More Effectively with Tasks and Priorities") for messages you are not working on immediately. Check whether there are three appropriate folders that work for you (delete quadrant 4 or D messages right away). You can process these folders at predetermined times or in the context of your email block after you have completely processed all newly received messages. Plan for taking care of very important and urgent Priority-1/A/ quadrant 1 messages by making an appointment with yourself in your calendar if you are unable to work on them immediately.

If you aren't sure whether you can delete a message right away:

- Ask yourself whether it requires a response, follow-up activity, or simple answer on your part (and whether it is really necessary).

- If not: Ask yourself whether you will need this message later on to look up information contained within it, and whether you would find this message again using your search criteria.

- If not: Delete the message.

> **CAUTION**   Make sure you adhere to your company's policies regarding archiving and storage of email messages. Maybe you are not allowed to permanently delete some (or, in extreme cases, all) of the messages this book is telling you to delete. In this case, create a folder called *Compost*, *Garbage Archive*, or something similar, into which you can move the messages whenever we recommend deleting.

File Email Messages Accordingly

To keep your inbox organized, follow these three guidelines.

- The required follow-up activity is clear or this message contains information that pertains to a specific appointment or deadline: Convert the mail into a task or appointment.

- The message requires an answer at a specific time in the future or further processing steps: Save the message in your folder structure and flag it for future processing (see the section "Flag the Messages You Still Need to Work On" later in this chapter).

- No answer or other follow-up activity is required of you, but you want to save the message for look-up later on: File it in your folder structure.

Convert Email Messages into Tasks and Appointments

Sometimes an email message is nothing more than a task (or several) that you need to perform. Others represent appointments (these also include flight or hotel confirmations) or additional information about an appointment (such as an agenda or driving directions).

If you are sending such messages yourself, it may be more practical to use a meeting request (to set up or update appointments, see Chapter 5) or use the Outlook functions for assigning a task to others. If you do it that way, the recipient just has to click one button to save the message in his task list or calendar.

> **CAUTION**   Be careful when using the feature to assign a task to someone else: Creating and delegating an Outlook task can seem authoritarian or presumptuous to clients, colleagues, and managers in other departments or companies. If you are not sure how your task delegation (for example, sending required data) will be received, it's better to write a regular email message.

If you receive such a message as a plain email message, you should convert it into a task or appointment so that you can find it again quickly when you need it.

How to create an appointment or a task from an email message

1. Right-click the message in your inbox and keep the mouse button pressed.

2. Drag the message to the **Tasks** or **Calendar** group button at the bottom of the navigation pane, and release the mouse button.

3. In the shortcut menu that is now displayed, click on the action you want: for example, select **Move Here as Task with Attachment** (see Figure 1-4). This automatically removes the email message from your inbox.

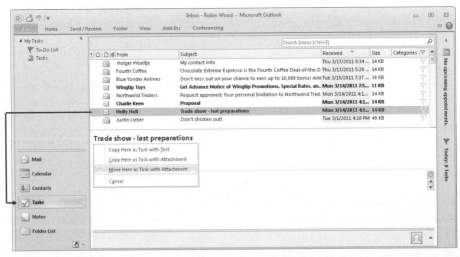

FIGURE 1-4 Move email messages by dragging them into the task list.

We recommend that you copy or move the email message as a task with attachment (instead of "with text"). Copying as a task with text inserts the entire content of the email message (including headers, such as the sender) as text into the note pane of the task. Inserting an email message as a task with attachment has the disadvantage that you can't read the text immediately but need to double-click the inserted letter icon instead. However, this method allows you to attach several messages at the same time, represented in a compact fashion. You can keep the original message with all its pictures and attachments (which are removed if you do a copy as text). After double-clicking the attachment, you can also use the **Reply**, **Forward**, and **Reply All** functions in exactly the same way as if you had opened the message in your inbox—or as if you had put the message into a follow-up file and given it a date, a priority and, if necessary, a reminder. It will later show up in your tasks. More about this in the next chapters.

4. Outlook opens a new task form and automatically uses the email message subject. Complete the entry by adding a due date and define a reminder if necessary.

5. Save and close the new task by clicking the appropriate button.

How to quickly create a new contact entry for the sender of an email message

1. While keeping the left mouse button pressed, simply drag the entire email message onto the **Contacts** group button at the bottom of the navigation pane (in this case, you want to copy the text).

   Outlook creates a new contact. It automatically uses the sender's address and name from the message, and the entire text of the original mail is displayed in the note box.

2. Select the entire text except for the signature.

3. Press Delete to delete the text, so that only the signature is left.

4. Select the company name (by double-clicking it if it's just one word, triple-clicking it to select the entire row, or just clicking in front of the first word and dragging over the whole company name until you reach the end of the name).

5. Click the selected text and drag the company name onto the **Company** text box.

6. Repeat steps 4 and 5 for all other relevant data, such as phone numbers.

7. After you have transferred the data (and deleted any superfluous data), save and close the new contact by clicking the corresponding button.

Create an entry in your Outlook contacts for each contact that might be relevant for you. After you have practiced this process a few times, it only takes a few seconds to create a new contact from an email message with a signature. The advantages of entering the contacts are:

- If the phone number or email address has been updated, you can always find the current data in your contacts (unlike in older messages that have the wrong number).

- You no longer need to search through dozens of messages if the sender does not continue to send the address data he sent in the first mail.

- The contact data will also be available in printed address lists and for your iPhone or BlackBerry, if you need it while you are traveling.

- You can provide your colleagues with the contact data by placing it into a public or shared folder.

How to create tasks and appointments from individual parts of a longer email message

If an email message contains multiple paragraphs, each of which represents an individual task or appointment, do the following:

1. Select the respective sections.

2. Release the mouse button, point to the selected text, and click it again.

3. Drag the selection to the corresponding group button in the navigation pane— **Tasks** or **Calendar**—and release the mouse button.

   Outlook opens a new appointment/task form and enters the selected text into the note field of the new entry.

4. Add a meaningful subject line and further information, if necessary.

5. Save and close the new task or appointment by clicking the corresponding button.

How to insert multiple email messages into existing tasks and appointments

You can also append individual or multiple messages (as well as appointments, tasks, contacts, and notes) to already-entered appointments, tasks, and contacts. You might want to do this with a message that contains access data for a phone conference and two messages with the new documents to be discussed there.

1. Open the entry by double-clicking the appointment in the calendar.

2. Outlook 2010/Outlook 2007: In the appointment form, select the **Insert** tab, and in the **Include** group select the **Outlook Item** command (see Figure 1-5).

   Outlook 2003: On the **Insert** menu, select the **Item** command.

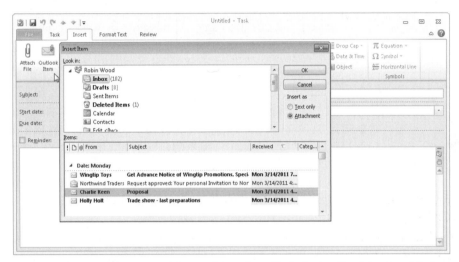

FIGURE 1-5 Insert email messages into appointments and tasks to view the data where it belongs.

3. In the **Insert Item** dialog box, select the corresponding folder in the **Look in** box and then select the message you want in the **Items** box.

4. Click **OK** to insert the message.

5. Save and close the changed appointment.

How to use a flag to mark an email message as a task in Outlook 2010/Outlook 2007

1. Right-click in the column with the flag (**flag status**).

2. Use the shortcut menu to assign a due date (**Today**, **Tomorrow**, and so on).

This automatically transfers the email message as a task into your To-Do List (see Chapter 2) and thus into the Task List (see Chapter 3, "How to Gain More Time for What's Essential with an Effective Week Planner," and Chapter 4). By using the shortcut menu, you can also flag the message as taken care of, delete the flag, or add a reminder (an "alarm," which in Outlook 2010/Outlook 2007 is also displayed when you move the message from your inbox into a different folder).

With the Set Quick Click command in the shortcut menu, you can specify the function of the flag when the column is clicked (for instance, setting the due date to Tomorrow or Today). After you have done this, only a single click in the flag column will then be enough to mark the message as a task that is due tomorrow. Another click marks the email (and therefore the corresponding task) as completed. The flags will even carry over to your BlackBerry: If you use BlackBerry OS 5 (introduced in 2009 with the BlackBerry Bold 9700) or higher versions, you can also flag your messages on the BlackBerry. Flags set there will also appear in Outlook and vice versa.

This method has the following advantages compared to dragging an email message onto the Tasks group button (as described earlier in this section):

- When you switch to your tasks, Outlook shows the original email message directly in your To-Do list. If you mark the email as completed in any email folder, you are also marking the task as completed—and if you check off the message as completed in the To-Do list in the Tasks view, you are also marking the email message in your inbox (and any other folder) as completed. If you delete the email from the To-Do list or the email list, it also gets deleted from the other location.

- Without any additional steps, you can now sort or filter your task list by the Icon field (see Chapter 2) to display the email messages always at the bottom or not at all in certain views, or maybe only the messages but no "regular" tasks.

The drag-and-drop method of converting email messages into tasks, which already existed in previous versions of Outlook, still has three crucial advantages:

- If you want to delete the message from your inbox to retain a better overview of your email but will need to respond to it later on, it will still be available as an attachment. (When you use the flagging method, the task is removed as well whenever you delete the email message. If you copy or move it into a task, however, you can decide whether to keep the message, and you can later independently delete the task that contains the email copy.)

- You are keeping all items that need to be taken care of later in one location: your task folder. If a few months down the road you are looking at an email message about a project and need to work on it, or you want to update presentation slides, get back in touch with someone over the phone, or need to order new printer cartridges, everything is there in your task folder. However, if you mark the email message with a flag, it becomes a different data source that does not display in certain Outlook views. Depending on the panes the user has displayed, this can lead to confusion in Outlook 2007/Outlook 2010. (We will spare you the technical details here, because they are version specific and quite complicated to explain.

In short: the drag-and-drop approach works better if you need to work intensively with email messages that require follow-up, especially if you need to adjust the subject line once in a while or add further information to the note field.)

■ When using the drag-and-drop method, you can, if necessary, add further and more extensive comments as well as additional email messages and data attachments in the note field of the task without changing the original message (as you might want to do, for example, when delegating).

In the end, it's up to you whether you prefer to use the time-tested drag-and-drop method for email messages even in the newer versions of Outlook or instead flag messages to convert them—it depends on how you work and how complex the tasks resulting from your email messages are. (Do you ever change the subject lines of messages that are flagged as tasks, or do you write subject lines that are so unambiguous to begin with that this is not necessary? Do you flag a lot of messages as tasks, and do you want to display them in several views separately? Do you use a BlackBerry with BlackBerry OS 5 or higher that will also show flags and synchronize them with Outlook?)

Create and Use Your Own Folder Structure

It takes approximately two hours to design and set up a meaningful folder structure for messages and to file the saved messages in the correct locations within them. Experience shows that it works best to use no more than seven main folders (in addition to *Inbox*, *Drafts*, and the other default Outlook folders). For each main folder, you can create subfolders. You should also try to keep your structure to no more then seven subfolders per level, so that you can later orientate yourself quickly and confidently.

The setup that works best for you depends on your area of work and your personal thinking style—each person's brain is wired differently. For example, if you are managing five large projects, you may want to create one main folder per project, thus sorting your messages by topic. Some users may prefer to sort by time, with folders such as *Completed*, *Reply by Tonight*, *Process This Week*, *Process This Month*, *Waiting for Reply*, and *Follow Up by End of Week*. You can also come up with a combination. For some teams, it may even make sense to have all team members use the same folder structure. There is no fixed rule that can be applied to every situation. Do what works best for you.

Try to find a structure that works for you. For example, get together with a colleague who has a similar working style as you—two heads put together sometimes come up with better ideas. Or you might ask someone who has already successfully cleaned up his or her inbox with a folder structure, to share experiences and give you tips.

The following lists some example criteria for how you can divide your folder structure:

- Persons/contacts (colleagues, clients, suppliers)
- Topics/areas of expertise
- Projects/products
- Priority (see Chapter 2)
- Locations (countries, cities, company locations, plants)
- Product numbers, reference numbers, customer numbers
- Deadlines (Must be completed by tonight, By this weekend, This month)

It might initially take you a little while to get used to this new structure. However, if after three to at most five weeks, you still find your structure to be cumbersome or unclear, and you continue to have a difficult time assigning or finding messages, you should revise your structure, taking your experiences into consideration.

How to set up new folders

1. In the folder list, right-click the desired parent folder you want (for example, the name of your inbox or **Personal Folders**) and then select **New Folder** in the shortcut menu. Alternatively, you can press the Ctrl+Shift+E key combination and then select where the new folder should be inserted.

2. In the **Create New Folder** dialog box, type an appropriate name into the **Name** box.

3. If necessary, change the entry in the **Folder contains items of type** list box to **Email and Provision**, if the dialog box was not opened from email view.

4. Close the dialog box by clicking **OK** to create the new folder.

TIP

Outlook automatically sorts your folders alphabetically. Start the folder name with @, z, or a number to place it at the beginning, the end, or a certain position in the list.

How to move messages into the correct folder

1. In your inbox (or any other folder), click the message you want to move.

2. Drag the message onto the target folder and release the mouse button to drop the message into the folder.

If you want to copy (not move) the message, right-click it and select the corresponding command in the shortcut menu after dragging. You can also press and hold Shift or Ctrl while clicking to select several messages simultaneously, and then move/copy them in one go by right-clicking and dragging the selection. If you want to move an entire folder within your folder structure (not just messages), simply click the folder and drag it into another folder or back onto the main level (into Personal Folders or your Microsoft Exchange Mailbox).

FAVORITES—QUICK ACCESS FOR YOUR MOST IMPORTANT FOLDERS

Use your *Favorites* folder to access your most frequently used folders quickly, without having to click through several folder levels each time (see Figure 1-6). Simply drag a folder or subfolder into the Favorites section. Because you can't see the parent folder levels in your Favorites section, it makes sense to add some form of identification to the folder names, either in front of or behind the name, such as *Technical data (product D)*. Just like all other folders, your *Favorites* folder can be opened by clicking it, or it can serve as a target for moving messages with the drag-and-drop method.

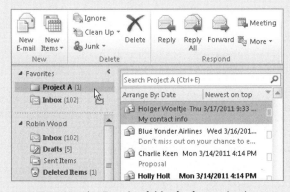

FIGURE 1-6 Use the *Favorites* folder for fast navigation.

How to customize message sorting for individual folders

Within the folders, you can sort and group the messages according to different criteria; for example, you can sort one folder by subject and another by sender, while all remaining folders are sorted by date. (You will learn more about sorting, grouping, and customizing views in Chapter 4.)

Click a column header to sort the items according to your chosen criterion. Clicking the column header again reverts the sort order, as shown in Figure 1-7.

FIGURE 1-7 Change the view of the items contained in the folder quickly and easily.

Flag the Messages You Still Need to Work On

To make sure that you don't overlook any required follow-up activities for email messages you haven't marked as completed yet, you can either create a task with a copy of the message as an attachment, as described earlier, or flag the message as pending (for example, if it's not worth creating an extra task for it, because the email needs to be taken care of very soon). Outlook supports you with message flagging—adding small colorful categories or flags to mark the messages. Messages that need to be taken care of later can also be converted into tasks, as described earlier, and you can use color flagging to group them and have certain messages always at the top of the respective folders (for example, important basic information in project folders).

Right-click in the Categories column to assign a category to an email by using the shortcut menu (or to remove previously set categories). By clicking in the Categories column, you can set or remove a category you have specified for quick clicking (set this to the category that you use most often). In Chapter 3, we will examine categories and examples for category systems in more detail.

Because one message can have multiple categories assigned to it (and a red flag for the due date), you can now use different colors at the same time to quickly find your message again by searching in the appropriate category. This is an improvement from the colored flags in Outlook 2003. In Outlook 2010/Outlook 2007, you can now, for example, have a red flag for "Due today" and also a blue square for "Product specs" at the same time.

How to assign a colored flag to a message in Outlook 2003

1. Select the message in the message list.

2. Click the **Flag Status** column (the flag icon) to assign the default flag to the message, or right-click the column, select the **Flag for Follow-up** command, and then confirm it by clicking **OK**.

    After you have processed a flagged message, you can use the shortcut menu to mark it as completed.

    You can also use the shortcut menu to remove the flag completely, or use the appropriate commands to select a different color for flagging, as shown in Figure 1-8. In the submenu of the Set Default Flag command, you can change the default color (which you can assign by clicking the flag column).

FIGURE 1-8 The shortcut menu contains options for colorful flagging of messages in Outlook 2003.

By the way, starting with BlackBerry OS 5, you can use different colored flags for message flagging on your BlackBerry. It gets completely and mutually synchronized with Outlook 2003 and can even display alarms.

Try to develop a system for yourself with up to six colors. For example, red could mean "Important and must be taken care of as quickly as possible," green tasks can wait until the end of the week, and blue tasks can wait until the end of the month. Yellow might mean that it is theoretically due by the end of the week, but that it's just something that's nice to have and could be deleted if you don't have time, and you only look at purple items if you have some extra time, but otherwise they will be deleted at the end of the month.

Don't Force Alarms on Yourself: The Reminder Functions of Outlook 2007 and Outlook 2010

In previous versions of Outlook, you were also able to flag email messages for follow-up and add a reminder to open a message window at a certain preset time. However, the older versions of Outlook show reminders only if the message is located in the *Inbox* folder at the time of the reminder. With Outlook 2010/Outlook 2007, you (or the recipient of your message) will also receive a reminder if the message is located in a different folder. You can now also set a flag with an alarm individually for yourself and a different alarm (or no alarm) separately for the recipients, as shown in Figure 1-9. For example, if you have sent an email message to Robin Wood, you can set a reminder to yourself for two weeks later, and politely check in with him if he hasn't sent you a reply yet—without an automatic reminder appearing in his Outlook Inbox.

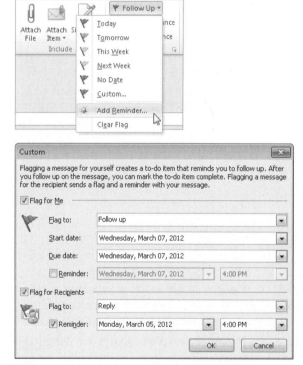

FIGURE 1-9 Flag an email message separately for yourself and the recipient to follow up with a reminder.

When writing an email message, on the Message tab, in the Tags group (Outlook 2010) or Options group (Outlook 2007), click Follow Up, and in the drop-down menu, click Add Reminder (Outlook 2010) or Flag For Recipients (Outlook 2007). You can now flag the message for yourself and the recipients separately so that Outlook displays a reminder at the set time. If you flag the message for yourself, it is automatically flagged as a task and is displayed in your To-Do List as well as in the task list.

Before you get all gung-ho about using this function for each message you send, please think twice. Imagine that you add a reminder to each message to your manager, who will now have unwelcome reminder windows popping up on her screen at inconvenient times, possibly even accompanied by an annoying sound.

In any case, this new separate flagging remains practical and discreet, if you flag a message just to yourself as a task while you write it—for example, to check a week later whether a reply with the requested data has arrived, or whether you need to follow up on it.

If you come to clear agreements with your team and take a reasonable approach when dealing with follow-ups and reminders for recipients, this function can be more useful than disruptive. For example, you could add a task flag for yourself for tomorrow to take care of important data for trade show preparation (so you will remember to work on it tomorrow), and you can set a reminder for Wednesday of the following week for a colleague who appreciates getting reminders and is out of the office until Monday. This way you both have a task or a reminder, so you will both remember to prepare yourselves in time for the team meeting on Friday.

If some senders begin bombarding you with "alarm messages" that open an unwanted reminder window, you have a means to defend yourself: the Rules Wizard, as shown in Figure 1-10 (see "How to set up and change rules with the Rules Wizard," later in this chapter). Create a new rule (Create Rule Without Template, Apply Rule To Incoming Messages, or Check Messages Upon Arrival) that removes message flagging for incoming messages. (See Figure 1-10: while creating a rule from a blank rule for messages you receive, select Flagged With Action, click the blue underlined text Action, and click OK to confirm the Any Action template; in the next step, select the Clear The Message Flag action. If necessary, define an exception as the last step—for example, if the sender is a colleague on your team who uses flagging for other recipients in a reasonable fashion.)

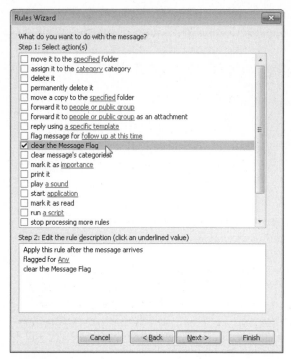

FIGURE 1-10 Use the Rules Wizard to defend yourself against sender-controlled reminders in your Outlook inbox.

How to add short notes and reminders to a message in Outlook 2003

1. In the shortcut menu of the **Flag Status** column of the message (see Figure 1-8, earlier in this chapter), select **Add Reminder**.

2. In the **Flag for Follow Up** dialog box (see Figure 1-11), assign a due date and time for an alarm, so that Outlook will remind you at that time.

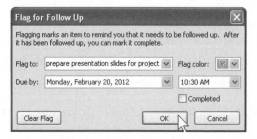

FIGURE 1-11 If necessary, add a note in the header area of the email message to identify it.

3. In the **Flag to** text box, you can enter any text you want. It will be displayed in the preview and, when you open the message, in grey or yellow below the info bar in the message header.

4. Close the **Flag for Follow Up** dialog box by clicking **OK**.

Unlike in Outlook 2010/Outlook 2007, in Outlook 2003 the reminder will open a window only if the message is located in the inbox at the time of the reminder. Therefore, only use this function for messages that you can't assign to a folder and thus have to keep in the inbox. Or you may want to avoid the reminder function altogether and instead copy or move messages into appointments or tasks to which you then add a reminder (see the section "Convert Email Messages into Tasks and Appointments" earlier in this chapter).

Keep All Items That Are Flagged for Processing in a Single View

With the help of search folders, you can search your complete mailbox (all folders in your Exchange account) or a complete personal folder file with all subfolders for email messages that have certain criteria, as shown in Figure 1-12. For example, you can see all messages that are flagged for processing in one view—even though they are located in different folders for different projects. After you have set up a search folder, you can open it with one click of the mouse, just like a regular email folder.

The search folder itself does not contain any messages, just links to them—you always see the messages that match the criteria in all searched folders. For example, if you open (in a search folder for messages that are flagged for follow up) a message that is located in the *Project C - Inquiries* folder, perform the still-pending processing step, and then mark it as completed, the message is removed from the search folder. However, it remains in the *Project C - Inquiries* folder, but it now has the Completed status. If you had deleted the message in the search folder, it would also have been removed from *Project C - Inquiries*. Therefore, even when working from the search folder, you are always working with the original message.

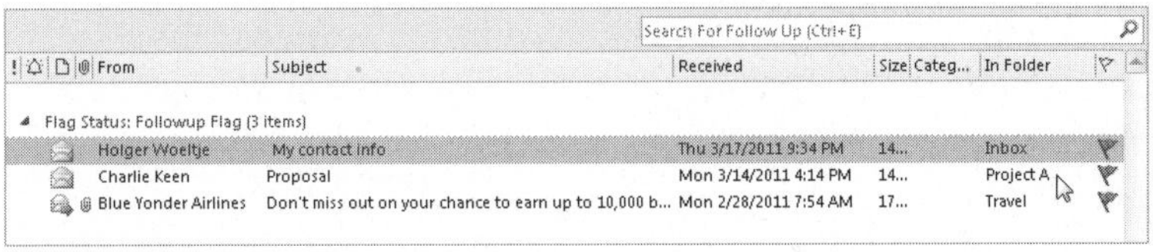

FIGURE 1-12 Use search folders to keep an eye on the folders containing email messages that still need to be processed.

How to create your own search folders

1. In the folder list (to the left of the navigation pane), right-click **Search Folders** (below the last folder in your mailbox in Outlook 2007, but sorted alphabetically with the other folders in Outlook 2010) and then select **New Search Folder** in the shortcut menu.

2. In the **New Search Folder** dialog box, in the **Select a search folder** list, select one of the predefined search criteria. For example, select **Categorized email** (under **Organize messages**) or **Messages flagged for follow-up** to get a result similar to what's shown in Figure 1-12.

3. In the **Search mail in** list, you can select the personal or public folder you want to search.

4. Close the **New Search Folder** dialog box by clicking **OK** to set up the new search folder. The folder will then be filled with the appropriate messages.

Now you can open your search folder like any other email folder by clicking it. If you don't see it in the folder list, you need to expand the search folder list. Click the small triangle or the plus sign next to Search Folders in the navigation pane. (To later close the list, click the minus-sign or click the triangle again.)

You can further refine your search—for instance, to display only messages from a certain sender that also have a red category or flag. To do so, in the Select A Search Folder list, select the Create A Custom Search Folder entry and then specify the desired criteria with the Choose button. (This works similar to the creation of filters for work views; more about this in Chapter 3). You can customize and rename your newly created search folder with the commands in the shortcut menu and add it to your Favorites (see Figure 1-6, shown earlier).

Let Outlook Presort Your Inbox for You

With its automatic filter functions, Outlook does some of the email processing for you. For example, you need the Movie Newsletter when you want to select a movie to watch—not on Thursday morning, when it arrives in your inbox and you have something else to do. By using the correct rule, you can make sure it gets automatically moved into the appropriate folder as soon as it arrives. You no longer need to move it manually, and you don't see it unless you feel like going to the movie theater and you open your *Private events/Movie news* folder.

How to set up rules directly from a message

It is quite simple to set up a rule directly from a message to which the rule applies:

1. Right-click the message on which the rule should be based, and in the shortcut menu, click **Rules/Create Rule** (in Outlook 2010) or (in Outlook 2007/Outlook 2003) click **Create Rule** directly.

2. Outlook will open a dialog box that provides a preselection based on the clicked message, containing the subject, sender, or recipient you may want to filter for. If you agree with these settings, select the action you want to execute in the **Execute the following** group box.

3. Close the **Create Rule** dialog box by clicking **OK** to apply the rule, or click the **Advanced Options** button to make further adjustments. Outlook opens the Rules Wizard and offers you a large number of options that are already adjusted to the selected message.

How to set up and change rules with the Rules Wizard

If you want to set up a rule and don't happen to have the right kind of message to use as a template, or if you want to change an existing rule, open an email folder and do the following:

1. Outlook 2010: On the **Home** tab, in the **Move** group, click **Rules/Manage Rules and Alerts**.

    In Outlook 2007/Outlook 2003: On the **Tools** menu, click **Rules Wizard** or **Rules and Alerts**.

2. In the dialog box that now opens, you will see all the rules that have been defined so far (see Figure 1-13). You can add new rules that will change the process order, delete rules, and change or copy existing rules, to use them as a basis for creating new rules.

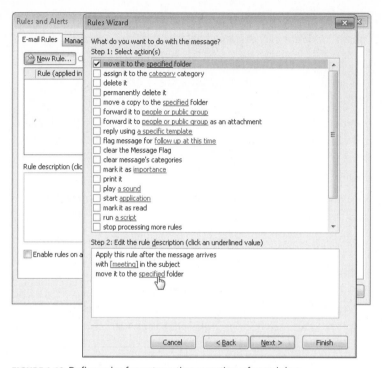

FIGURE 1-13 Define rules for automatic presorting of your inbox.

The Rules Wizard is quite self-explanatory as it leads you through the rule setup. Basically you just enable the individual actions or conditions (as shown in Figure 1-13) as you go through the individual steps. In the description box, you specify the details about the selected condition/actions by clicking the blue underlined terms.

With the Rules Wizard, you can automatically flag messages from your managers in color and move messages, for example, with the words *Project B* and *FYI* in the subject line into the *Project B – read* folder. For each message you send to your colleague Robin Wood, you can move a copy with *ToDo* in the subject line into the *Check back by end of week* folder. Take 15 minutes to look at your inbox, look at all the available options in the Rules Wizard, and think about which other rules will make your workday easier.

> **CAUTION** Using rules too hastily can lead to lost or overlooked messages. Take your time and think twice before defining a rule that deletes messages automatically or moves them unread into a folder that you don't check regularly.

Think Before You Communicate

If you keep a few guidelines for writing better messages in mind, you help others, because your messages can be processed better and more quickly. On the other hand, if
you compose and send each message at lightning speed without thinking, you end up
losing the most time by trying to win time. It pays to invest a little bit more time into
choosing your words wisely. In the end, you will find yourself coming up with more concrete and to-the-point answers, which lead to fewer inquiries and thus to noticeable time
savings on both sides.

Make Your Text Easier to Understand: Always Adjust It to the Recipients

When you are writing a message, try to put yourself in the position of the recipient:

- Is this message relevant to the recipient? Is he required to respond, or are you
  just providing important information for him? Are you sure he needs to be on the
  recipient list? Keep the number of recipients as large as necessary, but as small
  as possible. Nobody is happy about 30 additional email messages per day that
  "might just possibly interest her someday under certain circumstances."

- What is clear to you, but not clear to the recipient? Where do you need to explain
  backgrounds or circumstances?

- Did you add all the required information? For example, if you ask a colleague to
  contact "Mr. Smith," make sure to add the corresponding contact data.

- What kind of style does the recipient prefer? Will you receive an incomplete response if the message is longer than 10 lines? Or will he send you several inquiries
  if you don't send him a comprehensive message with all the details?

- Be careful with HTML formatting: Too much colored text and too many blinking
  backgrounds will distract more than they help. It'll also look strange if you play
  with font styles and sizes too much (especially on mobile devices).

Keep Your Phrasing Short, Precise, and Crystal Clear

Try to keep your text as short and clear as possible, and use blank lines between paragraphs as a design element. This will save time on the recipient's side and increases the
chance that your most important points won't get lost in the text. Keep in mind: The
longer your email text, the higher the probability that it won't be read entirely or that
something will be misunderstood. If you are about to explain complicated or unexpected
circumstances, announce briefly what the next section will be about ("first the heading,
then the article"). Some recipients reply to messages by paragraph—especially because

more and more people tend to read and answer a third of their email messages on smartphones—and thus might assume a different intent on your part.

State your expectations clearly. For example, include *FYI* in the subject line or indicate whether you are expecting a response, and when. (Please make sure you are polite, though.) Instead of "I wonder if this will work this way. Maybe we can do it differently," write the following: "I suggest that we do the following: ... What do you think?" Instead of writing "Wouldn't it be nice to eventually find out what's going on?", formulate clearly what you are referring to. If you need results, make sure the recipient knows what exactly you need and in which format; if necessary, give him an example. Using a sentence such as "Please send me a status report every Friday by noon; see attached template (one page only, please)" not only avoids 20 superfluous pages and some wasted hours for the other people, it also saves you from receiving a lot more data or answers and questions than you need.

There is nothing wrong with adding *ToDo:* in front of each item, or maybe *Please answer:*, or *FYI:*, as long as you don't come across as bossy. Avoid (or explain) abbreviations if you are not sure that the recipient knows them. (Oh, by the way: *FYI* means "for your information (only)"—so the recipient will know that you do not expect him to answer.)

If you are dealing with two completely different topics, it's best to write two separate email messages. This way the recipient can reply to one and save the other as information.

Use Well-Written Subject Lines to Make Everyone's Life Easier

Always add a short but very clear subject. This helps the recipient assess the content, importance, and urgency of your message before opening it, and helps to find it again more easily when searching for it later. This will pay off for you as well—recipients will answer faster and the response will fit your needs better.

To write a good subject line:

1. Start with the due date.

2. Continue with the project/customer/topic.

3. Add some keywords that summarize the topic.

4. Finish with what the recipient should do (take action? just send a short answer? just read or file the message and discuss the topic with you during the next meeting?).

Depending on your work situation, it might be useful to change the order. For example, consider whether it is better to put the due date first or last. For people who travel a lot on airplanes or spend a few days at a summit/conference, so they can only check their email twice a day, it's great to have the due date first. That way they can tell immediately if some messages require a response on the same day while others can be rescheduled for next week. But if most messages need to be answered during the next 24 hours, and none of them is more urgent than any other, the end of the subject line is a better place to put the due date.

You Try It

1. Check your response to email messages: How often do you check for new messages? Do you really need to do it that often? Disable the notification about incoming messages, if you don't have to answer everything right away.

2. Make an appointment for yourself to create your own folder structure to clean up your inbox, and file the first messages immediately. Depending on how full your inbox is, you might want to make a second appointment for yourself to go through all the remaining messages and delete or file them as necessary.

3. Find three messages in your inbox that are nothing but tasks or appointments (or do this exercise when the next appropriate message arrives) and convert them to tasks/appointments accordingly. Find an email message that includes the contact data of a person as a signature that might become relevant for you and that you haven't entered yet. Use this email message to set up a new contact by using the drag-and-drop method, and continue to do the same for all relevant new contact data.

4. Mark all messages that you can't (or don't want to) process immediately, but need to take care of by tomorrow at noon, with a red flag as their flag status.

   If you are working with Outlook 2003: Create a search folder that lists all flagged messages. Before noon tomorrow, take the time to open this search folder and process those messages. Then mark the ones that are due at noon the next day with a red flag, and so on.

   Alternatively, if you are working with a different version of Outlook, use the Categorize function to automatically color-code the messages from at least three senders from who you frequently receive important messages. Create a search folder to show all messages with the same color code (category), no matter which folder they are filed in.

5. Wait half a day and don't check for newly arrived email messages during that time. (If this is not possible right now, wait until after the next long meeting or do it on Monday morning.) Write down how many new email messages you have received. Use a stopwatch as you process all those messages, one by one, as quickly as possible according to the DANF System. (Measure the time again after you have used the DANF System for two weeks and have gotten used to it.) Determine a value for your mail processing by block—such as three times a day for 30 minutes—and, if possible, set fixed times in which you process your inbox by block (instead of whenever a new message arrives).

6. Check the messages in your inbox: Which subject lines leave you in the dark as far as content and importance, and are unclear about what response is expected of you? How would you have phrased the subject to make these aspects clearer? Then look through your *Sent Items* folder and check the subject lines of the messages you sent in the past month to see how you handled such issues.

7. Repeat step 6, but this time check the message body for style, (un)ambiguous phrasing, clear formulation of the expected response, and length of the text. Keep your conclusions in mind when writing future messages. You may even want to write a short summary about what you will change, and print it out.

CHAPTER 2

How to Work More Effectively with Tasks and Priorities

IN THIS CHAPTER, YOU WILL

- Discover how to set priorities.
- Use task lists.
- Define your own customized views.
- Use filters.
- Fine-tune your priorities.
- Use a To-Do List.

"Everything Is Important!"

DO YOU HAVE so much to do that a lot remains undone? So much that you forget something once in a while? So much that ultimately time runs short, because you just couldn't get started earlier? Do you sometimes get the feeling there just aren't enough hours in the day, and there is no way that you will get everything done?

People who scamper from one crisis into the next and still manage to keep things more or less under control feel as if they have accomplished a whole lot. "Wannabe action heroes" measure their productivity according to the amount of overtime they put in, the stress they are under, and the number of tasks they get done (quantity, not quality)—after all, people who are under so much stress must be especially important. At first glance, it actually does look like they really apply themselves and are enormously productive. And that's fatal, because they frequently get admired and applauded for their performance. In the long run, they don't achieve big results—but in the long run, you can always blame the bad economy, changing trends in customer behavior, or other lame excuses.

WHY WANNABE ACTION HEROES MANAGE TO GET EVERYTHING DONE LAST-MINUTE—OR JUST FAIL

Putting Out Fires

This morning, Robin Wood was supposed to turn in the marketing plan for next year. Four weeks ago, he suddenly remembered that it needed to be completed before the beginning of the new fiscal year. He could have continued working on it this morning, but he spent the past one and a half hours confirming five Facebook friendship requests and taking care of 40 email messages—hey, at least that gives you the feeling you got something done! The marketing plan is already 70 percent complete anyway. There will probably be a bit of trouble with his managers, and the entire budget will be delayed. But somehow Robin will manage this. After all, that's what he's so admired for: that he always gets everything done at the last moment—well, maybe not everything, and maybe not always.

Like the other day, when he just didn't manage to finish that sales presentation for this year's most promising new corporate client, which had been due for quite a while. "I work best under pressure," he had thought, and left everything for the final week. And then he had gotten sick that week and wasn't able to use that time to work on the presentation. The competition, however, had been fully prepared, and Robin lost the contract—but such things just happen....

You could call this modus operandi "the fun of putting out fires." How boring it is to implement "fire prevention measures" beforehand.... You seldom get accolades for that. Nobody notices that there is no fire! That's not exciting, because you are not preventing a crisis at the last possible moment. But there are some advantages: If you make your plans in time, and work on large pending tasks early on and get them done before the small stuff, you will not run into time trouble. And you will be under very little stress. You can usually leave work at a reasonable hour, and when something goes wrong you still have time to catch it.

We frequently get ourselves lost in all those little issues that grab our attention by seeming urgent. Tomorrow it could be too late to do them. Or perhaps somebody keeps nagging us about an issue. If you can't say "No," you will soon have no time left for important tasks that don't have a "voice" to keep pressuring you with—no time for preparing important projects or presentations well, no time to take command and act. All you will do is react.

Let's Get Started and Change This!

In this chapter, you will take your first steps toward more effective time management, the basics of weekly and daily planning:

- Write down your plans to gain a better overview of all pending tasks.
- Determine what tasks will get you ahead and how far.
- Start to focus on what has the greatest impact on your success.
- Begin to work early on long-term tasks with "high leverage"—even if they are not due immediately and nobody is pushing you to complete them.
- Find out what's more urgent and more important than the rest, to separate the wheat from the chaff.
- Say "No" to things that keep you from what's more important.
- Use task lists for flexible planning.

How to Run a Country Like the United States in the 24 Hours a Day Has to Offer—Set Priorities!

How does the saying go? "For everything we do, we miss something else, and for everything we miss, we gain time for something else." (Now all we need to do is perform the more valuable and important tasks, and miss the rest.) Effective time management means to make conscious decisions.

> **NOTE** If you feel that you just don't have enough time to get everything done, you are right—and you have recognized one of the most important basic principles of time management. Next you need to continue making yourself aware of this fact and base your decisions on it. What is valuable enough for you to devote your precious time to?

Even if your place of work fits your strengths and personality, and you are motivated, there is no magic bullet that gives you more time. Every person has exactly 24 hours of time each day. Whether dishwasher or millionaire, head of state or university student, department manager or engineer—each day they all have the same amount of time available to them. And in all occupational groups, some don't get their work done and complain about a chronic lack of time, while others with the same responsibilities and workload are not only successful in their profession, but also find time for family, friends, hobbies, and social engagements. The amount of time somebody takes to complete his tasks depends on his responsibilities or his occupation only to a small degree (30 percent at most). What's most important is his ability to identify the tasks that have the largest positive influence and to consistently take care of them—and to be disciplined enough to take care of them, even when it's no fun at all; to stick with them consistently, no matter what is trying to distract you, interrupt you, or urgently squeeze in.

> *The main thing is to keep the main thing the main thing.*
> — STEPHEN COVEY

Focus on What Matters Most (the Pareto Principle)

Toward the end of the 19th century, Vilfredo Pareto discovered a recurring mathematical behavior for the distribution of riches among the population of his country. It was calculably unbalanced: 20 percent of the people owned 80 percent of the money.

This phenomenon also appears in other areas of life and was later applied to process optimization and time management (see Figure 2-1). A typical distribution pattern may look like this:

- 20 percent of the customers create 80 percent of the revenue.
- 20 percent of the product line yields 80 percent of the profits.
- We wear 20 percent of our clothes 80 percent of the time.

Generally speaking,

- 80 percent of the effects are caused by 20 percent of the causes.
- 80 percent of the results are caused by 20 percent of the efforts.

And so on. Of course, this rule can also be applied to the distribution of our time and the achieved results. Usually, 80 percent of the value creates results from 20 percent of the effort, and the remaining 20 percent of the value comes from the remaining 80 percent of the effort.

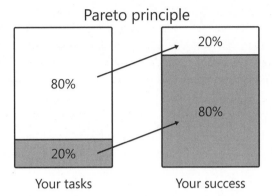

FIGURE 2-1 The Pareto principle: With 20 percent of the effort, you can frequently achieve 80 percent of the effect.

> **IMPORTANT** Concentrate on the few crucial items. To get ahead in life, you don't need to do absolutely everything or tackle all tasks. Filter out the most important things. Take the time you need by consistently saying "No" to other issues. Otherwise, you're in danger of getting distracted by the 80 percent of tasks that don't create much value but only keep you busy so that you miss the things that really matter. By focusing on the 20 percent instead, you'll actually achieve more by doing less.

Decide What's Most Important—Use the Eisenhower Matrix to Set Rough Priorities

General Dwight D. Eisenhower, who later became president of the United States, knew how important it is to set priorities. He developed a relatively simple but very helpful model that helped him run the United States. And just like us, he only had 24 hours available each day. His matrix has stood the test of time and has been used over and over for task planning. These days, it is even proving useful for processing email messages.

Find out which tasks influence your successes the most. To do so, it helps to set priorities. The Eisenhower Matrix combines the two criteria "important" and "urgent," creating four priority classes (see Figure 2-2). For your planning, you must analyze all pending tasks, compare them, and file them. Of course, much of what you are doing is important. But ask yourself: which tasks are more important than others? This way you can create a first rough ranking.

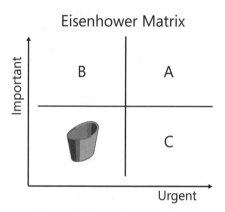

FIGURE 2-2 The first step is to set priorities with the Eisenhower Matrix.

- Tasks that are both important and urgent receive Priority A. You might call them crises: If you don't take care of them right away (depending on the time horizon and the complexity of the task, this can mean minutes, today, or this week), you end up with a bigger problem. (Examples are attending to important contract negotiations, dealing with the breakdown of a production machine, and finishing a project task that your colleagues need so they can continue working on the other tasks tomorrow.)

- B-Tasks are important, but not urgent. They are the key to effective time management—but unfortunately they are often neglected. Tasks that are not urgent but very important (B) receive a higher priority than purely urgent tasks because they are frequently responsible for producing important results or have a large influence on the entire performance. A good example is learning how to type with all 10 fingers in order to write your future email messages with twice the speed. One segment of the B-Tasks consists of the so-called "wandering tasks" (for example, a complex report for the board meeting or an elaborate proposal presentation for a large project), which become increasingly urgent if you don't look at them for a while and therefore eventually slide into the quadrant for A-Tasks.

- Extremely urgent tasks that, when compared to A-Tasks and B-Tasks are less important, get Priority C. Either they have to be taken care of soon (otherwise it's too late) or they need to be discarded right away to gain time for A-Tasks and B-Tasks. C-Tasks are also items that can be delegated easily but that you do yourself anyway, thus wasting time (you could have it done for you by someone else and have done something more important instead).

- D-Tasks are those that can be discarded most easily. Of all tasks, they are the least urgent and the least important. They are useless "escape tasks," and include the usual email messages with five people more than necessary on the Cc line, through which we often scroll aimlessly.

> **NOTE**
>
> Microsoft Outlook only recognizes three priority levels: high, normal, and low. You have three ways for dealing with them:
>
> - You can discard D-Tasks altogether without making notes.
>
> - You can combine C-Tasks and D-Tasks under the *low* priority.
>
> - You use an additional field for setting priorities. For example, some users divide the Eisenhower Matrix further into A1 to A4, and so on, up to D4, and simply add these letters to the subject line of the task. Others create categories and filter the view for them when necessary. We will use a new field for more detailed prioritizing of tasks in the day planner (see "Fine-Tune Your Priorities with the 25,000 $ Method," later in this chapter).

Say "No!" More Often—and Therefore "Yes!" to What's Important to You

Become aware that you will never have enough time to do everything you could do and everything others expect of you. Make sure you use your time for what's most important to you and gets you closer to your goals. You can only gain the time to do this by saying "No" to the less important items and omitting them.

Learn to give precedence to B-Tasks before C-Tasks and D-Tasks, and to sacrifice or discard those in favor of B-Tasks. You can save yourself a lot of stress and will generally produce better results. You will also feel that you have better control over your own time.

- Remember: Importance and urgency are two completely different issues. Important items get you closer to your goal, whereas urgent items require your immediate attention—but are they really worth it?

- Keep the right-of-way rule in mind: Importance before urgency. Not everything that's urgent must truly be done. Only this way will you avoid falling prey to the "dictatorship of urgency." The danger is that you might get bogged down in too many urgent but relatively unimportant activities.

Write Down Your Plans

"He who plans a lot falls under the tyranny of his own schedule." "Sometimes it's too much hassle to write everything down. Why not just do it right away? And besides, I don't want to be tied down. Written plans kill any kind of spontaneity." Such arguments are common, but they are not true. If you plan well, you actually make time for unplanned items and creativity.

> **IMPORTANT**   Planning is the best way to escape from the behavior pattern of just reacting, and to get the most important things done in time so that you can avoid a crisis. You can divide your time more freely and gain back control over your day.

Writing down your plans pays off:

- You will always remember the important things and won't forget them any longer: Just look at your plan and they'll be there.

- Planning gives you the freedom to use your brain power for concentrating on the current task or for being creative instead of always trying to remember things you must not forget.

- Written plans act as contracts with yourself and create obligations.

- You are more likely to take care of things.

- Planning makes you more accountable to partners who work as a team with you (see Chapter 5, "How to Schedule Meetings So They Are Convenient, Effective, and Fun").

■ Being accountable is a big step toward finishing tasks, to stop postponing and starting to do the stuff that gets you results.

■ Only a written plan gives you the possibility to look back and check what you did. You can find out why you got a lot less done than you had intended. Did you give preference to items with lower priority? Did you take noticeably longer than you had imagined (is there anything you can improve in order to complete such tasks more quickly, or is it more realistic to allow for more time in the future)? This is the basis for optimizing your way of working: reality checks, improvement potential, and learning about problems and their causes and getting rid of them.

TIP   Write down all tasks, appointments, and phone numbers/contact addresses immediately in Outlook or your smartphone. This way you stay on top of any situation and can focus on the essential. Your mental capacity is much too precious to waste on issues your computer can take care of. Write your plans down. This way, you can use your brain power for the most important things!

Use Task Lists to Plan Flexibly and Effectively

Outlook has great ways of helping you with your written plans for appointments and tasks. You can enter tasks even weeks before they are due. With the sorting and filtering functions of Outlook, you can reduce the displayed tasks to show only those that are due today or those that are pending for a certain project, and you can arrange them according to priority so you can get a quick overview.

However, working with tasks successfully requires a bit more strategy and consideration than just writing everything into a calendar, and of course it takes a little work and practice. In this chapter and the next two chapters, we will take the required steps together: we will cover the basics of working with tasks, priorities, setting up views, filters, weekly planners, categories and groups, daily planners, block building, Productivity Hours, the 25,000 $ Method, and the processing of task lists. This will provide you with a time-tested and (once you get used to it) relatively simple, flexible, and at the same time highly effective system for arranging your task lists according to your priorities and thus giving you a way to take control over the time available to you.

Tasks vs. Appointments

Make sure you differentiate between appointments and tasks:

- An appointment is bound to a fixed time window. It answers the question "When exactly will it happen?"

- A task, on the other hand, answers to the question "What exactly will I do?" (or "How important is it?"); sometimes with a due date, sometimes even without any time aspect at all.

Therefore, an *appointment* (for example, a phone conference with five people or a dentist appointment) takes place exactly at the time for which it was planned. However, it makes no difference when you complete a *task,* as long as you do so before the due date. This makes you more flexible when planning tasks, and you can select them according to importance and project. In certain cases, it might make sense to "set an appointment with yourself" to complete a task. (In the next chapters, you will find out when this is a good option.)

Tasks in Outlook

You can create a new task very simply and quickly without having to click through a lot of menus: Press Ctrl+Shift+K and then enter the data into the Task form.

WORKING SYSTEMATICALLY

Robin Wood teaches classes for interns. This time he decides to approach everything more systematically: A month ago he had set up a task for planning his teaching units, which is due today and which he has completed on time. He has divided the topic into three teaching units and set up a separate task for the preparation of each unit (duration: approximately 20 to 45 minutes).

Of course, for this week he only needs to prepare this week's unit. Therefore, each week gets its own task with its own part of the topic. Classes take place on Wednesday mornings. He needs to prepare them the day before, which means the task is due each Tuesday. If Tuesday is booked up with appointments or he has some extra time earlier during the week, he can do the preparation earlier, for example on Monday.

This section provides a short introduction to the most important elements of the Task form. (Figure 2-3 shows the Microsoft Outlook 2010 form, which looks different than the one in Microsoft Office Outlook 2003, but the important functions, commands, and data fields are almost identical.)

- First of all, you need to select a meaningful subject; don't just type "call Mike," but also indicate the goal of the call. Keep the subject line short, no more than one line. You can add more details in the large note field in the lower part of the task form. Choose the first two or three words of the subject in such a way that you can immediately tell what it is about (and also judge its importance), how long it will take, and how much effort is required (for example "Prepare 1hr class").

- You can use the Start Date field if you can't start a task until a certain date or to set the beginning for larger tasks that last several days. However, don't overdo it at the beginning and start using the task list only for things you can take care of in one or two hours; if something takes longer, split it into several tasks. If you need to create complex project plans with dependencies between subtasks, it's better to use a specialized software, such as Microsoft Project.

  Because the Start Date and Due Date fields are connected, changing the start date automatically changes the due date as well—and this can be fatal, if it makes you miss an important handoff date simply because you decided to prepare every-thing one week before the due date instead of the originally planned two weeks and Outlook automatically moved your due date out by one week.

> **CAUTION** The Start Date field frequently leads to more work and problems than benefits. It's best to leave it empty and just work with the Due Date field. If you want to start working on a project one week before the handoff date, enter this day (one week before) into Due Date—the day on which you want to have the task in front of you and begin working on it.

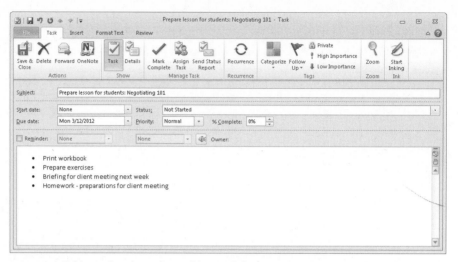

FIGURE 2-3 Robin teaches three classes this month for interns. In preparation, he has set up one task for each. The next class (which will take place on Wednesday) is due on Monday.

- Enter a due date into the Due Date field (in Outlook 2003, the Due Date field is located above the Start Date field; in Microsoft Office Outlook 2007 and Outlook 2010, it's the other way around). Just take a guess if you're not completely sure— it takes a while to get a feeling for setting a date, and you can still change it later. Feel free to set an earlier due date for a B-Task that isn't due until a few months from now or isn't due at all, if you want to take care of this task earlier. If next week is already fully booked, this week is still relatively open, and you can start on a task early, simply move the due date into this week. As part of the weekly planning process (Chapter 3, "How to Gain More Time for What's Essential with an Effective Week Planner") and the daily planning process (Chapter 4, "How to Make Your Daily Planning Work in Real Life"), we will refine what exactly you take care of and when. For example, you might set tomorrow as a due date for an A-Task (high priority) as well as for a B-Task (normal priority). This means that the A-Task isn't only as important as the B-Task, but it is also more urgent (making it A instead of another B). So if you only have time for one task tomorrow, you will take care of the A-Task and postpone the B-Task.

- Try to estimate the *priority* according to the Eisenhower Matrix from the beginning. Start by always setting it to low. If the task is part of your most important tasks, set it to normal. If it is also very urgent, set it to high.

■ For a larger task that you can't work on in one go, you can use the % Complete field to record how far you have gotten. However, it's easy to get confused this way or to drag out half-finished tasks (though the field is useful for tracking the status of larger tasks you have delegated). You should therefore initially divide bigger tasks into partial tasks of one to two hours. Enter them as individual tasks and complete them one at a time. You can also (or alternatively) add information into the Status field, such as "Waiting for someone else" or "Deferred" (for now). These fields are connected with each other and connected to a small check box in the task list: If you select the check box, Outlook sets % Complete to 100 and Status to Completed.

TIP   You can filter or group your task list according to any of these fields, for example to display all tasks that contain the value *Waiting for someone else* in the Status field and *start next month*. (You will learn more about filtering later in this chapter, in "Use Filters to Clean Up Your Views," and in Chapter 3.)

■ *Categories* (assigned via the Categorize button) are a very useful feature. We'll explain them in detail in Chapter 3. (In Outlook 2003, you can find the corresponding button as well as the categories text box in the lower-right corner below the large note field.)

■ In the large note field in the bottom part of the Task form, you can enter additional details, such as bullet points for performing the task. You can also insert copies of documents here that are related to the task. (In Outlook 2010/Outlook 2007, go to the Insert tab and select Attach File from the Include group. In Outlook 2003, go to the Insert menu and select File.) You can add another Outlook element—for example, a copy of an email message related to the task—directly by using the Outlook Item command button from the Include group on the Insert tab (in Outlook 2003, you need to go to the Insert menu and select Item). If you open the task again later, you can directly view the associated inserted files and email messages simply by double-clicking the file name in the note field. In Outlook 2010 and Outlook 2007, the text editor functions you know from Microsoft Word are available as a text editor in the note field. The Format Text tab allows you quick access to numberings, lists with multiple levels, quick format templates, and colorful highlighting to create clear and easy-to-read notes. You can use the Review tab to access proofing tools, or Start Inking to insert handwritten notes and sketches on tablet PCs.

How to insert links to files instead of copies

If you want to insert a very large file without taking up too much space in your Outlook Inbox, or if you always want to make the latest version of a file available from the Outlook task (for example, a Microsoft PowerPoint file you have stored on your local file system, which you will edit a few more times before starting the task), you can simply insert a link to the file instead of the file itself.

1. Open the task.

2. Go to the **Insert** tab and click **Attach File** in the **Include** group (Outlook 2003: the **File** command on the **Insert** menu).

3. Find and select the file you want in the **Insert File** dialog box.

4. Click the arrow to the right of the **Insert** button.

5. In the menu that now opens, select **Insert as Hyperlink** (see Figure 2-4).

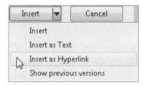

FIGURE 2-4 To save space, insert a link instead of a file.

You can also insert email messages and files into appointments (for example, a PDF file with an e-ticket and flight data) and into contact entries (for instance, driving directions).

The Text Editor in Outlook 2010/Outlook 2007

If you open a task (or email message, appointment, or contact entry) in its own window by double-clicking or using Ctrl+Shift+K, the editor in Outlook 2010/Outlook 2007 will be displayed. It offers you various advanced functions.

The Insert Tab

Apart from inserting files, elements (in the Include group), and hyperlinks (in the Links group), you can now take advantage of many additional functions from Word 2010/Microsoft Office Word 2007 by simply clicking the Insert tab in Outlook. The Quick Parts (in the Text group) and the tables are especially useful. If you are looking for the Paste command from the old Edit menu (to insert the Microsoft Office Clipboard content), it is now located on the Format Text tab, in the Clipboard group. (The Ctrl+V key combination still works.)

Select frequently used long words, sentences, and paragraphs (for example, by dragging over the text or triple-clicking the paragraph). In the Text group on the Insert tab, click Quick Parts and, on the menu that appears, select Save Selection To Quick Parts Gallery. You can now enter a name for the Quick Part and select several other options (for example, for dividing your Quick Parts into categories such as promo email messages, meeting invitations, and more). From now on, you can insert the text that has been saved in this manner by clicking Quick Parts (in the Text group on the Insert tab) in the current message or in the note field of the task, appointment, or contact.

The editor also works for tables and Quick Tables (like the Quick Parts just described, except that you insert a complete table with all its content, instead of text). When preparing a meeting, you can set up a standard checklist as a Quick Table (one column with preparation steps, such as "review documentation," "order lunch," and similar; and next to it a column in which you enter an x for a completed step). Whenever you are preparing a meeting, seminar, customer visit, interview, and so on, you can simply click Insert/Table/Quick Tables and select the entry you have just created to insert your complete checklist.

The Format Text Tab

The Format Text tab allows you to remove all text formatting in the note field of a task, an appointment, a contact, or an email message (Delete Formatting—the eraser icon in the Font group); to highlight text in color (as with a marker pen); to change the text color or font size; and much more with one quick click. Some of these features have already been around in the Format menu and on the Format toolbar, but many new features have been added; for example, styles and outlines (lists with multiple elements).

Listing all the functions of the Outlook editor would take much more space than we have available in this book. We'll therefore conclude this editor overview with two functions that help you when entering text in multiple languages and save you many mouse clicks if you work intensively with text formatting.

Format Text with Fewer Mouse Clicks: Take Advantage of the Mini Toolbar

If you select text in an email message or in the note field of an element by using the left mouse button (or by double-clicking or triple-clicking), a barely visible (almost completely transparent) bar with buttons on it appears to the right or left above the selected text. Move the mouse pointer a bit to the left or right toward this bar to make it completely visible. You now have the most frequently used text formatting commands at your disposal, right next to your selected text, and can access them with just one click.

In Outlook 2007, you may need to enable this Mini Toolbar first (unless your IT department has done so for you): Click the Office button (the round button with the Office logo in the upper-left corner of the default Task form) and then on the Editor Options button in the lower-right corner. This gets you to the Editor Options dialog box in the Popular category. Select the Show Mini Toolbar On Selection check box and click OK.

Take Advantage of the Multilingual Spelling Checker and the Foreign Language Dictionary in Outlook 2010

Here Outlook 2010 looks very different from Outlook 2007. If you are using Outlook 2007, see the next section.

On the Review tab of a task (or an appointment, contact, or email message) that is open in its own window, you get access to the thesaurus and the foreign language dictionaries. In Outlook 2010, you are working with Word as your (seamlessly integrated) editor for the individual Outlook elements. You can take advantage of Word's multilingual spell-checker not only when writing email messages, but also when you have inserted a large amount of text into the note field of an element (for example, for text that contains both English and German sections). If you want, while you are writing, Outlook can underline text that was not found in the dictionary. If you want to switch the spelling checker on or off or customize the AutoCorrect options that operate while you are writing text, click the File tab and select Options. In the Outlook Options dialog box that opens, click the Mail category on the left and then the Editor Options button (very close to the upper-right corner). On the left side, you can now choose between Display (options), Proofing (options), and Advanced (options) for the editor. Don't get confused, because from the menu path it sounds like you only change the option for email messages—the settings you specify here also apply to task note fields, appointments, and contacts.

In older versions of Outlook, the Tools/Research command leads (after several clicks) to translation and formatting support for selecting a foreign language dictionary or thesaurus. In Outlook 2010, you can perform a lookup much more easily and quickly: Select a word (for example, by double-clicking it) in the note field of an element (a task, appointment, or contact opened in its own window) or in the text of an email message. Go to the Review tab and retrieve the respective dictionary either in the Proofing group via Thesaurus or in the Language group via Translate. With Language/Translate/Choose Translation Language, you can select the target language with just one click (or disable the function), and from that moment on always display a translation when you point to a word for more than one second. After a while, the translation disappears—if you need it again, simply point to a different word and then back to the original word. The translation is only shown if you have mapped the text to a language different than the specified target language. (For example, if you are writing in English, and the language for the translation is set to English as the target language, you won't see a translation.)

Take Advantage of the Multilingual Spelling Checker and the Foreign Language Dictionary in Outlook 2007

Outlook 2007 looks very different from Outlook 2010 here. If you are using Outlook 2010, please read the previous section.

In a task (or appointment, contact, or email message) that you have opened in its own window, you will see a rather Spartan-looking group called Proofing with the Spelling (Spelling & Grammar) command at the right end of the Task tab. If you click the Spelling button arrow , you get access to the thesaurus and foreign language dictionaries. In Outlook 2007, you are working with Word as your (seamlessly integrated) editor for the individual Outlook elements. You can take advantage of Word's multilingual spelling checker not only when writing email messages, but also when you have inserted a large amount of text into the note field of an element (for example, for text that contains both English and German sections). If you want, while you are writing, Outlook can underline text that was not found in the dictionary. If you want to switch the spelling checker on or off or customize the AutoCorrect options that operate while you are writing text, click the Office button (in the upper-left corner of the default Task form), click the Editor Options button on the lower-right, and then select the Proofing category on the left side. Don't get confused because the Editor Options dialog box only mentions the content of Outlook email messages—the settings you specify here also apply to task note fields, appointments, and contacts.

In older versions of Outlook, the Tools/Research command leads (after several clicks) to translation and formatting support for selecting a foreign language dictionary or thesaurus. In Outlook 2007, you can perform a lookup much more easily and quickly: Select a word (for example, by double-clicking it) in the note field of an element or in the text of an email message. Go to the Task tab, click the Spelling button arrow, and retrieve the dictionary you want by using Thesaurus or Translate from the shortcut menu. With the Translation QuickTip command (from the same menu), you can select the target language with just one click (or disable the function), and from that moment on always display a translation when you point to a word for more than one second. After a while, the translation disappears—if you need it again, simply point to a different word and then back to the original word. The translation is only shown if you have mapped the text to a language different than the specified target language. (For example, if you are writing in English, and the QuickInfo for Translation is set to English as the target language, you will not see a translation.)

Define Your Own Views (Outlook 2003, Outlook 2007, and Outlook 2010)

Being able to define your own views in Outlook is very helpful when you are working with tasks. You only enter each task once but are virtually defining different task lists for which Outlook selects the entries you want and hides the others. For example, you can choose to only display tasks that are due this week or today. With just one click, you can switch to only those tasks that are due for a particular product this month (see also "Filter and Group by Category" in Chapter 3). This way you can keep an overview of a large number of tasks, even if you have entered them weeks before their due date.

How to set up a new view

After you have defined a new view, you can display it with exactly the same criteria any time with one or just a few mouse clicks (see Figure 2-5).

1. From any task view in the main window of Outlook 2010, go to the **View** tab, click **Change View** (in the **Current View** group), and select **Manage Views**. In Outlook 2007, go to the **View** menu and choose **Current View/Define Views**. In Outlook 2003, go to the **View** menu and click **Arrange by/Current View/Define Views**.

2. In the dialog box that appears, you can use an existing view as a template by clicking the **Copy** button and then editing this view to your liking. If you don't want to use an existing view as a template, click **New**.

3. Give the view a new name (for example, **Due this week—unfinished**), keep the default setting for the **Type of view** as **Table**, and then click **OK**.

4. You can confirm the settings in the next dialog box by clicking **OK**, and choose **Apply View** to create the new view.

You can also keep the dialog box open and define the filters next (see the next section, "Use Filters to Clean Up Your Views").

Outlook 2010 enables the reading pane in the right part of the window by default for new views. It also shows comprehensive notes about a task as a preview without you having to open the task by double-clicking it—but this takes up a lot of space, which limits the space for displaying your entire task list. When working with email messages, the reading pane is useful for reading the whole message without opening it in a separate window. For tasks, however, the subject line should be enough to help you decide what to do. It's better to use the space for a larger view of your task list. Disable the reading pane on the View tab, in the Layout group, in the submenu of the Reading Pane button, by choosing Off (see Figure 2-6).

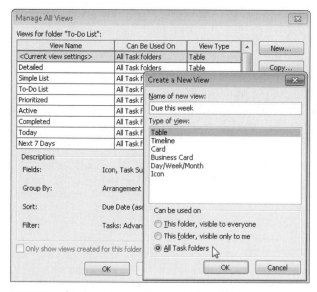

FIGURE 2-5 Create your own views to get a quick overview.

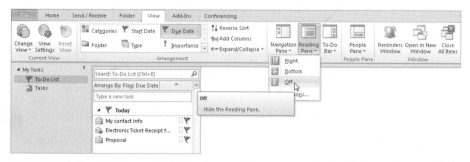

FIGURE 2-6 Outlook 2010 enables the reading pane in new views—hide it for the tasks.

Use Filters to Clean Up Your Views

Filter can help you clean up your views so that only certain tasks are shown. Only the tasks that meet the criteria established by you can pass through the filters.

How to set up a simple filter for your view

1. If the dialog box for customizing the view (from the last step for creating new views) is no longer open, or if you want to change a view some time after creating it, click **View Settings** in the **Current View** group on the **View** tab in Outlook 2010. In Outlook 2003 and 2007, simply click the **Customize Current View** link in the left part of the navigation pane to open the same dialog box.

2. Click the **Filter** button in the **Advanced View Settings** dialog box to open the Filter dialog box (see Figure 2-7).

3. Now you can specify the criteria. For tasks due this week, set the **Due** value in the **Time** list and the **This Week** value in the list next to it.

4. Close all open dialog boxes by clicking **OK**.

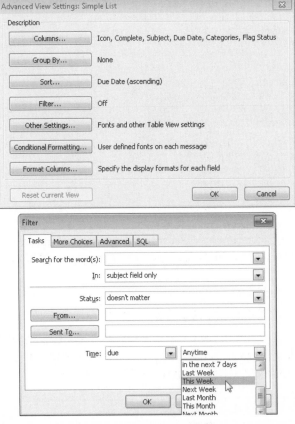

FIGURE 2-7 You can clean up your views with filters.

How to hide all completed tasks

1. Repeat steps 1 and 2 in the previous procedure for setting up a filter.

2. Click the **Advanced** tab (in the **Filter** dialog box, as shown in Figure 2-8).

3. Click the **Field** button. In the list of frequently used fields, select **Complete**.

4. In the now-activated **Condition** and **Value** lists, select the condition **equals** and the value **No,** and then click **Add to List**.

5. Close all open dialog boxes by clicking **OK**.

Now Outlook only displays tasks that are not completed yet. As soon as you set a task to 100 percent completed (or set the status to Completed or select the small Complete check box), the task is no longer visible in this view.

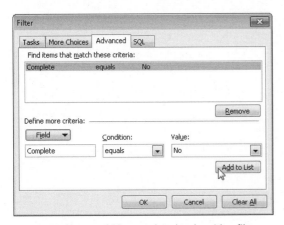

FIGURE 2-8 You can hide completed tasks with a filter.

In Chapter 3, you will learn about additional filter options, as well as the grouping of views as an alternative or supplement to filters, and you will also see how to remove filters.

Fine-Tune Your Priorities with the 25,000 $ Method

The 25,000 $ Method is optimally suited to further refining your planning after setting "raw priorities" with the Eisenhower Matrix first. It is an old time-management technique that is still as effective as it was 100 years ago—it just works!

THE 25,000 $ METHOD

After having been president of one of the largest corporations in the world—the United States Steel Corporation—Charles Michael Schwab took over Bethlehem Steel, which he took to the stock market in December of 1904. Bethlehem Steel later became the second largest steel corporation in the world. Charles Schwab hired Ivy Lee, a management consultant, as his personal coach. The fee agreement sounded fair: "Show me how I can make better use of my time. If your tips work, I'll pay you any fee you like within reasonable boundaries."

Ivy Lee gave him a piece of paper—unfortunately Outlook wasn't yet available back then—and told him: "Simply write down everything you need to get done tomorrow. After you have listed all the tasks, compare them according to priority. If tomorrow suddenly some machines became defective, bringing the whole production to a standstill, and you needed to take care of the problem immediately and would therefore only have time left for one single task from your list, which one would you choose? Which task would you decide on, if you could only do one task from the entire list? Write the number 1 in front of that task.

"Which one of the remaining tasks would you choose if you would still have enough time left to fit in just one more? Give this task the number 2. And so on until you have established a priority ranking for the entire list. Tomorrow, start with task number 1 as soon as you begin your work day. Do nothing else until you have finished this task. Then check your list again. Has anything changed in the meantime that caused your number 2 to move down in priority? Did something happen that's so important that you should take care of it immediately, thus making it your new number 2? If necessary, adjust your list and continue with number 2. Do nothing else until you have completed this task. Then take a short break and afterwards continue with number 3, and so on.

"Even if you didn't get everything done by the end of the day, it's no big deal. Such is life. But with this method, you have at least completed the most important tasks instead of leaving them sitting around—that's what really counts. The key to success it to do this daily: List your tasks and rank them according to their relative importance as you compare them with each other. Create a daily plan by deciding priorities, and stick with it. Written prioritization is also a very important step towards more self-discipline when it is implemented consistently. Take care of the most important tasks first and keep doing it as long as the priorities don't shift. Make this your daily habit. Try it for as long as you want. Once you are convinced of the effectiveness of this system, send me a check and decide for yourself how much this tip is worth to you."

A few weeks later, Charles Schwab sent a check for $25,000 to Ivy Lee. Later he said that this was the most profitable lesson he had learned in his entire management career.

(From *The Time Trap* by Alec Mackenzie, Amacom, 1972)

How to define a 25,000 $ view

After you have set up a view (as explained earlier in "Define Your Own Views"), you can use it for planning with the 25,000 $ Method. Insert a custom field called, for example, 25,000 $ (see Figure 2-9).

1. Switch to the new task view in Outlook 2010 by going to the **View** tab. In the **Current View** group, click the **Change View** button and click the name of the new view (for example, 25,000 $) in the submenu. In Outlook 2007/Outlook 2003, click the name of the view in the left part of the navigation pane (below the **Current View** headline).

2. Right-click one of the column headers of the view, such as **Due**, and select **Field Chooser** from the shortcut menu.

3. In the **Field Chooser** window, click the **New** button.

4. Type **25,000 $** into the **Name** field, select **Number** in the **Type** list, and click **OK**.

> **TIP**
> When creating the new field, make sure to select the Number option from the Type list—otherwise the task with the entry 12, for example, will later be sorted between 1 and 2 (or you would need to enter 01, 02 and so on each time). The Number type makes sure the sorting is correct.

5. Drag the **25,000 $** field from the **Field Chooser** window next to one of the other column headers in the task view; for example, next to **Task Subject** or **Subject** (see Figure 2-9).

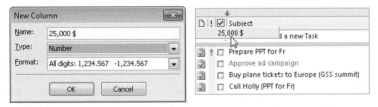

FIGURE 2-9 Select the Number type for the field, and insert the field into the view as a new column.

TIP

You can very easily get rid of any fields shown in your view if you don't need them: Drag any superfluous fields such as Start Date and Reminder Time from the view into the Field Chooser window. Now the fields are no longer shown—if necessary you can drag them back from the field chooser into the view any time in order to show them again.

6. Close the **Field Chooser** by clicking the **Close** button.

7. Finally, sort the view in ascending order according to the newly inserted column: Click once on the **25,000 $** column header.

How to use your 25,000 $ view for refining your priorities

You can now work with your new view and begin refining your initial rough Eisenhower Matrix classification to create an absolute task order (see Figure 2-10).

1. Imagine: If nothing went according to plan and you only had time for one of your tasks today, which one would you definitely want to get done? For this task, enter the number **1** into the **25,000 $** field.

   As soon as you click a different task, the task you just marked with 1 is moved down. Outlook will later sort task number 2 behind it (one position below). All tasks without a number are displayed at the top of the list.

2. Which of the remaining unnumbered tasks is now the most important? This task gets the number **2**, and so on.

NOTE

By the way, your other task views will not be changed by your 25,000 $ field and will behave just as before, independent of the values you have entered into the field.

3. Maybe you are now wondering which task might be the next most important one. Don't waste too much time on guesswork. Just make a decision. There is no "100 percent correct" solution. You are just trying to establish an approximate task ranking by comparing importance. Practice makes perfect. Maybe you will notice

a task and immediately realize that it is the least important of all the remaining unnumbered tasks, and you want to put it at the last position right away. Which number should it get? In this case, you don't even have to care about the total number of tasks, simply give the task the number **99** (assuming you don't have 150 tasks listed for today...). The next, slightly less unimportant task gets the number **98**, and so on. Even if you only have 17 tasks for today, Outlook will still sort them correctly this way.

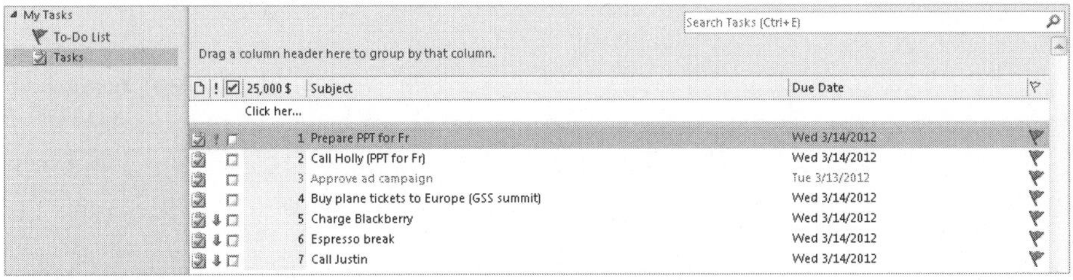

FIGURE 2-10 Create a 25,000 $ view to decide which task comes next.

We will further refine the 25,000 $ Method as part of the daily planning process (see Chapter 4), but before we get there, we will first tackle weekly planning (see Chapter 3).

OTHER WAYS TO USE THE 25,000 $ METHOD

If you like detailed planning, this method is also well suited to an extensive prioritization of your task list for the whole week or for a particularly large project, for example. As previously explained, you can create additional views (for example, "25,000 $ Project A") and retrieve them with just one click. Insert a 25,000 $ field into these views as well, with a correspondingly detailed name (for example, "Proj. A 25,000 $ Prio"). This way you retain an overview even with complex situations: One task can be number 1 regarding the project, number 5 regarding the week, and number 2 regarding the current day. This tip is for those readers who want to delve deeper into the details of planning, after having learned about the tips and simple methods just described. All others should remember not to go overboard with the planning, otherwise the positive effect might reverse itself. Especially in the beginning, one 25,000 $ view is enough (preferably just for the day). Keep it simple.

The To-Do List—View Tasks from Multiple Folders and Email Messages at the Same Time

Outlook 2010/Outlook 2007 helps you eliminate the two biggest hurdles when you are working with multiple task folders. Outlook now displays reminders/alarms for tasks regardless of which folder they are located in. (In previous versions, alarms were only displayed for tasks in the default *Task* folder.) You can finally view all tasks in all task folders simultaneously, and not just the tasks in a particular folder. This really helps you keep track.

If you go to the Tasks module in Outlook and, for example, work with different views (see "Define Your Own Views," earlier in this chapter), you only see the tasks of the current task folder you have selected right now (the To-Do List will show all tasks from all folders instead). Just like for email messages, you can create new and therefore multiple folders for tasks (see Chapter 1, "How Not to Drown in the Email Flood")—for example, to individually adjust access rights to your tasks for your team for each folder and thus for all tasks therein (one folder just for you, one with read permissions for your whole team, and a third task folder you only share with your administrative assistant). Or you could use folders to have an additional level for sorting and dividing your tasks (other than the categories)—for example, private and professional tasks that pertain to a particular project/product and are then grouped by category within the folder. However, working with several task folders can easily lead to confusion, and therefore continues to be a mere matter of taste—only occasionally it can be quite useful. In general, we recommend that you work with one task folder only (and hide the tasks you don't need by using filters).

If you go to the My Tasks pane in the Outlook tasks and click the red flag with the word To-Do List next to it (directly above the list of possible views in the navigation pane in Outlook 2007, or directly below the ribbon in Outlook 2010), Outlook displays all tasks from the folders listed below. You will also see all email messages you have flagged for follow-up as task elements (with a more or less red flag depending on the due date; see Chapter 1). The To-Do Bar on the right side of the screen (see Chapters 1 and 4) also displays email messages marked as tasks and the tasks from all of your task folders, just like the To-Do List.

| NOTE | You can only see the marked email messages in the current task view if you have selected the To-Do List instead of an individual task folder. If you only want to see the tasks from a certain folder, go to the My Tasks pane and click the name of the folder. |

You Try It

1. Think about which tasks really get you ahead. Which tasks would turn out to be extremely profitable because they save time and money or increase efficiency in other areas (for example, creating email folders, cleaning up the inbox, marketing/website improvements, or continued education)?

2. Create a B-Task for at least one such activity (something you've been meaning to do for a long time—for example, cleaning up your email inbox) and set a realistic due date for it within the next three weeks.

3. If you are not working with Outlook tasks yet, start managing your task lists in Outlook. Enter 20 tasks (each with a meaningful subject) that you want to or have to get done next week. (If you are already using tasks, display the ones due next week.)

4. Set the Priority for all to Low. Look for no more than three A-Tasks and change their Priority to High. Look for no more than five B-Tasks and change their Priority to Normal. Complete these tasks before all others (on the due day at the very latest). The fewer tasks you rate as more important or more important and urgent than others, the higher the probability that you will actually complete them all during the week.

5. Sort the task list by priority, display only the tasks due this week (by using a filter), and hide all completed tasks.

6. Create the 25,000 $ view for Today that only shows tasks due today, insert the 25,000 $ field, and sort by this column.

CHAPTER 3

How to Gain More Time for What's Essential with an Effective Week Planner

IN THIS CHAPTER, YOU WILL

- Use categories.

- Track important categories.

- Filter and group by category.

- Apply the Kiesel Principle.

- Prepare a task list for a week.

- Plan tasks and appointments in Outlook.

"I Don't Have Time for That!"

UNLIKE NEXT month, the next week is close enough already to plan appointments and tasks specifically and realistically. At the same time, a week is long enough to allow you to keep your balance by including tasks for all areas of life. A day can get much too short very soon if something goes wrong (more about that in Chapter 4, "How to Make Your Daily Planning Work in Real Life"). A week, in contrast, is long enough to make up for a day plan that has gotten out of control or was just too full. You can use the week as a period for comprehensive planning. And you can effectively accomplish this task by planning in Microsoft Outlook.

Did you set your priorities, but have certain B-Tasks that still don't have a due date and therefore continue to remain undone? Does your day-to-day business leave hardly any room for the task list?

ROBIN HAS NO TIME AGAIN...

Robin Wood has no energy and feels totally exhausted. The persistent summer heat and all the traveling.... When he was younger, he had a much easier time dealing with all that. He used to go running regularly and played basketball. His colleague, Holly Holt, is on a wellness trip these days and maintains that all is connected. He should start doing exercise, she says. That way he'd become fitter again and would also be able to work better. "It would make just as much sense for you as taking a typing class, considering how much you type," she quips. Easy for Holly to say! In any case, he has no time left for that right now. Maybe next year....

His department has 152 customers—10 of whom make up 56 percent of the revenue—and they are very satisfied. Back in February, he resolved to look for ways to support those 10 even better and to provide additional individual solutions. After all, this not only means progress for his customers, but also more revenue and profit for his department. But none of that has to happen today, and during daily business there just isn't any time left for it right now.

He really likes telephone conferencing, though, which is easy to do from the conference room next door with his wireless headset—less traveling, plus such talks are usually better organized and more quickly ended than old-fashioned meetings. His wife, on the other hand, recently complained that conference calls are obviously becoming his preferred and soon-to-be only mode of communication with her, too....

What Really Matters—and Why Does It Continue to Remain Undone?

Unlike when tackling your daily email or your daily planning, where something always remains undone in the evening, the problems with weekly planning are not immediately obvious. Many people don't do any weekly planning at all: They use plans for the year or the quarter (if any), and only for their professional life. Whatever you enter weeks or months in advance will show up in Outlook in the month, week, and day view anyway. So why plan the week separately?

Weekly planning is the key to achieving long-term goals, a balanced life, and the completion of your B-Tasks, even if they don't have a due date. If they remain undone for an indefinite period of time, effective weekly planning is the best way to counteract this problem. If, for example, you continue to neglect your private life or your health because of your profession, or if you only pursue short-term plans and goals, use weekly planning to also include private and long-term goals.

Even to workaholics who have decided to make their career their purpose in life, the results of the scientific studies in this area still apply: People who exercises (run, swim, dance, and the like) three times a week and have a balanced personal life with time for friends and family not only achieve more per hour but also more in the long run. This means that they actually get more done in a 55-hour week than an out-of-balance workaholic gets done in a 70-hour week. These people are also more creative, work more reliably, and have an easier time dealing with crises.

Let's Get Started and Change This!

In this chapter, you'll discover:

- How to use Outlook categories to sort all your tasks by project or work/life area.
- How to come up with your own category system and thus keep an overview of the week.
- How to balance the different areas of your life.
- How to plan your professional and private life together.
- How to use key tasks to get ahead in all areas on a continuous and long-term basis.
- How to block times in your calendar for these key tasks so that you will regularly find time for things that are important to you, even without an urgent due date and during stressful times.

> **TIP** ✓ Set aside approximately 20 to 30 minutes each week to do your weekly planning. You will notice that it will pay off with more balance, contentment, improved performance, and long-term successes (not just professionally) after a few months.

Take Advantage of Categories to Combine Tasks

Before showing you how to plan your week with the help of categories and the Kiesel Principle, we will cover the basics of categories first. Categories are very useful for keeping track of multiple tasks in different areas and to retain a balance and an overview.

They help you assign "themes" or "keywords" to tasks. This is where they are the most helpful. After you are comfortable with them, you can also use them for other Outlook entries, such as appointments. You will find examples for categories later in this chapter, in "Set Up Your Own Category System."

Gain Perspective with Categories

Before we begin filtering and grouping by category, let's take a look at how to assign and select categories with the help of a few examples. In Microsoft Office Outlook 2007, the category system was extended with new functions, and in many instances the handling (for example, the techniques for assigning categories) was changed. But the strategies for working with categories remain the same in all Outlook versions. However, the steps shown for Microsoft Outlook 2010 and Outlook 2007 on the next pages are different for Microsoft Office Outlook 2003. Also, in Outlook 2003 not all additional functions are available (such as Quick Click and customizable shortcut keys for assigning individual categories). We will therefore show you the category system for Outlook 2010/ Outlook 2007 first, and later the category system for Outlook 2003 (see "The Category System in Outlook 2003: How to Assign Categories" later in this chapter). From the "Set Up Your Own Category System" section onward, we will explain practical strategies for working with categories that are the same in all versions. If you are working with Outlook 2003, please skip the next few pages and continue reading with "The Category System in Outlook 2003: How to Assign Categories."

In Outlook 2010/Outlook 2007, you can no longer click in a table view or just start typing in the Categories field of a task (or appointment or contact) in its open window or in the corresponding column of a table view to assign a category as you used to be able to do in previous versions. But in newer versions of Outlook, the use of customized category lists has become a lot easier.

How to Assign Categories to Tasks

The categories are no longer located in the lower-right corner of the default Task form—the corresponding command is now represented by a square with four colors (Categorize), which is located in the Tags group (Outlook 2010) or Options group (Outlook 2007) on the Task tab (see Figure 3-2, later in this section). By clicking this command button, you can assign new categories and change the currently assigned ones. (All Categories at the end of the list of names takes you to the category list, which we will cover in more detail later in this chapter.)

All assigned categories are now displayed directly above the task subject in the bar, which is colored according to the category.

In a list view of the tasks, right-click the Categories column in the row that belongs to a task to directly assign a new category from the list with just one click on the corresponding category name, or to remove a previously assigned category from the task.

"QUICK CLICKING" WITH THE MOUSE

If you right-click the Categories column, the Set Quick Click command is displayed in the shortcut menu (see Figure 3-1). Use this command to select your most frequently used category. You can then set this category directly by clicking the Categories column of the clicked task, or click again to remove it.

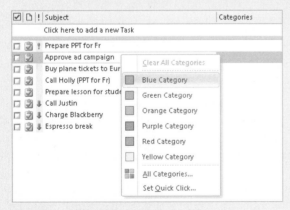

FIGURE 3-1 Assign categories to tasks with the right mouse button, or use Quick Click to do it with just one click in the Categories column.

How to Assign Categories in the Calendar

After you have opened an appointment (for instance, by double-clicking it) in its own window, click Categorize on the Appointment tab, in the Tags group (Outlook 2010, see Figure 3-2) or in the Options group (Outlook 2007), and select the category you want from the menu. All of the other steps (accessing the category list and viewing the assigned categories directly via the subject line, for example) are the same as for tasks.

In the Day/Week/Month view of your calendar, right-click an appointment and select Categorize from the shortcut menu.

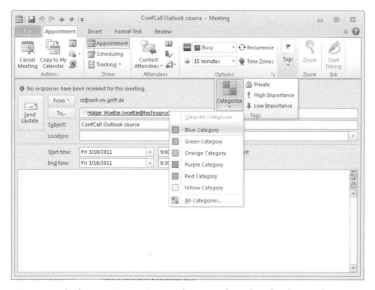

FIGURE 3-2 Assign a category to appointments by using the Categorize command in the Tags group.

How to Assign Categories to Email Messages

In your Outlook 2010/Outlook 2007 inbox (and other email folders), you can now assign categories to email messages quickly and easily via the corresponding column—just like for tasks, as described previously.

After you have opened an existing email message (for instance, by double-clicking it) in its own window for editing, you can find Categorize (for received email messages) directly on the Message tab, in the Tags group (Outlook 2010) or in the Options group (Outlook 2007). However, if you are in the process of writing a new email message, go to the Message tab and click the small arrow (the so-called "dialog box launcher") to the right of the Tags or Options group name to open the Properties dialog box (Outlook 2010) or Message Options dialog box (Outlook 2007).

You can find the Categories button in the lower-left corner of this dialog box (and a list of currently assigned categories next to it).

The Master Category List in Outlook 2010/Outlook 2007

Unlike in the previous versions of Outlook, the list is only initialized with the names of a few primary colors (Blue Category, Yellow Category, and so on). To assign a category, open the shortcut menu (just like previously described for tasks, appointments, and email messages) and select All Categories to open the master category list in the Color Categories dialog box. In this dialog box, you can select or clear the appropriate check box to add the category to the current entry or to remove it again. In Outlook 2010/Outlook 2007, you can directly edit the master category list by using the New button (see Figure 3-3) or, after selecting an already listed category name, by using the Rename and Delete buttons as well as the Color and Shortcut Key lists.

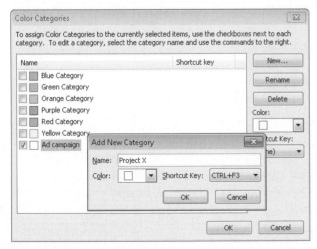

FIGURE 3-3 The master category list in Outlook 2010/Outlook 2007 allows you to assign colors and shortcut keys.

How to use shortcut keys to quickly assign your most important categories

You can assign shortcut keys from Ctrl+F2 through Ctrl+F12 to an existing category in the list by using the Shortcut Key list.

After you do so, you can use these key combinations to assign categories to a task you clicked in the list, a selected appointment, or an element opened in its own window. Pressing a shortcut key again removes the category from the element. The shortcut keys don't work when you are writing a new email message (only when opening a received mail), because they are caught by the editor and interpreted differently (for example, Ctrl+F2 would open the page view).

How to fill the list with your own categories

1. In the **Color Categories** dialog box, click the **New** button.

2. Type the name of the category you want into the **Name** field in the **Add New Category** dialog box.

3. If necessary, select a color and a shortcut key for your new category by clicking the lists, and then close the dialog box by clicking **OK**.

4. Repeat these steps for all additional categories you want to add.

5. Close the master category list by clicking **OK**. You can find examples for some of the categories in "Set Up Your Own Category System" later in this chapter.

How to revise the master category list

It's worthwhile to customize the displayed category list. This way you can later assign your own categories with just one click and don't need to scroll through long lists with lots of categories you don't need. If you want to keep the Blue, Yellow, Green, Purple, Orange, and Red default categories for coloring your appointments (see the next section), just leave them in the list. If you don't need those categories, it's best to delete them:

1. In your task list, right-click the row belonging to the task (it does not matter whether the mouse pointer is on the **Categories** column or another column), and then select **Categorize/All Categories** from the shortcut menu. If you have opened a task in its corresponding form (for instance, by double-clicking to open it), replace this step with a click on the **Categorize** button (in the **Tags** group in Outlook 2010 or the **Options** group in Outlook 2007) and select **All Categories** in the menu that appears.

2. Click the first category you don't need, unless it is already selected (for example, **Purple Category**), then click **Delete** (see Figure 3-4).

3. Repeat step 2 for all categories you don't need, and then close the master category list by clicking **OK**.

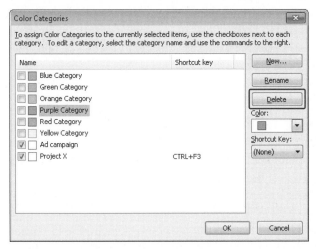

FIGURE 3-4 Delete entries you don't need from the master category list and add your own.

Keep Track of Your Most Important Categories by Using Colors

In Outlook 2010/Outlook 2007, entries that belong to a category automatically receive colors. Just a quick glance lets you know which category an entry belongs to without having to read the name; when you are skimming through task lists or email lists, you can gain a quicker overview this way.

How Outlook 2010/Outlook 2007 Displays Category Colors

If you have opened an element in its own window, the categories and the colored bars are displayed directly above the subject (or the headers of a new email message or the name of a contact). When you are writing a new email message, the categories are hidden in the Properties dialog box (Outlook 2010) or Message Options dialog box (Outlook 2007, see "How to Assign Categories to Email Messages" earlier in this chapter).

In table/list views (such as your task list or the email messages in your inbox), a colored square is displayed in the Categories column, followed by the category name. If an entry belongs to multiple categories, you will see all colored squares next to each other and, to the right of them, the category names. If the Categories column isn't wide enough, the information is truncated at the right border. First the names disappear, and if the column is quite small but has many categories, the squares furthest to the right disappear as well. The order is not alphabetical or hierarchical—whenever you assign a category, the category you assigned last is added on the left. In order to make a certain category appear on the very left (and therefore ensure its visibility in narrow columns), you need to remove it and assign it again, so that it gets displayed to the left of the previously assigned category.

In the To-Do bar (see Chapter 1, "How Not to Drown in the Email Flood" and Chapter 4) and in the Daily Task List, which is displayed below the appointments of the day in the calendar views (see Chapter 4), there is very limited space, and therefore the Categories column is so narrow that there is only enough space for one colored square. Unlike for an extremely narrow Categories column in other views, Outlook now doesn't restrict itself to the color that is furthest to the left, but instead condenses the color icons: Instead of squares, Outlook now shows two or three smaller bars next to each other. If there are four or more categories, you still only see the three most recently assigned colors.

How Outlook 2010/Outlook 2007 Colors Appointments According to Category

In the Day/Week/Month view of your calendar, an appointment has as a background the color of the category that was assigned to it last. Any additional categories assigned to it are displayed as small colored rectangles in the lower-right corner (only in the Day and Week view, not in the Month view). As soon as an appointment is assigned to any category—even if this category has the color None—the color belonging to the category overrides the results of all conditional formatting rules (Outlook 2010) or automatic formatting (Outlook 2007) rules for the Day/Week/Month view (see "How to automatically color your appointments by category," later in this chapter).

How to Avoid Problems with the Category Colors

In order to work with categories in a meaningful way, you need to think about a color system. Simply assigning a color to each category can easily lead to chaos, because the category assigned last determines the color. This makes it a pure game of chance whether you will be able to see the categories important to you in the currently set column width.

Just one thoughtlessly assigned category can be enough to ruin the result of conditional/automatic formatting for appointments. In Outlook 2010/Outlook 2007, you can use any criteria to automatically specify the color of an appointment in the Day/Week/Month view (see "How to Automatically Color Your Appointments" later in this chapter). For example, if you are constantly traveling between four different cities, you may want to color your external appointments according to the value entered in the Location field: green for Seattle, yellow for San Diego, red for Los Angeles, and purple for Denver. Or you can book meeting rooms while planning many meetings at short notice and therefore color all appointments red for which you have entered the Location value of *Still to book a room for*, and orange if you have used the abbreviation *ConfCa* for conference calls. As soon as you accidentally assign a category to such an appointment (even if this category does not have a color), the result of the conditional/automatic formatting is overridden; if you are just taking a quick glance, you might overlook the fact that you still need to book a room or that the appointment is an external appointment in a city far away from your office.

> **NOTE**   Outlook is not consistent with "colorless" categories (set with the None color): For example, if you are coloring an appointment red via a category and add a green category, the appointment is displayed in green. If you then add a category without a color, the appointment color stays green. However, if you add a category without color to an appointment that was colored yellow via conditional/automatic formatting, Outlook displays the appointment without a color (in the background color of the calendar) instead of yellow until you remove all categories from this appointment.

Here is how to avoid shooting yourself in the foot: If you want to color according to criteria that are not coded in categories but set the color via automatic/conditional formatting instead (see previous examples), your only option is to *not* assign any category to any of your appointments. As soon as just a few of your appointments have only a single (colorless) category, it will destroy the result of the conditional/automatic formatting. In order to take advantage of the automatic formatting, you must therefore do without categories for appointments. However, coloring via a category is usually easier to understand and quicker to set up than conditional/automatic coloring. For example, if you want to color according to projects, record the project for an appointment by category, and require each appointment to belong to only one project, simply remove the color of all your categories (assign the None color) and assign a color only to the individual project names. This way you will reliably recognize the associated project by its color, and another color can't accidentally override the project color.

The final option is manual coloring (for example, if that is what you are used to from the obsolete Label field in Microsoft Office Outlook 2002 and Outlook 2003): Assign the None color to all categories in your master category list. In addition to your already existing categories, now add the Red category, Blue category, and so on, each with the correct color (some color names are already available as categories by default if you haven't deleted them; see Figure 3-4 shown earlier in this chapter). This way you can use the categories to color-mark your appointments, tasks, and more, quickly and simply, without creating color chaos by accidentally assigning other categories for projects and other areas of your life.

KEEP YOUR COLORS ON TOP

If you are working with an extensive master category list, add a prefix to your color categories so that a particular category always appears at the top or at the bottom of the list and there aren't dozens of other categories between all of your color categories (see "Set Up Your Own Category System," later in this chapter). If you are editing the master category list in Outlook 2010/Outlook 2007, newly created categories usually appear at the end of the list initially. As soon as you close the list after editing, the list gets sorted alphabetically again.

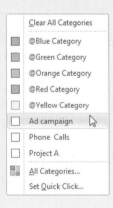

If you are using Outlook 2010/Outlook 2007, you can skip the next few pages and continue reading with "Set Up Your Own Category System." The rest of this section focuses on the category system in Outlook 2003.

The Category System in Outlook 2003: How to Assign Categories

1. In the task list, find the task to which you want to assign new/different categories.

2. Click in the **Categories** field belonging to this task (in the **Categories** column; see Figure 3-5).

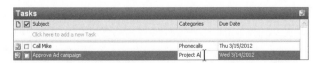

FIGURE 3-5 The Category field of a task allows direct editing.

3. The blinking cursor is now located in the **Category** field of the selected task entry, so you can start editing directly. If you want to assign multiple categories at the same time, separate them with a semicolon.

4. Click a different task or switch to a different view (such as the calendar) to have your changes saved automatically.

> **NOTE**   If you have opened a task in its Task form by double-clicking it, you will see the Categories field in the lower-right corner next to a button of the same name. Here you can also directly enter and edit categories.

The task's subject, due date, and so on, can be changed in the same manner. Also, individual fields for appointments shown in the list view (more about these in Chapter 4) can be quickly updated this way.

However, this manner of changing and assigning categories also has its disadvantages:

- With longer category names (such as "Supplier contract design template"), it can be a bit cumbersome to always enter the entire name.

- If you make a typo when entering a category name, the associated filters can no longer find the task, and when you later group by category, this entry appears in a separate group.

- As you begin working with categories, it will take you some time to get used to uniform names. You might enter "Meeting" one time and "Meetings" the next time, or "Conference" or "Conferences," which could lead to problems with filtering or grouping.

Alternatively, you can use the master category list to avoid these problems—and to assign categories more comfortably.

How to assign categories using the Outlook 2003 master category list

1. Right-click the row that belongs to the task (it doesn't matter whether the mouse pointer is in the **Categories** column or in another column), and then select **Categories** from the shortcut menu.

   If you have opened a task in the associated Task form instead, replace this step with a click on the **Categories** button (in the lower-right corner of the form).

2. Assign the category in the **Categories** dialog box by selecting the appropriate check box (see Figure 3-6); clear the check box to remove the assigned category.

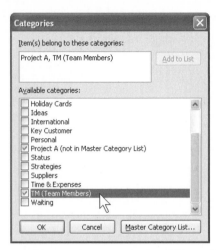

FIGURE 3-6 Assign categories by clicking—this avoids typos or mix-ups between singular and plural.

3. If a category is not in the list, you can add it in the **Item(s) belong to these categories** field. Any category you have added here can be inserted into the master category list by clicking **Add to list**.

4. Close the **Categories** dialog box by clicking **OK**.

How to clean up the Outlook 2003 master category list

It is worthwhile to customize the displayed list of categories. This way you will be able to assign your own categories later on with just one click and no longer need to scroll through a long list with lots of categories you don't really need.

1. Right-click the row that belongs to the task (it doesn't matter whether the mouse pointer is in the **Categories** column or in another column), and then select **Categories** in the shortcut menu. If you have opened a task in the associated Task form, replace this step with a click on the **Categories** button (in the lower-right corner of the form).

2. In the **Categories** dialog box, click the **Master Category List** button.

    If you haven't yet customized the master category list or your company hasn't pre-allocated the entries for you, you should first delete the default entries so that you can replace them later on with your own entries that better fit your way of working.

3. Click the first entry in the list.

4. While keeping the Shift key pressed, click the last entry in the list.

    Now all entries are selected and are displayed with a blue background (see Figure 3-7).

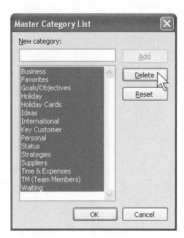

FIGURE 3-7 Delete unneeded entries from the master category list and add your own.

5. Click the **Delete** button.

How to fill the Outlook 2003 master category list with your own categories

1. In the **Master Category List** dialog box, type the name of the category you want into the **New Category** field.

2. Click the **Add** button.

3. If you have made a typo, select the entry and then click **Delete**.

4. Repeat these steps for all additional categories you would like to add.

5. Close all open dialog boxes by clicking **OK**.

You will find some examples for what your own categories could look like in the next section.

Set Up Your Own Category System

Take a quiet half an hour (ideally together with a colleague who has similar tasks and a similar way of working) to think about which categories work best for you. Set up a customized master category list, as described earlier. Try to define the categories in such a way that you can assign all your tasks without trouble.

In this section, you will find a few examples; apply any ideas that work for you, and add further categories of your own.

It almost always makes sense to create categories for your most important projects, functions in your company, and areas in your life (see Figure 3-8, and also "Seven Days, Seven Hats..." later in this chapter).

FIGURE 3-8 Create categories for your most important projects and areas of life.

> **NOTE** Don't allow the number of categories to get too large, so you can still keep track. Try to create no more than five to nine entries per area (for example, per project or function in your company). The fewer the better.

Maybe you can take care of certain tasks only at certain times of the day (such as calling colleagues in faraway time zones); set up the corresponding criteria for them.

You could also consider setting categories based on location. For example, if you work from different offices, are responsible for various construction sites or technical installations in buildings, usually purchase from several warehouses, are a weekend commuter, or due to a lot of business trips spend 10 to 20 hours per week on airplanes, it makes sense to add additional categories for certain locations (see Figure 3-9). Which tasks can you only take care of in the office, which ones just as well on the plane? (This might be even better for some tasks, because there are fewer opportunities for distraction and fewer people walking by than in your office.)

FIGURE 3-9 Take advantage of categories for times and places if it helps for your area of work and working method.

GROUP YOUR CATEGORIES

If you are working intensively with this "location principle" and assign a location to most of your tasks, you should also set up an Everywhere category, so you don't confuse or overlook tasks to which you have forgotten to assign a location and those that do not belong to any particular location.

To make sure times and locations don't get sorted alphabetically in between the other categories, you can use an "order sign" at the beginning (see Figure 3-9). Outlook lists categories with the same signs and letters sequentially and sorts them directly to the beginning or the end of the list. When your category list becomes more extensive, you can use these characters to sort thematically related categories you need to access frequently, to move them to the top of the list. The @ sign is displayed before numbers and letters. You can also use numbers to move several thematic groups in a particular order to a specific position in your list (for example, mark projects with a 1 in front, family obligations with a 2, and so on) Outlook sorts the exclamation point before the period, and the period before the @ sign. Entries with a *z* are moved to the bottom of the list—and those with two or more leading *z* characters even further down.

Are you managing several colleagues and keep taking care of tasks belonging to one particular colleague? Even though you can delegate tasks to this person, it might make sense to create corresponding categories (see Figure 3-10). Maybe you don't want to display them in a view grouped by "delegated to" but instead together with other categories, or maybe you want to see the delegated tasks together with those you take care of yourself and that belong to a particular colleague, his projects, or certain clients. Or you might be taking care of tasks for several of your managers without them sending you these tasks as delegated Outlook tasks.

FIGURE 3-10 Create categories for your team members and the most important mid-year goals.

It also makes sense to create categories for your most important long-term and medium-term goals, if they have a lot of subtasks and you want to keep the goal in view. Leave other goals out of the category list and limit yourself to no more than five so that the list does not get too full. (Or you may decide not to add goals as categories. You will learn more about goals in Chapter 6, "How to Use OneNote for Writing Goals, Jotting Down Ideas, and Keeping Notes.")

| CAUTION | Be careful with separator characters such as the comma (,) or semicolon (;) in category names, even though they seem practical, especially for goals as category names. Commas and semicolons trigger a separation in Outlook 2003, creating two categories (one with the first part of the name and the other with the second part). In Outlook 2010/Outlook 2007, commas and semicolons in category names are therefore no longer allowed. Permitted separators are periods (.), colons (:), and hyphens (-). |

Especially for freelancers, a category separation into activities often makes sense (see Figure 3-11).

FIGURE 3-11 Activity-related categories, such as this one for a freelance journalist can be useful for freelancers.

Take the suggestions you just read and combine them with your own ideas to build a category list that works for you. Don't use too many categories in the beginning. If you are working with categories for the first time, you shouldn't use more than 15. After you become accustomed to working with them and have ideas for further categories that would be practical for you, you can gradually add those over time.

Filter and Group by Category

Filtering and grouping helps you view only certain entries from your entire task list. By combining filters and groups, you can create more detailed views that allow you to get a quicker and better overview of the tasks that are relevant at the moment.

Filter Your Views

With filters, you only display entries that meet the filter criteria. You can choose between "category contains" and "category doesn't contain," which creates two practical filter types: Positive filters (which show only certain entries) and negative filters (which show everything but certain entries; in other words, it hides them).

With negative filters you can, for example, hide all tasks in the "A.M." view that have the category @PM assigned to them.

- If you are working in Los Angeles, it makes little sense to call your business partners in Singapore between 8:00 A.M. and 12:00 P.M., because it's the middle of the night there. Therefore, such entries should be hidden.

- Tasks without a specific "time category,"—for example, the next installment of your slide show preparation, which you can work on at any time—should continue to be displayed. Therefore, a positive filter for the @AM category would make little sense—not only would it remove the tasks planned for later, but also all those that have no time assigned to them, such as a task that you can take care of at any time.

How to define positive filters for categories

1. Open any task view, right-click one of the column headers (such as **Due date**), and select **View Settings** (or **Customize Current View**, in the versions before Outlook 2010) in the shortcut menu. Alternatively, you can click **View Settings** in the **Current View** group on the **View** tab in Outlook 2010. In Outlook 2007/ Outlook 2003, you can also click the **Customize Current View** link in the navigation pane on the left.

2. Click the **Filter** button in the **Advanced View Settings** dialog box.

3. Click the **More Choices** tab, and then click the **Categories** button in the **Filter** dialog box (see Figure 3-12).

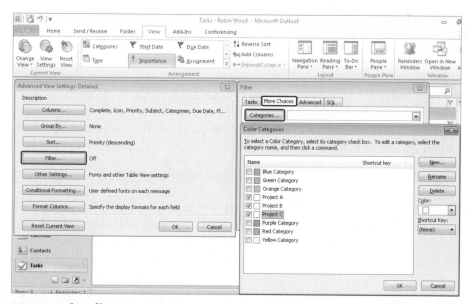

FIGURE 3-12 Set a filter to see only those tasks that are assigned to a project.

4. Select the check boxes of the categories you want to display (for example, all of your projects).

5. Close all open dialog boxes by clicking **OK**.

Your view now only shows those tasks that are mapped to a certain category (in the example, all of your tasks that belong to one of your most important projects).

HOW TO REMOVE A FILTER

If you made a mistake when defining a filter (especially if it contains other criteria in addition to the categories) and have lost track, or if it starts getting a bit "scary" because you suspect that the tasks you actually wanted to see were filtered out as well, you can just remove the filters specified for the current view.

1. Go to any task view, right-click one of the column headers, and select **View Settings** (or **Customize Current View**, in the versions before Outlook 2010) in the shortcut menu. Alternatively, you can click **View Settings** in the **Current View** group on the **View** tab in Outlook 2010. In Outlook 2007/Outlook 2003, you can also click on the **Customize Current View** link in the navigation pane on the left.

2. Click the **Filter** button.

3. At the bottom of the dialog box, click **Clear All**. (Don't worry, this just clears [deletes] the filter criteria, nothing else.)

4. Close all open dialog boxes by clicking **OK**. Now you can build the filter based on the initial state (or leave the view unfiltered).

How to create negative filters

Negative filters for hiding certain entries (showing all entries that do not meet certain criteria) are defined slightly differently.

1. Open any task view, right-click one of the column headers, and select **View Settings** (or **Customize Current View**, in the versions before Outlook 2010) in the shortcut menu. Alternatively, you can click **View Settings** in the **Current View** group on the **View** tab in Outlook 2010. In Outlook 2007/Outlook 2003, you can also click on the **Customize Current View** link in the navigation pane on the left.

2. Click the **Filter** button.

3. Click the **Advanced** tab.

4. Click the **Field** button, and from the shortcut menu, select **Frequently-used Fields**. Finally, select **Categories** (or a different field for which you want to filter; if that field is not contained in the list, you can locate it in the **All Task Fields** list).

5. In the **Condition** list, select **doesn't contain**.

6. Enter a value in the **Value** field. For example, enter **Project** (or **@AM**) into the field.

 **NOTE** All categories that contain this word as part of their name are hidden. Typing *Project* in the Value field therefore hides *Project A* and *Project B*, but also *Projectmanagement software*, *Book Project*, and *Theater Project* (even though you might only want to hide your work projects right now).

7. Click **Add to List** to add this criterion to the filter (see Figure 3-13).

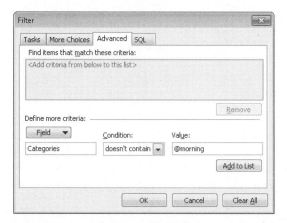

FIGURE 3-13 Don't forget to add the filter criteria to the list after defining them.

8. Close all open dialog boxes by clicking **OK**. All tasks are now hidden in this view if they have a category assigned to them that has a name containing the word you defined.

ADVANCED FILTERING WITH SQL

If you define multiple criteria within the same filter that checks the categories, Outlook uses *or* to link the conditions. (The same goes for applying multiple criteria to the same field, for example if you are using both Not Started and In Progress for Status Equals, in the same filter.) Outlook links different fields with *and* (for example, Due This Week and Status Not Complete).

Advanced users who know their way around databases or query languages can also define detailed criteria by directly editing the SQL statement:

1. In the **Filter** dialog box, click the **SQL** tab (see Figure 3-14).

2. Select the **Edit these criteria directly** check box.

3. Edit the SQL statement to which you now have access (for example, when linking multiple category criteria, you can replace **OR** with **AND**).

4. Close all open dialog boxes by clicking **OK**.

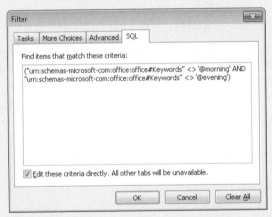

FIGURE 3-14 For advanced users, there are still more options available by directly editing the SQL statement of the filter.

If you want to use the other tabs again for this filter instead of the SQL statement, clear the Edit These Criteria Directly check box.

Work with Grouped Views

By grouping views you can, for example, pool entries thematically, show or hide them quickly, and sort them by category. Grouping is very useful if:

- You want to sort your tasks by priority, but at the same time you would like to see tasks with normal priority for an especially important project before all other tasks of a comparatively less important project. Or maybe you just want to keep a thematic overview. For this purpose, you sort by priority and group by category. This way each category forms a group that displays all associated tasks within this group, sorted by priority.

- You want to quickly check which tasks are pending for your 10 current projects (defined as single categories). It would be too much work to define 10 different filtered views or toggle between filters each time. Instead, you can group by category, collapse all groups (that is, hide the group entries), and then show or hide all tasks belonging to a certain project with just one click (expand or collapse the group).

- You want to sort your entire task list by categories. However, this is not possible with the sort function in Outlook, because one entry might belong to multiple categories (and it's not even possible if you map each entry to only one category). If you group by category instead, a task appears in all groups/categories it belongs to. Because group names are sorted alphabetically, you have now sorted your tasks alphabetically by category.

How to group your tasks by category

- Open a task view, right-click the **Categories** column header, and select **Group By This Field** in the shortcut menu (see Figure 3-15).

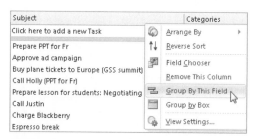

FIGURE 3-15 Group your task list with the help of the corresponding shortcut menu command.

Or you can use a drag-and-drop technique:

1. If necessary, show the **Group By Box** (see "How to Show or Hide the Group By Box," just after this section).

2. Click the **Categories** column header and drag the field into the **Group By Box** (see Figure 3-16).

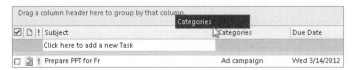

FIGURE 3-16 Drag the column header into the Group By Box to group by the desired field.

 TIP To undo the grouping of the task list, all you need to do is drag the field (in our example, Categories) out of the Group By Box—the field will appear to be crossed out with an X.

How to Show or Hide the Group By Box

Don't worry—existing groupings will not be removed if you do this:

- Open a task view, right-click any column header, and then select **Group by Box** in the shortcut menu (see Figure 3-17).

FIGURE 3-17 To group with the drag-and-drop technique, show the Group By Box. You can later hide it for more space in your view.

NOTE Some predefined views are automatically grouped according to arrangement. To change the Group By settings for such a view, you first have to choose View Settings (Outlook 2010) or Customize Current View (Outlook 2007/Outlook 2003) from the shortcut menu (see Figure 3-17, the menu item below Group By Box). In the dialog box that opens, click the Group By button and clear the Automatically Group According To Arrangement check box.

How to Expand or Collapse Your Groups

- Click the small triangle (the plus/minus symbol in Outlook 2007/Outlook 2003) in front of the group name in the group header (for example, the graphic shown below). Outlook then expands the group (that is, shows all its entries) if the group had previously been collapsed, or collapses it (that is, hides all its elements) if the group had previously been expanded.

> ☐ Categories: Ad campaign (2 items)

- To expand or collapse all groups at once, right-click the small triangle (in Outlook 2007/Outlook 2003, the plus/minus symbol) or directly on a group label and select the corresponding command from the shortcut menu (see Figure 3-18).

FIGURE 3-18 Collapse all groups at once so you can focus on only one group afterward.

If you combine these steps, you can, for example, first expand all groups and then collapse some groups in order to quickly hide them (see Figure 3-19). Or you can collapse all groups and then expand one or several in order to focus on the entries therein, without being distracted by any other groups.

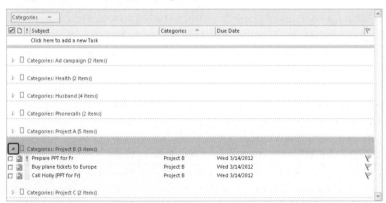

FIGURE 3-19 Expand individual groups while keeping the others collapsed to get an overview of all the tasks for a specific project.

> **NOTE**
>
> Because you can assign multiple categories to one task, an individual task that has multiple categories assigned to it appears in each group separately (the other categories of this group are no longer displayed in the Categories field). For example, you may see the Sample Task task that is assigned to the Department Manager and Project A categories once in each of these groups, but it is the same task. Therefore, if you set the due date for Sample Task in the Department Manager group to next Wednesday, the Sample Task displayed in the Project A group also gets the new due date (because it's the same task, which is just separately displayed in each group).

The Kiesel Principle—Gain More Time for What Matters Most Each Week

Take about 30 minutes to plan your week. Initially it might take you longer, but after a few weeks, you will get used to it and it will become a routine. This will really start to pay off soon, because you'll assign time slots to what matters most to you while still having some time left in your calendar, thus preventing the urgent small stuff from distracting you from the more important stuff that still has some time until it's due, but that will remain undone forever if you don't make it due in the near future by assigning a time slot to it.

Keep Your Life in Balance

Do you know what it's like to feel like you have hardly any time left for your friends, your significant other, your family, and yourself? Even if examined purely from a work performance perspective, it makes sense to keep one's life in balance. Of course, you can totally concentrate on your work for a few weeks and neglect everything else. However, after a few months at the latest, your performance will decline significantly. If you prefer to spend a few hours less in the office, you actually get more done in less time due to higher motivation, better mental balance, and resistance to stress. The speed and quality of your work increase and you make better decisions.

> **IMPORTANT**   Make sure to regularly devote time to all areas of your life.

Plan Your Professional Life and Private Life Together

Plan your work, your private life, all other areas of life, and your activities together so that you avoid conflicting appointments, don't get confused, and don't forget anything.

KEEP EVERYTHING IN ONE PLACE

If you are planning in Outlook, plan everything there—unless private planning is prohibited on your office computer or you don't have access to it on the weekend or in the evening. If you don't have a smartphone that syncs with Outlook, and access to a desktop PC without a possibility for mobile data retrieval or synchronization is the problem, you can print out day planners, a current month planner, and task lists for the weekend, so you can make notes of tasks and appointments for that time. On Monday morning, transfer all newly planned appointments and tasks consistently to Outlook and then immediately destroy all handwritten notes to avoid getting confused on what is the latest, up-to-date version. This approach requires a lot of discipline, however: You must make very sure not to plan appointments multiple times and not to forget them altogether (if they are entered in a calendar you are not looking at while using another one). Alternatively, you can keep a private or family calendar online and then synchronize it with Outlook (assuming this is permitted by your company and not prohibited by security guidelines).

The times when people worked in their offices every day exactly from 9 to 5 are over, just like the times when average citizens got married in their mid-twenties and one of the spouses took care of job and finances while the other stayed home with the kids, took care of the household, and organized private activities. Professional and private time no longer have the same fixed time slots every day but are (at least partially) mixed and distributed differently:

- Suddenly you need to take over a few tasks for a colleague who will get in a few hours late due to a snowstorm, and therefore you'll need to stay three hours longer in the evening. This actually works out great for you, because you had promised your daughter for the day after tomorrow that you would watch her school theater performance at 3 P.M., and can therefore compensate for the extra time by leaving the office early.

- A dentist visit, dropping off your car at the auto repair shop, or picking it up does not require a whole day off, but it interrupts your work time.

■ In the next week, you will be traveling on business for four days and have a few appointments late in the evening. You therefore plan a phone call home for the late afternoon. And it works out well that you will finally be in Chicago again, because it gives you a chance to meet up with your old friend Mark. So you make a two-hour appointment with him before your first meeting and his flight to Frankfurt, Germany.

PLAN YOUR PRIVATE LIFE, TOO!

This might seem strange initially, but it doesn't mean that you should only talk to friends if such a conversation is in your schedule. For busy people, the problem is actually quite the opposite. If you are forced to end a welcome but unexpected phone call or visit early, for example, because there is still so much else you need to get done, immediately plan an appointment in the near future to continue this call or visit and make sure you have enough time.

You should take a date with your significant other and leisure activities with your children just as seriously as a project meeting with your team. Reserve time for it in your schedule early on, and keep it free, together with the necessary buffer time beforehand. Setting up regular hours just for a conversation without any special activities has done wonders for many extremely busy spouses and improved the quality of their relationships immensely.

Early and binding planning does not devalue your private life; on the contrary, it enhances it. You avoid forgetting or postponing time with loved ones or friends, and you don't keep cutting this time short or end up canceling it due to your job or other activities.

Separate your activities into various "life hats"; different subareas of your life (see "Seven Days, Seven Hats..." later in this chapter) instead of dividing them just into professional and private, and make sure to keep a balance between the four areas of life.

The Four Areas of Life for a Life in Balance

The four areas of life (see Figure 3-20) are:

■ Work

■ Contact (loved ones, friends)

- Purpose (Why am I doing what I'm doing? Is there a higher power or a God, and what does that mean for me? What can I do for the good of my fellow humans, so that this world becomes a little bit better and a little bit more beautiful?)

- Myself (sports, recreational activities, hobbies, self-improvement outside of the work environment)

If short-term heavy pressure in one area of life is driving you crazy, you are able to counterbalance it with the energy derived from other areas. The correct balance between all areas of life not only makes you feel better, but you also become more productive in all areas. It isn't necessary (and frequently not even possible) to divide your time exactly into equal parts for all areas. The quality of time is experienced differently—a quiet 45-minute walk at dusk around a lake, or a dance class with your spouse can easily balance out a four-hour nerve-wracking contract negotiation in the office.

The four areas of life

FIGURE 3-20 With a balanced week planner, you can keep all four areas of life in balance. This is not only more comfortable but also is the basis for long-term (professional) success.

Seven Days, Seven Hats...

The concept of "life hats" helps you retain enough time and energy for all areas of life in your hectic day and to concentrate on your key tasks. In the long run, it pays to take care of each area regularly. Otherwise, large deficits in one area will eventually affect your happiness and productivity in the other areas as well.

A "life hat" is simply a name for a subarea that is important to you. Find your important life hats, but choose no more than seven, so you can wear each of them equally well. Each life hat describes (technically speaking) a certain function you fulfill, kind of like a hat you are wearing.

To keep a balance, take all areas of life into account. Life hats could be, for example:

- Department manager, employee organization, specialist for your chosen area, supervisor, colleague

- Boyfriend/girlfriend, spouse, mother/father, daughter/son, brother/sister

- Volunteer at a drug prevention project, driver for "Meals on Wheels," helper with the Red Cross

- Hobby photographer, golfer, cook, outdoor sports enthusiast (for example, climber, trekker through the Rocky Mountains, or mountain biker through the Alps)

Remember not to let private activities (especially sports) become an additional source of performance pressure (unless you need this kind of challenge and can handle it well). Above all, take care of your relaxation and your psychological balance. Also keep your long-term professional development and your personal finances in mind.

The life hats help you keep these areas in view (just like a project) and allow you to devote time to them, even if no urgent task is pending right now. Let's assume you made the following resolution (and are immediately implementing it): "If my kids have problems in school, I will always be there for them, support them, and if necessary postpone job-related tasks." What if your children never have any problems in school? If you specify in such a way when you "will be there," you may notice months or even years later that these urgent and special cases never happened and that you were never "there." So it's better to devote time regularly to each area. If you are behind schedule with an important work project, soon a customer, a colleague in your team, or a manager will complain. In your private life, however, you frequently notice too late that you have deeply neglected one area—with time it becomes more and more difficult to compensate for it and, unfortunately, from a certain moment on it sometimes even becomes impossible. Especially for the relationships with your loved ones and your friends, as well as your relaxation and your health (exercise and eating right) it's important to regularly invest time.

The life hats help you to pay attention to all areas of life even in hectic times. You should also define two professional hats; for example, for your own continuing education and career planning, and if you are a manager, to regularly give yourself time for personal interaction with your employees and their advancement (even if neither evaluations nor the delegation of tasks, a reprimand with a change of direction, a special recognition, nor a promotion are pending).

Regularly Take Time for What Really Counts

Every day you have 24 hours available to you that you can fill similarly or completely differently. The various life hats/areas will switch, merge, and fuse partially for different activities. For example, if you play soccer with your son and have a long talk over ice cream, you haven't just enjoyed time with your son in your "Father" or "Mother" life hat, but at the same time you have also done something for your health and relaxation. When you are trying to regularly devote time to all life hats, the Kiesel Principle (see sidebar that follows) is helpful.

You can use the Kiesel principle for all kinds of plans; for example, for a first rough division of long-term projects. It has been especially successful for weekly planning, for which we will use it next. If you are familiar with Steven Covey's approach to time management (as detailed in *First Things First* by Stephen R. Covey, A. Roger Merrill, and Rebecca R. Merrill, Fireside, 1995), you might have noticed that our approach is similar to his, so you can easily apply the things you've learned from him to Outlook with this book you're reading. He calls this tactic "big rocks first," his "roles" are similar to your "life hats," and our whole approach goes well with his.

Use the Kiesel Principle to stay in balance. Define seven life hats. Each day, devote about one or two hours to one of your hats for one or two B-Tasks. Plan one B-Task per life hat—your so-called key tasks for this week and this particular hat. Using the Kiesel Principle, you can thus make sure that you take care of each life hat at least once per week. If a day is much too full (and there is no way that you can spare an hour), make up for that hour on another day in the same week. The week is long enough to even out such effects.

Of course, it's much better and nicer for you if you can devote more than just one hour per week to each life hat. The Kiesel Principle is not meant to represent an upper restriction. It's just meant to help you get at least one hour's time a day, even if your schedule is very full and you have a lot to get done in the office.

One hour per week and per life hat—seven hours per week for the things that are most important to you: You can always take this much time, if you really want to. It pays off in the long run.

THE KIESEL PRINCIPLE

Metaphorically speaking, a typical day for our hero, Robin Wood, goes something like this:

Imagine a very large glass jug—about the size of a bucket. This is what Robin does:

1. He pours a lot of water into it.

2. Next he pours a bunch of sand into the water.

3. Then he adds a few handfuls of gravel (*Kiesel* in German).

4. In the end, he still wants to add two large bricks—but the jug is almost completely full. Sometimes he manages to add one brick halfway, if he's really careful, but other times the muddy mixture he has created so far runs over. The second brick doesn't fit at all.

So how can we improve this situation? Whenever Robin doesn't know how to go on, he asks his assistant, Melissa MacBeth, who has the following tip for him:

1. When the jug is still empty, just go ahead and add two or three bricks without worrying about it—if there is nothing else in the jug, they'll fit just fine.

2. Then add the gravel, which will fill the gaps.

3. Then add the sand.

4. And finally add the water. This way around is much cleaner and creates a lot less stress.

Even though this way not everything always fits, whatever is left outside is just a bit of sand and part of the water. The bricks (the big chunks) are completely accommodated.

You are probably guessing what this image illustrates: simply going with the flow compared to a planned approach, where you accommodate and complete the most important tasks with the highest leverage. The Kiesel Principle helps illustrate an important maxim: *The largest chunks first, because that way they'll fit*! (This means the *most important* tasks, not those that take the most time.)

So why is it called "the Kiesel Principle" and not "the Brick Principle"? Simply because we think "the Kiesel Principle" sounds better and you'll have learned a new German word now, too.

How to Plan Your Week with Outlook

With these basics, it's now easy to create a rough weekly plan in Outlook, from which we will build more granular daily plans in the next chapter.

When exactly you sit down to plan your week depends on your personal taste and work rhythm or your work environment. Some people have a bit of quiet time in the office on Monday mornings and find it easy to take this time to plan the upcoming week right at the beginning of it; others may prefer to take care of the weekly planning on Friday afternoon the week before, or at noon on Saturday from home (and maybe take this opportunity to plan the week together with their partner).

What's important is that you plan your week before it starts, or at the very latest on Monday morning. When you are trying to find the ideal time, keep the following in mind: If you want to align private or business appointments as part of your weekly planning (and haven't done so before), the people concerned should of course be available at your chosen time; you may need to swap out the appointment planning—for example, coordinate business appointments during business hours on Friday in the office before you plan your week on Saturday, or align private appointments you haven't yet specified for the week at home the preceding evening, before you plan the rest on Friday morning in the office.

Prepare Your Task List for the Week

For the following steps, we will assume that you've already read and understood the instructions for filtering and grouping from the earlier sections, as well as all of Chapter 2, "How to Work More Effectively with Tasks and Priorities" (how to define views, work with tasks, and set priorities) and thus will provide you with shorter instructions instead of detailed step-by-step directions.

Start Your Weekly Planning by Evaluating the Previous Week

If you just want to check how much you already got done (normally we hide this immediately in our customized task views, so we can concentrate on what's ahead), do the following:

- Define a view called **Completed This Week** that only shows the tasks you completed this week or the previous week, if you are planning your week on Mondays (see Figure 3-21). (Outlook automatically records the completion date of a task in the **Date Completed** field. If the task is open in its Task form, you can find this field after clicking **Details** in the **Show** group on the **Task** tab or, in Outlook 2003, after a click on the **Details** tab.)

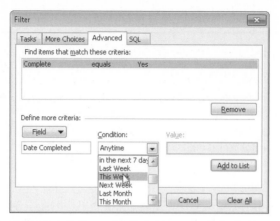

FIGURE 3-21 Define a view that shows you all the tasks you completed this week.

If you also group this view by category, you can quickly see whether you have neglected a certain area or have completed an especially large number of tasks for another area.

> **NOTE**
> The following information also applies to the rest of this section: Whenever we talk about "this week" as a filter criteria for Outlook, we mean that you are planning the following week at the end of the current week. So "next week" shows the tasks for the week you are planning and "this week" shows tasks for the week that's almost over. If you are planning your week at its beginning on a Monday, please replace filters for "this week" with "last week" for the entire section that follows, because on Monday the new week has already started. (The same goes for "next week," which you then need to replace with "this week.")

Plan the Incomplete Tasks from the Previous Week Again

Define a view for the tasks due this week or switch to it if you have already created it. After all, this week is almost over. Look through the list for tasks you didn't manage to get done yet (and won't be able to get done in the time left until the weekend):

- Is this task so important that you must or want to get it done no matter what?

- If Yes: Set a new realistic due date.

- If No: Remove it.

- There are tasks that might be important but that don't need to be completed soon or don't belong to your key tasks. Maybe you had originally planned such a task as "due this week," but then it became too much. If the completion of this task is not due for a long time, there is no specific due date, and the coming weeks are completely booked:

  - Assign it the Master Task List category. (If necessary, set it up in the master category list.)

  - Delete the due date (this also hides the task in all views for daily and weekly planning, which filter for "due today," "due this week," and so on).

  - Set up a view that only shows your master task list, and look through it once a month, for example (add it as an appointment in your calendar), if checking it once a week as part of your weekly planning is becoming too much. Think about which tasks of the master task list you want to specify an upcoming due date for.

Plan your tasks for the next week

1. Switch to a view for the tasks due next week.

2. Think about which tasks you haven't entered yet, and add them. (It's best to enter everything as soon as you think of it!)

3. The next step is to define and plan your key tasks (see "Plan Appointments with Yourself to Concentrate on the Essential Tasks," later in this chapter). Perform this step at this point to avoid postponing the key tasks in the next step.

4. Go through the list and check the calendar as well, to gain an overview of your appointments. Then think about whether the number of tasks is realistic:

   - Which tasks can you remove because their importance has changed?

   - Which tasks can you remove (or postpone) because there are just too many? In the first step, cut less important tasks; and in the second step, check how many tasks you can postpone—not all of them, otherwise you may end up procrastinating.

- Or maybe it's the other way around: There are very few tasks pending or suddenly some tasks and appointments have been canceled. Take a look at your master task list and switch to a view for the tasks due this month or next month. What is especially important? What can you get done this week already? This makes room in the coming weeks to catch any changes, or maybe you won't have to delete so many tasks. Set the due date of the selected tasks to the appropriate day next week. There is nothing wrong with taking care of a task that is neither important nor urgent, but that is just simply fun.

5. In the final step, prioritize your tasks for the following week again. (After all, some of them were entered a few weeks ago, and the priority is always assessed against all your other tasks, many of which you didn't know about back then.) Look through all tasks and use the Eisenhower Matrix (see Chapter 2) to decide which ones get high, normal, or low priority. The more tasks get a low priority, the fewer get a normal or high priority, and the better the chance that you will get all your tasks with high and normal priority done this week, no matter what goes wrong.

Plan Tasks and Appointments Together in Balance

In the Daily Task List in your calendar, Outlook 2010/Outlook 2007 displays the tasks due (or, if you prefer, completed) for that particular day below the day and week view. This new view uses the available space better than the task block of older Outlook versions and is especially practical for week planning:

- You can see for the whole week whether the tasks are distributed well and if there is enough time between the fixed appointments for the tasks, or whether you need to redistribute (for example, if Monday is full of appointments and has 30 tasks, while Tuesday and Wednesday only have two short appointments and only five tasks).

- If you want to even out an imbalance, you can use the drag-and-drop technique to directly move individual tasks (or multiple tasks selected together) from one packed day to a more open day.

- In Outlook 2010, the Daily Task List Tools tab opens as soon as you click a task in the list. Now you can use the buttons, for example to mark the task as Completed or change the priority.

DO YOU HAVE AN EYE ON EVERYTHING?

Depending on the screen resolution, Outlook window size, and height and width of the area for the Daily Task List you are working with, you might only see the first one or two words of the task subject and, for example, only the first 5 of 15 tasks pending for the day (see Figure 3-22). If the first part of the task subject is not enough to remind you what it means, point to the corresponding task and wait briefly. Outlook will show a kind of "sticky note" with the entire subject of the task for a few seconds. If you want to see this information again later on, point away from the task and then back to it. A scroll bar to the right of the Daily Task List tells you whether there are additional tasks in the list below the ones shown. If there is a scroll bar, you know that there are further tasks that didn't fit on the screen. Scroll down to view those tasks. If there is no scroll bar to the right of the Daily Task List, all tasks due this week are shown. The same applies to the tasks displayed in the task bar.

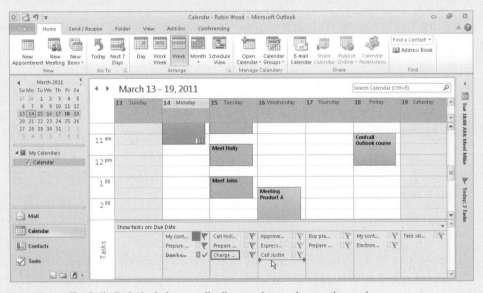

FIGURE 3-22 The Daily Task List helps you distribute tasks evenly over the week.

How to Show or Hide the Daily Task List

Switch to the week view of your calendar. Click the small arrow in the upper-right corner of the Daily Tasks List to minimize it, or in the minimized list on the arrow at its right border to expand it back to the size you used last time (see Figure 3-23). On the View tab in the Layout group, click Daily Task List and then select Off in the expanded menu to hide the list permanently (which gives you about one more line of space for appointments). In Outlook 2007, go to the View menu and select Daily Task List/Off.

If you don't see the task list below the appointments, switch it back on by choosing View /Layout/Daily Task List/Normal in Outlook 2010 or View/Daily Task List/Normal in Outlook 2007.

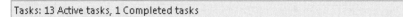
Tasks: 13 Active tasks, 1 Completed tasks

FIGURE 3-23 The minimized task list saves space and can be expanded to its full size with one click.

How to Customize Your Daily Task List

Point to the upper margin of the area that contains the Daily Task List (the dividing line between the calendar and the tasks; see Figure 3-22) and resize the list as desired by dragging the border (this doesn't work in the minimized view, only in the normal view, when the arrow in the upper-right corner of the list points down). If you right-click the header of the list (for example, on the Show Tasks On text), you can specify whether you want those tasks to be displayed in the list on the day of the assigned start/due date and whether you also want to see completed tasks (to see how much you got done today).

Plan Appointments with Yourself to Concentrate on the Essential Tasks

Create a category for each of your life hats. In this section, we will cover the planning of key tasks in more detail:

1. Switch to a view for the tasks due next week grouped by category. (If you have no problem working with many views, just create a new one that only shows the tasks for one of your life hats.)

2. If there is a life hat with no B-Task due this week, try to come up with one. For example, as a B-Task you could insert the planning and preparation of a surprise trip to Las Vegas with your significant other or a weekend on the beach.

3. Now that each life hat has at least one B-Task for this week, find one per life hat and assign it the **Key Tasks** category. (You have to create that category before assigning it for the first time.)

4. Switch to the calendar to make appointments with yourself for these key tasks.

How to create the appropriate task view for week planning in your calendar

1. From the calendar, switch to the **Work Week** view or the **Week** view by clicking the corresponding button on the **Start** tab (Outlook 2010) or clicking in the default toolbar (Outlook 2007/Outlook 2003). Switch to the next week (remember, it's Friday and we are planning your next week).

2. Outlook 2010/Outlook 2007: If you don't yet see your tasks to the right of your appointments, go to **View/Layout/To-Do Bar/Normal** (Outlook 2007: **View/To-Do Bar/Normal**). Outlook 2003: If the TaskPad is not shown, go to the **View** menu and select **TaskPad**.

3. Enlarge the To-Do bar or the TaskPad, if necessary, by dragging the dividing line between the calendar and the tasks to the position you want.

4. Outlook 2010/Outlook 2007: In the To-Do bar (on the right) above the task list, right-click the **Arrange by** heading and select **View Settings** (Outlook 2010) or **Custom** (Outlook 2007) from the shortcut menu. Outlook 2003: On the title bar of the TaskPad, right-click the word **Taskpad**, and then select **Customize Current View** from the shortcut menu.

5. In the dialog box that opens, click the **Group By** button and clear the **Automatically group according to arrangement** check box.

6. In the **Group items by** list, select **Categories**.

7. In the lower-right area of the **Group By** dialog box, in the **Expand/collapse defaults** list, select **All collapsed**.

8. Close all open dialog boxes by clicking **OK**, and then expand the **Key Tasks** group in the To-Do bar or the TaskPad on the right side of the Outlook window next to your appointments (as shown earlier in this chapter in "Work with Grouped Views"). You could also set a filter to only show tasks due next week next to your calendar, but because we already selected only tasks that are due next week as Key Tasks, working just with that group of key tasks works just as well for the next steps we are describing here.

You can now see the present appointments for next week (see Figure 3-24), and next to them your key tasks for next week. Now you can plan fixed times for completing these tasks as appointments with yourself. Plan a task for each day. If a day is too full and there is no time for the task, put two tasks on a day where there is more time. They can be converted quickly and easily into an appointment, as described next.

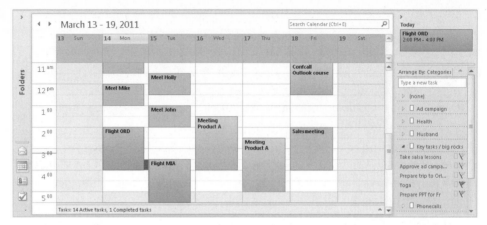

FIGURE 3-24 Plan appointments with yourself for your key tasks according to the Kiesel Principle.

How to convert entries from the To-Do bar/TaskPad into appointments

1. Click a task (or, in Outlook 2003, on the small task icon in front of the task) to select it without switching into editor mode for one of the fields. The task now has a blue background.

2. Press Ctrl+X to move the entry to the Microsoft Office Clipboard.

3. Look for an appropriate time slot in the calendar (for example, in the **Work Week** or **Day** view) and then click (very briefly so no blinking cursor appears, but only so that the time is selected) on the beginning—for example, in the column for **Wednesday** at **11:00 A.M.**

4. Press Ctrl+V to insert the entry from the Clipboard. In Outlook 2010/Outlook 2007, an appointment with the subject from the task is now entered. Outlook 2003, however, opens an Appointment form.

   Outlook has already entered some information for you into the newly created appointment:

   - The new appointment was created for the selected time on the selected day.

   - The task subject was copied to the subject of the appointment.

   - All categories that were assigned to the task were copied to the appointment.

   - The entire task is moved to the appointment as an attachment. You can find it in the note field of the appointment form and can now open it by double-clicking it to view any further information you might have entered into the task.

- If the task was marked as private, the new appointment is also private (see Chapter 5, "How to Schedule Meetings So They Are Convenient, Effective, and Fun").

- The task was deleted from your task list. If you don't want that to happen, maybe because it is necessary to log the completion, just press Ctrl+C instead of Ctrl+X in step 2. However, with Ctrl+C, the task will not be inserted as an attachment; only the text from the task is copied into the appointment. (Alternatively, you can drag a task into the calendar by keeping the right mouse button pressed and then select Copy Here As Appointment With Attachment. In Outlook 2003, you need to click the desired target time in the calendar first before copying and pasting by dragging.)

5. In Outlook 2003, you can edit the subject of the appointment, if necessary, and close the form by clicking **Save and Close**.

6. Go to the bottom margin of the newly created appointment, click on the lower margin of the appointment, and drag downward until the duration of the appointment is reached, such as 10:00 to 12:00. Release the mouse button to set the appointment to this duration.

7. Repeat these steps until all your tasks have been planned.

ALLOW YOURSELF A DAY OF REST FOR NOTHING BUT PRIVATE THINGS

This also applies to freelancers: Give yourself one day of rest per week! Leave all your work behind that day, and with that we mean the whole day (so no little one/two-hour exceptions).

It doesn't have to be Sunday—especially on Sundays you might be able to work without being disturbed. The idea of Sunday as a day of rest has a certain advantage, though: It is the day when most people have time for friends and activities, especially if they are bound to regular working hours. Therefore, think hard and try to find a better alternative, instead of planning your Sundays for professional activities.

It doesn't even have to be the same day each week—however, a certain regularity and a fixed pattern help many people relax much better and truly rest. So try to always keep your day of rest to the same day of the week.

How to automatically color your appointments

If you want to be able to see at a glance (and without having to read the text of all of your appointments) when you need to catch a plane or be in a meeting, for example, in a full week or month view (see Figure 3-24, shown earlier), the function for conditional/automatic formatting of the Day/Week/Month view for appointments can help. (Outlook 2010 and Outlook 2007 automatically color by category but can also do automatic formatting by other criteria as long as you haven't yet assigned a category to your appointments.)

1. Use the **Work Week** button in the calendar to switch to the correct view (for Outlook 2010, you'll find it on the **View** tab in the **Arrangement** group).

2. In Outlook 2010, on the **View** tab, in the **Current View** group, click **View Settings** and then, in the newly opened dialog box, click the **Conditional Formatting** button. In Outlook 2007/Outlook 2003, just open the **Edit** menu and select **Automatic Formatting**.

    The **Conditional Formatting** dialog box (or the **Automatic Formatting** dialog box in Outlook 2007/Outlook 2003) now opens, within which you can define new color rules for the current view. (Alternatively, you can open this dialog box in Outlook 2007/Outlook 2003 from the **Customize View** dialog box by clicking the **Automatic Formatting** button.)

3. Click the **Add** button to create a new rule.

4. In the **Name** box, enter **Conference Calls**, for example, and then click the **Condition** button.

5. In the **Filter** dialog box that now opens, define the criteria for the appointments you want to color according to this rule (in the same way you have set other filters for the Outlook views). For example, if you select the **ConfCall** value in the **Search for the word(s)** field (next line: **In: subject field only**), all appointments that have *ConfCall* in the subject field are colored.

6. Set the filter by clicking **OK**.

7. In the **Conditional Formatting** dialog box (or the **Automatic Formatting** dialog box in Outlook 2007/Outlook 2003) that now opens, select the color you want in the **Color** list (or the **Label** list, in Outlook 2003)—for example, Red.

8. Close the dialog box by clicking **OK**.

From now on, all appointments to which the rule applies are colored accordingly in the current view.

To the right of the color name, Outlook 2003 shows labels that you can change as you wish. To do so, go to the Edit menu and select Label/Edit Labels directly after step 1 of the instructions just provided.

In Outlook 2003, you can specify a color for each appointment entry individually via the Label field by right-clicking the appointment (in the open appointment under Subject, to the right of Location). Outlook 2010/Outlook 2007 colors the appointments according to the category that was assigned last. A color that has been specified manually or according to category in this way always takes precedence over all conditional/automatic formatting. Even if you assign a category that has no color (Color: None), it'll overwrite the conditional/automatic formatting. So in Outlook 2010/Outlook 2007, you must not assign categories to make this kind of coloring work.

You Try It

1. Engross yourself in the first two tasks from Chapter 2. Which long-term task that would have a huge impact on your other work/personal life areas have you been postponing forever, simply because you "just don't have time" or because "it takes too long" (or whatever other excuse you come up with)—there is no such thing as "no time," only different priorities. Therefore: If the task is important enough to you—what's stopping you? Examples: finally start jogging again or clear out your office and create a filing system (such as hanging file folders) to eliminate chaos in the future and make sure that required paper documents can be filed away with one single move and can easily be found again.

2. Now divide this "mission" into small key tasks with a realistic due date (for instance, find a helpful colleague, take two hours with him or her to come up with a good system, procure and prepare the necessary materials such as hanging file folders and garbage bins, take two days in August when it's more quiet in the office to clean it up, and then have your helpful colleague check the progress resulting from this new system on a monthly basis and, if necessary, have your colleague correct it).

3. Develop an appropriate category system (empty out the main category list beforehand).

4. Map the appropriate categories to your tasks. (In the future, do so as soon as you create new tasks.)

5. Define your seven life hats (at least one per area of life), create categories for them, and come up with tasks for each hat that you will tackle in the near future.

6. Create a view of the incomplete tasks that are due next week, and group them according to category. Show the To-Do bar (the TaskPad in Outlook 2003) in your calendar and set up this view with the same filters and groups.

7. Plan your upcoming week as described in this chapter (delete outstanding tasks or change their due date, enter new tasks, if necessary, and adjust the priorities). Take advantage of the Kiesel Principle (plan key tasks for life hats, and enter appointments with yourself into your calendar for these tasks).

CHAPTER 4

How to Make Your Daily Planning Work in Real Life

IN THIS CHAPTER, YOU WILL

- Learn the basics of successful day planning.

- Combine similar tasks into blocks.

- Use appointment lists.

- Fine-tune your day planner.

- Use the To-Do bar in Outlook.

"Things Always Turn Out Differently Anyway"

YOU HAVE created your task list, have given the tasks a due date and prioritized them (see Chapter 2, "How to Work More Effectively with Tasks and Priorities"). You have planned your week with long-standing appointments and newly updated meetings as well as your "appointments with yourself" according to the Kiesel principle ("schedule big rocks first"; see Chapter 3, "How to Gain More Time for What's Essential with an Effective Week Planner"). Confident and full of energy, you start your day—and then suddenly it's evening already. You were able to keep most of the appointments, but the majority of the items on your task list have not been taken care of....

Not everything in life works out perfectly. Nevertheless, many people assume that things will always turn out as they had hoped, because more often than not, they actually turn out that way, which gives them room for more planning. Besides, there's no fun in constantly assuming the worst. However, if you assume that what worked out perfectly without any glitches in record time with a lot of luck will continue to do so in the future, you shouldn't be disappointed or even surprised if it doesn't work out quite so perfectly next time.

A TYPICAL DAY AT ROBIN'S OFFICE...

It's already 9:26 A.M. when Robin Wood enters the conference room in a bad mood to begin his work day. Usually it's fine to leave the house at 8:10 A.M., usually his commute to work will take exactly 50 minutes. But today one lane was closed due to landscaping—at this time of day, go figure!—and to make things worse, traffic was especially heavy...

"Sorry, I got stuck in rush-hour traffic," he mumbles.

"Which is the same every morning at this time," his boss replies with obviously little sympathy.

"But it's really not my fault. This sort of thing just happens—especially to me. Why does it always happen to me and Fred, but hardly ever to the others?" Robin muses. At least his colleague Holly Holt greets him good-naturedly, and her smile cheers him up a bit. The next hours are proof, in his mind, that it's impossible to plan your day well, no matter what: Once again, the meeting lasts an hour longer than scheduled. Afterward he was going to finish the presentation for his talk at tomorrow's trade show. But when he's back at the computer, he first takes a "quick look" at the new email messages instead.

Forty-five minutes later, he is interrupted by a colleague who needs help with a problem. Of course, the phone doesn't stop ringing. Suddenly he realizes that he has another meeting in 15 minutes. This meeting, however, takes place in a different building, and it takes him 20 minutes to get there, a fact he had not taken into consideration when glancing at the "3:30 P.M. meeting" request. At least this meeting ends on time, and on the way to get there he was able to grab something to eat at the hotdog stand—three hours past lunchtime.

Back at his desk, he could finally get started on the presentation—theoretically, anyway—but there are a few other things he should get done beforehand, so he's trying to squeeze those in really quickly. After a while, he becomes aware of how quiet everything is around him. It can't be past 6 P.M. already, can it? It sure can be. OK, let's do this. Finally Robin starts designing a new slide. As this task begins to get tedious, he checks his Microsoft Outlook inbox and answers a few requests, which shouldn't take too much time. Afterward, he follows a couple of exciting links for special rental car offers. Oops! It's 7:30 P.M. already. Robin realizes that he won't finish the presentation today—at least not in the office. Oh, well. Who cares. Wouldn't be the first time he's taking work home.... "So, what's the point of planning? Things always turn out differently anyway!"

Trying to halfway catch up on today's completely impossible schedule of too many tight appointments by working overtime or by distributing tasks and appointments to the upcoming (and equally packed) days, while being totally stressed out, is even less fun than assuming that some things might go wrong or take a little longer.

You can protect yourself against some of the disturbances, interruptions, and distractions. You don't need to let yourself get distracted by everything—but you can never completely turn off all distractions. These include unexpected chances and opportunities that really do require immediate action and are important enough to postpone other things. Reasonable daily planning is geared toward reality and takes such situations into consideration—within certain limits.

Realistic daily planning—or rather, its implementation, taking action accordingly—is a difficult and immense challenge. Hello, long-term plans and goals (and weekly planning): allow me to introduce you to the harsh reality of life. The challenge is to combine the two without getting lost in short-term distractions and all the exciting or urgent but unimportant stuff. Above all, you have to make consistent decisions to just say "No," and by doing so, say "Yes" to what really matters to you, your company, your boss, your clients, your family, and your friends. Really implementing your goals and B-Tasks, putting your plan into action at the moment of choice, requires a large amount of self-discipline. At this point, time management either works out or fails.

The following often stand in the way of planning your day and implementing your plan—the top reasons why people fail:

- The desire to do everything at once.

- Delays, slip-ups, and things that "just go wrong." (This happens occasionally, but you always have to plan for and be prepared for it to happen. Most people just assume that everything will always work out as planned.)

- Overestimation of your own capabilities or poor planning of time requirements.

- Only reacting, performing C-Tasks first, failing to hold yourself accountable, being defensive and trying to blame someone else for your failures.

- Unexpected disruptions and interruptions, distractions, fluctuating levels of concentration.

- An acute aversion to some tasks, no self discipline, listlessness and "procrastinitis": doing all the unimportant, easy, and fun D-Tasks first, thus wasting time and procrastinating on the more difficult, sometimes boring or riskier, but much more important tasks.

Let's Get Started and Change This!

For effective day planning, you should take the following steps into consideration:

- Plan for delays, glitches, disruptions, and interruptions. They will happen, so try to prevent them, find a strategy to protect yourself against the ones you can avoid, and still leave some room to catch up with your work if some of them still happen.

- Concentrate on what's essential, plan that first, and then take care of it consistently.

- Estimate the time requirements and your own performance realistically.

- Find a way to bundle the smaller tasks and leave free time slots in your plan as buffer zones.

- Tackle an issue and take responsibility, hold yourself accountable, and practice self-discipline to do boring and hard stuff when necessary to gain more time for tasks/activities that are fun afterwards, reach your goals, finish your work on time, and get home earlier (you can make a difference; see Chapter 7, "How to Truly Benefit from This Book").

Now that we have compiled the requirements of a solid schedule, it's high time to get started with implementing it.

The Basics of Successful Day Planning

Build time blocks to pool similar tasks, and process them in a concentrated fashion in a single stretch (see the sidebar "What Is a Block?" in Chapter 1, "How Not to Drown in the Email Flood"). Learn to estimate the actual time requirement of a specific task correctly— many people try to rely on their intuition and come up with unrealistic values.

Use your daily performance curve in combination with your disruption curve (you'll learn about these later in this section) to figure out the best time of the day to isolate yourself against disruptions and to focus on the most important tasks of the day. Combine phone calls and minor daily tasks into categories, so you can perform them as a block or during waiting or idle times, and thus take optimal advantage of intervals between bigger tasks.

Combine Similar Tasks into Task Blocks

How much time do you waste with the little stuff? A "quick" phone call here, a "short" email message there, and before you know it, 20 minutes have gone by. You should combine such similar small tasks into task blocks.

Doing so has the following advantages:

- You will make faster headway, because you don't need to get started again with a different kind of work every time (for example, when you switch to email from editing a report, you need two to three minutes to really get up to speed for answering messages. If you just answer one or two and then do something else, you'll need the three minutes again when you come back to email). Working on 10 five-minute phone calls or email messages at a stretch takes a lot less time than working on 10 different email messages 10 times in between other tasks. The effect is amplified by your ability to see the big picture. For example, you will automatically keep your phone calls short, if all the important issues have been addressed for that one call and you know that you still need to get eight more phone calls done within the next half hour.

- Unlike when you "just really quickly take care of some small task in between larger tasks," creating blocks allows you to see exactly how many email messages you get done in 30 minutes or how long it takes you to make five short phone calls. If you watch yourself for a while, you can come up with a good average value that allows you to estimate the time requirements more realistically and thus plan more effectively. You will also have an easier time finding out in which areas it makes sense to optimize processes, cut reserved time shorter, or invest more time.

- If you schedule your blocks at approximately the same time each day, you also gain the additional benefits of a routine. The whole issue becomes a kind of ritual and gives your day a firm structure. Such recurrent actions at the same times of day have a positive effect on your work performance. They keep you grounded as you move through your day, and help you center yourself more quickly.

- You will find it easier to concentrate on your big, important tasks, and it also becomes easier to prevent distractions from items that you will later take care of in the block. For example, if you realize that it would be necessary to make a phone call, but it doesn't have to happen at this very moment, you just add it to the list. Therefore, you won't be distracted for very long but can continue to concentrate on the task at hand.

Use Categories When Creating Blocks

Think about the areas for which you can create meaningful blocks. There are some tasks for which it makes sense to plan one or more blocks per day (for example, reading and answering email). For others, one to three blocks per week are sufficient, if not enough tasks accrue per day, if the tasks can wait a few days, or if you simply can't take care of an issue every day. Certain blocks even make sense monthly or quarterly—for example, expense accounts.

TIP

Add the *Block* suffix to the Outlook category name of each block building category (you'll learn more about block building toward the end of
the chapter, in "Hide the Tasks Intended for Block Building in the Week/
Day Views"). This is the most practical way to avoid frustration and other
problems when you work with block building categories and want to use
filters later.

Enter the names of the blocks that will come up more frequently—such as Calls (Block)
for phone calls that are longer than three minutes—into your main category list (for
more about working with categories, see Chapter 3). Now, if you think of a new task that
you would like to mark for the next block, just press Ctrl+Shift+K, for example, to create a
new task right from the middle of editing an email message. Enter the details (see Chapter 3) and assign the corresponding block, such as "Calls (Block)", as category.

Whenever you need to—for your daily schedule, for example—you can then switch comfortably to a view that is sorted by category, collapse other categories, and filter the view
by due date, to see your call block with all phone calls that must happen in the next five
days, for example (see Figure 4-1). Setting the corresponding views is covered later in this
chapter in "Order Must Prevail."

FIGURE 4-1 With a few mouse clicks, you can set the task list so you can only view the tasks that are
pending in the next few days for the corresponding block (group by category).

A Special Task Block: The ActionList

What to do with all the small items, which only take up to 10 minutes, max? Combine
them into a special block under the "ActionList (Block)" category. This block is an exception in that you don't work through it at a single stretch, because it includes diverse
smaller issues from different areas. Instead, you always call it up when you have short idle

times, for example, 10 minutes before the start of a meeting in the conference room or 8 minutes before an important phone appointment, when there is no other larger task you want to start yet. This way you can take care of these things quickly in between larger tasks and are filling short waiting or idle times.

For Advanced Users: Take Advantage of the Journal for Semi-Automatic Time Protocols

To save you from having to constantly switch between different applications and continuously look at your watch, the journal function of Outlook can help you create a time protocol (see Figure 4-2).

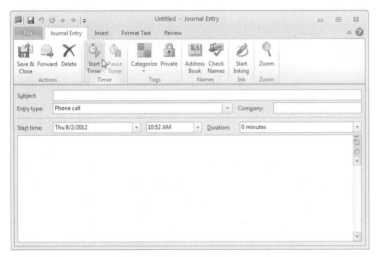

FIGURE 4-2 The journal function of Outlook has automatic time recording that can help you with your time protocol.

Whenever you begin a new task, just press Alt+Tab to switch to Outlook (press Tab again and release it while keeping Alt pressed and continue pressing Tab again until you have reached Outlook—unless Outlook is already open in the foreground). Then press Ctrl+Shift+J. Outlook will open a form for creating a journal entry that already contains the current date and time. Enter a unique subject. The Entry Type list contains all of the tasks that Outlook can automatically protocol. Ignore this field, because you can't customize it by adding entries, and you'd therefore be too limited. Instead, click Categorize (or, in Outlook 2003, the Categories button in the lower-right corner) and select the appropriate categories from the list.

LOOK THE TRUTH IN THE EYE: TIME PROTOCOLS

Keeping time protocols—or, more specifically, time use protocols—is a simple routine with a huge impact:

■ After completing a task and keeping track of the time, you can estimate the time required for other tasks that come up in a similar way much more accurately.

■ You will recognize individual issues and how much time they actually took you to accomplish—these values frequently differ slightly or even dramatically from the values you would have estimated. In combination with the creation of blocks, you might notice that "answering four short customer requests," which you would have estimated to take at most 20 to 25 minutes, in reality took a whole hour.

■ After a while, you can see quite clearly for which areas you need to allocate and plan for more time, and for which you can reduce the allotted time. You will recognize which tasks take most of your time and where it makes sense to investigate possible ways for optimizing your work.

Creating a time protocol is simple: Take a few very typical work days, and just track everything you are doing—everything that takes more than 10 minutes. If there are a few shorter tasks to perform, such as "8 min. for 3 short phone calls from ActionList," you should protocol those as well. What's important is that you always carry your time protocol with you, measure the time exactly, and enter everything immediately, as soon as it's done. (You don't need to run around with a stop watch, but you should take a look at your watch at the beginning and end of each task.) It's up to you whether to record your time protocol on paper, enter it into Microsoft Excel Mobile on your smartphone, or use the journal function of Outlook with automatic time recording.

In the simplest version, you just enter the start and end time of the task and a detailed description (in other words, not just "call"). Exceptions are blocks with many small activities at a stretch, where a collective name is sufficient (such as "email block"). Details in a further column are always helpful; for example, "10 messages deleted immediately, 5 small ones answered quickly, and 3 large ones taken care of." That's enough in the beginning. The protocol becomes more meaningful (albeit more complex) if you prioritize the task according to the Eisenhower Matrix (see Chapter 2); insert a column for the duration in minutes; in one column enter what you had planned for this time slot and in another column document your evaluation of this task (for example, "great: 100% correctly done as planned, but went much faster" or "wasn't really necessary right now and took a lot of time"); or even record your physical or emotional state in yet another column ("tired and having a hard time concentrating," "wide awake and very creative," "still tired, but routine stuff going well and quickly").

If your problem is procrastinating important tasks, getting easily distracted by other things, or fighting a lack of self-discipline, the time protocol can help you. If you look at your plan, see "write report for board meeting" but are entering something like "15 minutes spent aimlessly clicking around in the inbox," instead, you will realize right there and then, while entering these remarks, that you are shirking the actual task. This should shake you awake and hopefully cause you to quit postponing this unpleasant but nevertheless very important task.

Keep a time protocol consistently for at least three, or preferably five, representative work days, and enter each task of 10 minutes or more. Even though it might not be a lot of fun, it's worth it!

Then click the Start Timer button (or, in Microsoft Office Outlook 2003, press Alt+M). With Alt+Tab, you can switch back to the window that was open before you established the journal entry, while the journal window with activated time recording stays open. After you have finished the task, press Alt+Tab to move back to the open journal entry, and click Stop Timer (in Outlook 2003, just press Alt+M again). Outlook has now automatically added the duration. Enter any additional comments into the note field before saving and closing your journal entry. Because you probably won't need the Company field for your time protocol, you can use it to note something else instead, such as the priority or your level of satisfaction with the completion of the task, so you can later sort for this criterion and use it for evaluation purposes. Here you can also add remarks about the project or the part of your life this current task belongs to (see Chapter 3).

To evaluate your daily protocol, switch to the Entry List view. The typical Timeline view of the journal might not be very practical when dealing with many short tasks instead of task blocks. You should therefore define a new view of the type *Table*, which you can arrange or group, for example, by category or duration, to see which of your tasks take the most time or which type/category of tasks you use the most time for. You can also write the journal entries into a Microsoft Excel file, to add up the time for further evaluation, create diagrams for a quick overview, and much more. To do this in Outlook 2010, select Options on the File tab and then, in the Outlook Options dialog box, select Advanced. In the Export pane, click Export, and follow the instructions. In Microsoft Office Outlook 2007/Outlook 2003, select Import And Export from the File menu.

Take Your Performance Curve and Your Disruption Curve into Consideration

Some people are wide awake and absolutely fit early in the morning; others take a while to get going and then reach their highest potential with maximum performance and concentration when others are already getting tired, worn out, and have a hard time concentrating. Everybody has his or her individual performance curve, linked to his or her circadian rhythm. If you keep this curve in mind while planning your schedule, you can adjust your times of maximum concentration with high creativity and speed, combined with high quality of work, to target your most important tasks.

The performance curve is overlaid by other effects. Anyone who gets out of a mammoth meeting at 11:30 A.M., where negotiations went on for three hours without a break in a badly ventilated room, would be rather exhausted, of course, even if this person would otherwise have reached top form at that time of day. As long as at least half of your work days begin with a similar pattern, you will experience a similar performance curve. Therefore, you must consider one of your strongest overlays: your disruption curve, which usually is also quite regular. Maybe you have been able to work at your best between 10:00 and 11:00 A.M. when everybody else was on vacation. However, you can no longer use this time freely when, during regular work days, colleagues and clients constantly approach you with requests, and your boss keeps dropping by with new tasks for you.

Just go ahead and draw your own performance and disruption curves. It doesn't need to be an elaborate scientific chart—maybe you can even do it impromptu (see Figure 4-3). Or combine your experience with the time protocol, if you want to watch it a little more closely: Add a column for your performance capability and the amount/intensity of disturbance. If necessary, you can do an evaluation as to whether the interruptions can be moved to a different time slot. You can describe it in words or just use a number on a scale from 1 through 10, which makes later evaluation much easier.

Hourly productivity / interruptions

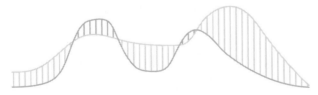

AM 6 7 8 9 10 11 12 PM 1 2 3 4 5 6 7 8 9 10 11

FIGURE 4-3 Draw your performance and disruption curves to determine the optimal times for Productivity Hours.

Focus on Your Important Tasks Without Interruptions During Productivity Hours

It's quite amazing how much you can get done during times when there are no interruptions of any kind. Especially if the amount of possible distractions you might take advantage of to escape unpleasant tasks is much smaller during that time. For example, if you are on a business trip to Brisbane, Australia, and there are no business dinners at night, you suddenly have a lot of time after 5 P.M. All your friends and colleagues who you might want to call are asleep. (If you're from Miami, Florida, in the United States, it's 3 A.M. there when it's 5 P.M. in Brisbane. If you're from Europe, a flight to the United States will do the same for you.) Because in Australia businesses are closing right about now, your inbox is no longer filling up—except for the occasional automatic newsletter (as well as a bit of junk mail that will be mostly filtered out). So what to do, if you're not up for exploring unfamiliar towns? Suddenly, after two or three days, you have finished the complicated and rather unpleasant but very important marketing plan—which is due in two weeks, and which you have been putting off for eight weeks....

But you don't have to go as far as flying to Australia once a month or locking yourself in your office on the weekend. Just set up one or two Productivity Hours per day (ideally 45 to 90 minutes), and focus on what's really important during that time. This will also help when traveling does not (if your customers and business partners are scattered all over the world, someone will always be working...).

For your Productivity Hours, try to find the time when your performance curve is considerably higher than your disruption curve. You will usually get "adjusted curves"; in other words, you would automatically rate your performance lower during times of frequent disruptions, so that in the end, your performance high points are located in times of a low disruption level. If the disruption high points coincide with the performance high points, try to move the disruption curve. For example, you could ask your very cooperative boss whether she might consider moving the briefing to an earlier or later time slot. (Or, if absolutely necessary, move the performance curve—for example, if your boss says no, maybe you can get up an hour earlier and start on your task sooner.)

Defend Your Productivity Hours

Rigorously block one or, if possible, two Productivity Hours each day:

- Enter your Productivity Hours as a recurring appointment into your calendar, so you don't accidentally (but only very consciously, if there is no other way) plan something else and won't get any meeting requests for those times. It would be best to talk to your colleagues about what you are doing, setting core times for meetings (see Chapter 5, "How to Schedule Meetings So They Are Convenient, Effective, and Fun") so that everyone can secure his or her Productivity Hours outside of those times and the Productivity Hours are generally respected. Otherwise, mark these times as private or just don't enter any text at all. Have courage: frequently a brief friendly explanation with the request to respect these times is all it takes.

- If a meeting request shows up anyway, suggest a different time or decline the request (unless there is really no other possibility).

- Try to select a time when it's quite normal for someone to be unreachable. For example, if your performance curve is high in the morning, just go to the office early. Lunchtime, between 11:00 A.M. and 2:00 P.M., can also work well (depending on how early or late you start). Anyone who can't reach you at 7:30 A.M., noon, or 5:30 P.M. wouldn't consider that strange under normal circumstances, but rather would try again at different times.

- If you are not expecting an extremely urgent and important phone call in the next few minutes, log off your phone with the central switchboard for the duration of your Productivity Hour or switch your phone to voice mail. Turn your cell phone off as well.

- Remember that the first three weeks are the most important. Remind your colleagues politely but firmly of the times when you are not available. At first, your colleagues will tend to disregard these times, even if they like the idea and are trying to respect it—it always takes time to change old habits. The consistency with which you fend off interruptions during these first weeks determines whether your quiet times will work out in the long run. If necessary, ask your boss for permission or choose a time when she isn't in the office yet, or not any longer, if she refuses to respect these times.

- Make sure you don't distract yourself:

  - Ignore your inbox during your Productivity Hour.

  - Focus completely on the planned A-type or B-type task you have planned for this time. Start on it immediately and get used to doing nothing else during your Productivity Hour (see also "Fine-Tuning Your Daily Planning," later in this chapter).

  - Whenever you would like to "quickly look up or write" (or answer, or order) something, do it before or after, but never during your Productivity Hours.

- If you travel a lot, and fixed appointments for your Productivity Hours are not possible, make use of these travel times. The fact that you don't need to come up with explanations to cut yourself off makes it even easier. Drive to the airport or the train station an hour earlier (or book the return trip for an hour later) and sit down in a lounge or coffee house, where you can work in peace. Turn off your cell phone and resist the temptation to "check email really quickly." If you are driving a car, you can just leave a little earlier (or return a little later) and along the way choose a rest stop or a café that offers a favorable environment.

Order Must Prevail

One of the major advantages of using Outlook for your time management is the enormous flexibility you have with the views. You only need to make your entries once, but you can still see the tasks for the current week, the current day, or even the entire quarter for a certain project with one click. Automatic marking with different colors helps you to keep other criteria in view (for example, you could show a list with all the tasks for a certain project, where tasks that are due this week are marked in blue). Or you could switch to a view that shows you all future appointments arranged by town—so you can see quickly when you will be in Los Angeles or San Diego next time, in case somebody asks you whether you "might have an hour to spare if you are in town sometime in August or September."

The three configuration examples in this section, which most users find very useful, will show you further tips for fine-tuning your Outlook views, now that you have learned how to set up new views, customize the displayed fields, sort, and group, and now that you understand basics of filtering as covered in the previous two chapters. This way you can always keep an overview and find information relevant to you.

Hide the Tasks Intended for Block Building in the Week/Day Views

While building the blocks, we have combined similar tasks to perform them at a single stretch—and not in between other tasks or at different times. This way you don't have to take too many single items into consideration while planning. For example, just hide the individual short phone calls reserved for block building (which can wait until the next call block) so they don't keep popping up between all the other tasks in your list. You will have an easier time keeping an eye on the remaining tasks.

How to hide all tasks belonging to block building categories

1. Define a new view (see Chapter 2) called **Tasks Without Block Building**. Or instead, change the current view accordingly. To do this, from your tasks in Outlook 2010, go to the **View** tab and, in the **Current View** group, click **View Settings**. In Outlook 2007/Outlook 2003, click the **Customize Current View** link (in the navigation pane on the left).

2. In the open dialog box, click **Filter**.

3. In the **Filter** dialog box, click the **Advanced** tab.

4. Click the **Field** button, and then select the **Categories** option in the **Frequently-used Fields** list.

5. In the **Condition** list, select **doesn't contain**.

6. Type **(Block)** into the **Value** field (see Figure 4-4).

7. Click **Add To List**.

8. Also hide any tasks you have already taken care of and marked as completed (see "Use Filters to Clean Up Your Views" in Chapter 2).

9. Close all open dialog boxes by clicking **OK**.

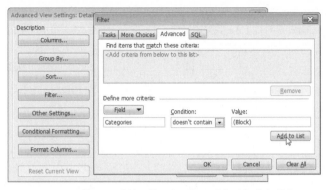

FIGURE 4-4 Use filters to hide all tasks allotted for block building.

Mark Tasks That Are Due Today and Tomorrow in Color

Perform the following preparations first: Define a new view based on the view you just filtered and call it Current Week. Arrange it according to priority in descending order (see Chapter 2). In the Filter dialog box, on the Tasks tab, filter for Due: This Week by using the two Time list fields, and then close the dialog box by clicking OK.

How to color tasks by using automatic color formatting

1. In the still-open dialog box, click **Conditional Formatting** (Outlook 2010) or click **Automatic Formatting** (Outlook 2007/Outlook 2003) to customize the view. The Conditional Formatting dialog box opens (see Figure 4-5).

FIGURE 4-5 Define rules for coloring your tasks.

BE CAREFUL WITH FILTERS!

Take a close look at the filter conditions you have specified and make sure you know exactly what they do when you are using your own custom filters. Otherwise the entries you were trying to view can easily "get lost," and you might overlook something.

For example, a filter Categories / Doesn't Contain / Call consistently hides all tasks that have been assigned to the Call category—even if the task also belongs to other categories, too. If you want to plan a phone call that should not take place within a call block (for example, because it takes a lot longer or is particularly important and should therefore be handled earlier and preferably outside of the block), it must not contain this category. Instead, thematically assign it to Project C, for example. Or use a different name for block building, such as Call (Block), so that you don't get confused if you tend to assign the category "Call" to each call, or if you often have calls that take place outside the call block.

Therefore, only assign tasks to the block building categories that you would like to take care of exclusively in the context of block building. To avoid confusion during filtering, just give all the corresponding categories the suffix (Block) at the end of their name and then filter for this word. This method may seem strange to you in the beginning, but it has certain advantages:

- The parentheses prevent you from unintentionally filtering categories that happen to contain the word *block*; for example "Project City Block."

- This keyword is less confusing than having to watch out for individual category names for block building (see previous example with the Call category name).

- If you set a negative filter that hides certain categories, it becomes relatively complicated to hide multiple categories at the same time, such as ActionList and CallBlock. If you simply list them one after the other in the Filter dialog box, Outlook will create a "show all that don't contain ActionList *or* don't contain CallBlock" filter—in other words, only hiding the tasks that belong to both blocks at the same time. As you can tell, it's getting more complicated.... The simplest way to solve this problem is to put (Block) into the name for each block building category and to just filter for "doesn't contain / (Block)".

2. Click the **Add** button.

3. Type the name of the new rule into the **Name** box; for example, **Due tomorrow**.

4. Click the **Condition** button.

5. On the **Tasks** tab, in the two **Time** lists, select **Due:Tomorrow** and close the **Filter** dialog box by clicking **OK**.

6. Click the **Font** button, select a color from the **Color** list (for example, Blue), and then close the **Font** dialog box by clicking **OK**.

    Now you have defined a rule that shows all tasks that are due tomorrow in a blue font.

7. Repeat steps 2 through 6 to create a new rule named **Today** in red (the color red is already reserved for overdue tasks in the default settings) to display tasks that are due today in red as well.

8. Close all open dialog boxes by clicking OK. The resulting view will look similar to the example shown in Figure 4-6.

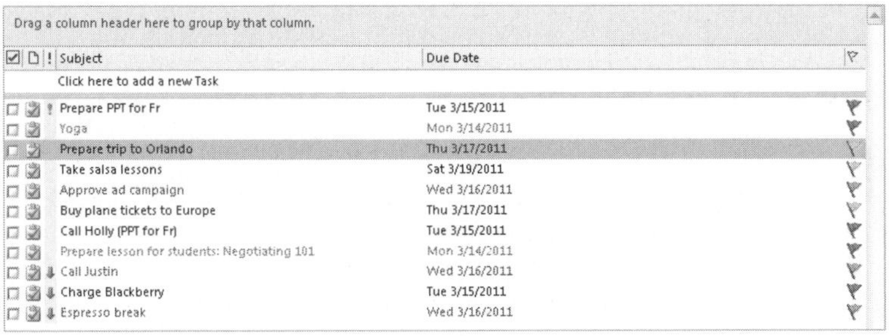

FIGURE 4-6 Define a view for your tasks that colors each entry automatically according to the rules you specified, such as overdue tasks in red and tasks due tomorrow in blue.

As you plan your day, this new view helps you decide which important tasks (of those that are due today, tomorrow, or during the coming week) you should plan to get done today, if tomorrow is a particularly packed day, for example. This way you can avoid having these important tasks be postponed because of less important tasks that are due a day earlier.

For advanced users: If you want to color your tasks according to criteria other than due date/time (for example, according to category), you need to keep in mind that a task can have only one color assigned to it. Make sure you color your tasks in such a way that only one color rule takes effect at one time if there are several categories per entry, and only mark your tasks according to a single criterion (such as by due date/time or by category); otherwise it could happen that one task is colored blue according to its category but then changes to red because of its due date, thus messing up the system you are trying to create.

How to turn off the red color marking for overdue tasks to avoid such color conflicts

1. In the **View settings/customizing the view** dialog box, click the **Conditional Formatting** button (Outlook 2010) or **Automatic Formatting** (Outlook 2007/ Outlook 2003).

2. In the **Rules For This View** list box (shown earlier in Figure 4-5), select the **Overdue Tasks** check box. If you just want to remove the red color for overdue tasks by deactivating the rule, simply clear the check box in front of this entry and proceed to step 5. Otherwise, continue with step 3 to adjust the settings in detail.

3. In the **Properties Of The Selected Rule** area, click the **Font** button.

4. In the dialog box that now opens, select **Automatic** from the **Color** list. If you want to, you could assign another formatting instead of the color, such as another font or size, to still see which tasks are overdue.

5. Close all open dialog boxes by clicking **OK**.

Gain a Better Overview by Using Appointment Lists

You are probably accustomed to looking at appointments in the day, week, or month view. However, Outlook can also display appointments in a table view, similar to what you are used to from your task lists. This view is practical when your main priorities are not questions such as "What do I have to take care of next week?", "Where will I be on the 20th of July?", or "When in November will I have three days available for a business trip to...?" Many of us have gotten used to such questions and not much else when working with the calendar—purely thinking along the lines of the time aspect, which used to be the only way to access appointments with the good old paper appointment planners.

If you consistently supply your Outlook appointments with information about categories and the location, as long as it is outside the immediate area of your office or home (see Chapter 3), you can arrange, group, and sort your appointments comfortably according to these criteria.

The following example shows how to create a new view that answers questions such as "When will I be in Seattle or Portland next time?" by showing appointments grouped by location.

How to create new calendar views as thematically grouped appointment lists

1. From any calendar view in Outlook 2010, go to the **View** tab and, in the **Current View** group, click **Change View**. In the menu that now opens, click **Manage Views**. In Outlook 2007, select **View/Current View/Define Views**, and in Outlook 2003 select **View/Arrange by/Current View/Define Views**. The **Manage All Views** dialog box opens (see Figure 4-7).

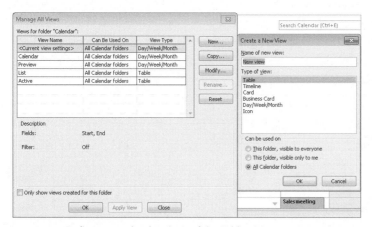

FIGURE 4-7 Define new calendar views of the Table type to sort appointments thematically.

2. In the **Manage All Views** dialog box, you can use an existing view as a template for a new view by clicking **Copy**. If you don't want to use any existing views as templates, click **New**.

3. Give the new view a name (for example, **Locations**), keep the default setting for the **Type of view** as **Table**, and then click **OK**.

4. In the dialog box that opens now, click the **Group By** button.

5. In the **Group Items By** list, select **Location**.

6. Close the **Group By** dialog box by clicking **OK**.

7. If necessary, you can now define filters or rules for conditional formatting.

8. Close the dialog box for the **Advanced view settings/Customize View** by clicking **OK**, and then the dialog box for **Managing all views/Custom View Organizer** by clicking **Apply View**.

You have now created your calendar view grouped by location (see Figure 4-8).

When you click the small triangle (Outlook 2010) or the minus/plus symbol (Outlook 2007/Outlook 2003) in front of one of the group headings, you can collapse or expand (hide or show) the entries of that group. When you right-click the symbol and then in the shortcut menu select Collapse All Groups, you will see only the different locations instead of the individual entries, and then you can click the small triangle or the plus symbol to view all appointments for the currently relevant location.

In case you are wondering why there are already several entries for the United States in the newly created location view: When you are using the Outlook function for the automatic insertion of holidays, Outlook assigns the location from there. (When you enter holidays for other countries, Outlook will record the corresponding country names.)

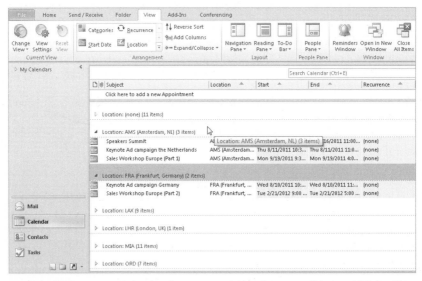

FIGURE 4-8 Create a new calendar view to see quickly when you will be at which location.

How to help yourself quickly, if you have accidentally entered duplicate holidays and now want to get rid of them

1. It is safer to group by category than by location (in case you have assigned **United States** to other appointments by yourself). You will find instructions on grouping in Chapter 3.

2. Select the first entry of the **Holiday** category.

3. Hold down the Shift key and click the last entry of the **Holiday** category to select all entries. (You could also just right-click the heading/name of that category and choose Delete from the shortcut menu, but this can go wrong quickly if you move the mouse a little and delete all the entries of another category by accident. It's safer to select everything you want to delete first so you can double-check your selection.)

4. Press Delete to clear all entered holidays at once.

If required, you can now solve complex questions as well, by combining the possibilities just shown. For example, you can create a colored view that only shows appointments belonging to your five most important projects for the next two quarters, grouped by project, arranged by date and location (conferences, trade shows, presentations, client visits, and more) so that Seattle is displayed in green, Los Angeles in orange, Denver in blue, Miami in yellow, and New York in red. (Filtering and automatic coloring via the automatic formatting of the list view works similarly for appointments as for task lists.)

After you get used to this approach of using themes (categories) or locations, such appointment views become extremely useful. Just go ahead and create a view grouped by category (make sure to assign the categories consistently to the appointments, which can be done quickly by choosing from your category list with two clicks; see Chapter 3). Looking at your view grouped by category, you may find out in retrospect that as Account Manager you had 22 internal meetings, but only 4 client appointments....

To get back to your customary calendar view, in Outlook 2010 go to the View tab and click Change View in the Current View group. In the menu that opens, click Calendar and then, in the Arrangement group on the View tab, click Week. In Outlook 2007/Outlook 2003, click Day/Week/Month in the navigation pane if you have your list of views displayed there, otherwise select Day/Week/Month via the View/Current View menu command (Outlook 2007) or View/Arrange by/Current View (Outlook 2003).

Fine-Tune Your Daily Planning

You have planned your week (see Chapter 3), added the Productivity Hours, created categories for block building, and assigned those categories to the corresponding tasks. You have created different views for your daily planning in Outlook, and maybe you've even been keeping a time protocol for the past few days. Read on to find out the final steps for successful daily planning.

Plan Pending Tasks with the 25,000 $ Method

You entered those appointments with a fixed date and time as soon as you made them. You also entered your Productivity Hours, as well as an appointment with yourself for a B-Task according to the Kiesel principle (see Chapter 3) into your daily calendar. Whatever is left to do belongs in your task list. In the next step, you must decide which of these tasks you want to do when. The 25,000 $ method (see Chapter 2) helps you to focus on what's essential during your workday.

How to fine-tune the 25,000 $ view (created in Chapter 2) for your daily planning

1. Navigate to your tasks. In Outlook 2010, go to the **View** tab and click **Change View** in the **Current View** group, and in the menu that now opens, click 25,000 $. If you are working in Outlook 2007/Outlook 2003, simply click the list of available views in the navigation pane on the left to get to the 25,000 $ view defined in Chapter 2.

2. In Outlook 2010, on the **View** tab, click **View Settings** in the **Current View** group. In Outlook 2007, go to the **View** menu and select **Current View/Customize Current View**.
    In Outlook 2003, use the **View/Arrange By/Current View/Customize Current View** menu.
    In Outlook 2007/Outlook 2003, you can also go to the navigation pane on the left and simply click the **Customize Current View** link.

3. Set a filter that hides the tasks you have already finished. Hide the ActionList as well as, for example, any tasks intended for the call block (see "Hide the Tasks Intended for Block Building in the Week/Day Views," earlier in this chapter).

4. Set a filter that only shows the tasks that are due today or overdue from the last few days: Go to the **Filter** dialog box, and on the **Tasks** tab select the **Due:in the last 7 days** options in the two **Time** lists (see Figure 4-9).

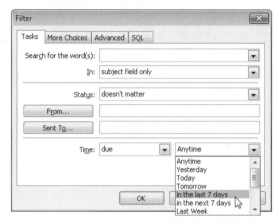

FIGURE 4-9 In the new view, only show all unfinished tasks from the past seven days, including today.

5. Close all open dialog boxes by clicking **OK**.

TIP   It's best not to set the filter to the due date of Today, but instead to In The Last 7 days. This way you can see all those tasks that you weren't able to get done in the previous days together with those due today. When something didn't get done for almost a week, you can try to determine a more realistic due date or decide to give up on it altogether when planning your next week. This way you won't lose track of tasks you don't get around to finishing for a few days.

How to plan your day (with the new view) according to the 25,000 $ method

1. Switch to the newly defined 25,000 $ day view, so that the tasks of the last few days that are overdue and the tasks that are due today but are unfinished are displayed.

2. Go through the list and delete the tasks that are no longer necessary. The more you delete, the more time you will have for the remaining tasks.

3. Switch to the view of tasks due this week (which you defined earlier in this chapter in "Mark Tasks That Are Due Today and Tomorrow in Color"). Briefly look through the most important tasks and those due tomorrow. Maybe tomorrow is a particularly full day, and today is relatively quiet. Or is there an important task that you'd rather get done today? Click the corresponding due date and enter **today**. (Override the existing text with the text **today**. Or click the arrow that appears

next to the due date after you click it, and select today in the date navigator. This may sound complicated, but after you have done it a few times, it will go quickly and easily.)

4. When you're done, switch back to the 25,000 $ view.

5. List any additional tasks you may have come up with today but haven't yet entered. (Ideally there shouldn't be any, because you've been entering each task as soon as you thought of it.) When something takes a very long time—30 hours, for example—divide it into smaller units of one to two hours, and think about which of those units you can get done today.

6. Now number the tasks according to importance, as shown in Figure 4-10 (see "Fine-Tune Your Priorities with the 25,000 $ Method" in Chapter 2).

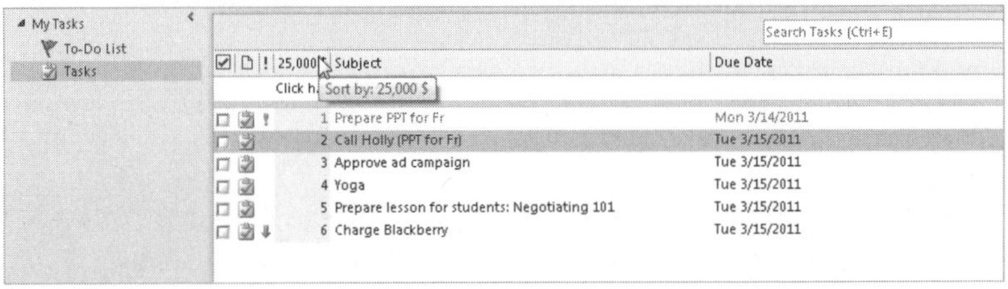

FIGURE 4-10 Use the new 25,000 $ view to determine which task is due next.

If your day doesn't start with a fixed appointment or a time with a high disruption curve and a low performance curve, display the 25,000 $ view and take care of task number 1 first.

But beforehand, make sure that you have time for this task. If you get to your office half an hour before an important meeting, but task number 1 takes one and a half hours and requires you to fully focus, or if this task can't be interrupted or is very difficult to get back into after an interruption, you'd better start with a task further back in the list that fits more easily into the time available.

Don't do anything else until this task is finished. Only look at your email at times you scheduled for your email block. When you have finished this task, briefly check whether something has changed and your priorities need to be adjusted. (For example, see whether a new A-Task has turned up; the importance of a task has suddenly increased or decreased dramatically; or a task has suddenly become completely unimportant, has been taken care of by somebody else, can wait a week, or you won't be able to start it until a week from now, because a crucial report has not arrived yet.) Then continue with the next task in order of importance.

Whenever there is no pending appointment (or email block) in your calendar, work on the next task in the list in order of importance, as long as there is enough time. If only a few minutes are left, and that's not enough time to finish a task, take care of a task from your ActionList. During times with a lot of unavoidable interruptions, focus on an email block, your ActionList, or less important tasks that are not seriously impacted by interruptions.

As a last resort, use your Productivity Hours to take care of task number 1—or assign it to your Productivity Hours on purpose right away, if you need to be able to concentrate extremely well, would have a hard time getting ahead otherwise, or the quality would be greatly compromised if you did not devote your Productivity Hours to it.

More Steps for Successful Daily Planning

Now you are prepared to complete your daily planning and give it a final polish. In the beginning it might all seem a little complicated and like a lot of work, but soon it will come easy to you. After you understand the principles, you will need about 15 to 20 minutes for planning in the beginning. After about three weeks of consistent implementation, the procedure will become a habit. It will become much easier for you, you will be able to estimate much more precisely, and you will only need five to eight minutes per day for preparation.

How to estimate the duration of pending activities

This is where time protocols come in handy, and then practice, practice, practice.... In time your estimations will become more and more precise. Outlook can help you, for example, in adjusting the 25,000 $ view.

How to adjust the 25,000 $ view in Outlook

1. Switch to the 25,000 $ view you customized in the previous section.

2. Right-click any column header and select **Field Chooser** from the shortcut menu.

3. Drag the **Total Work** field from the **Field Chooser** window up to the column header row and drop it next to another header, such as **Subject**.

4. Close the **Field Chooser** by clicking the close button (x) in the upper-right corner.

5. Now you can already enter an estimated duration for all of today's tasks into the **Total Work** field. Even if the field is pre-allocated with 0 hours, you can just override this value with, for example, 10 minutes. If necessary, you can add the **Actual Work** field, into which you can enter the time it actually took after the task has

been completed, as shown in Figure 4-11. (When a task is opened in the corresponding task form, both of these fields can be found in the **Details** section.)

☑	☐	!	25,00...	Subject	Total Work	Actual Work	Due Date	⚐
				Click ...				
☐	📄	!		1 Prepare PPT for Fr	1 hour	0 hours	Mon 3/14/2011	⚐
☐	📄			2 Call Holly (PPT for Fr)	10 minutes	0 hours	Tue 3/15/2011	⚐
☐	📄			3 Approve ad campaign	2 hours	1 hour	Tue 3/15/2011	⚐
☐	📄			4 Yoga	30 minutes	0 hours	Tue 3/15/2011	⚐
☐	📄			5 Prepare lesson for students: Negotiating 101	30 minutes	0 hours	Tue 3/15/2011	⚐
☐	📄	↓		6 Charge Blackberry	0 hours	0 hours	Tue 3/15/2011	⚐

FIGURE 4-11 Insert additional fields for more detailed planning, to estimate the duration for the task beforehand, and to keep track of the actual duration afterward. This helps control and estimate your time.

Make Further Appointments with Yourself

If you usually have to deal with disruptions at certain times of the day, plan appointments with yourself for your most important tasks during times with a low disruption ratio at the start of your work day (see "Weekly Planning" in Chapter 3). Also, if you can only take care of a certain task at a certain time or in a certain time window (for instance, you need to solve a complicated issue over the phone with a colleague who is located in a different time zone), create an appointment with yourself during your daily planning process.

Keep an Eye on Buffer Times

In real life, even a well-thought-out plan will never be executed exactly as planned—something will always come up, or take longer, or turn out differently than expected. A good plan catches this with buffer times. Therefore, use the 60:40 rule to plan: For example, if you have a 10-hour work day, fill only 6 hours of it (60 percent) with appointments and tasks that have to be done that day (you can include some more that would be nice to finish today, but are still fine if you don't get them done until tomorrow or the day after tomorrow). If everything runs smoothly, take care of the other tasks from your 25,000 $ view during the remaining time. If something takes longer, or an unexpected issue pops up that you must take care of immediately, you still have enough buffer time to meet your fixed appointments and take care of the tasks you assigned as appointments to yourself. You should use this rule for your entire day, including travel times and private plans: for example, plan 9 hours and leave 6 open, if you have 15 hours between finishing breakfast and getting ready for bed. This way you avoid having a conversation after hours—which took a bit longer than expected, combined with a traffic jam during rush hour—mess up the evening at the movies you had planned with your son.

Start with the 60:40 rule—plan out no more than 60 percent of the available time. Try to stick with it for three weeks. This kind of planning will soon become a habit and simple routine. After three weeks, slowly work up or down to the value that fits your work environment the best: For some people it works better to plan 70 percent of their time; for others, 50 percent planned and 50 percent buffer make the most sense.

Use the To-Do Bar to Keep Upcoming Appointments and Tasks in View

Although in the Outlook versions before Outlook 2007 you were able to display your tasks next to the calendar by using the TaskPad, the new To-Do bar in Outlook 2010/Outlook 2007 now helps you to always keep an eye on the upcoming appointments and tasks—whether you are working in a completely different week in the calendar and want to show upcoming appointments (in addition to all tasks that are due today); have filtered for and are only viewing tasks for a certain project, the trade show preparation, or next week (see Chapter 2) but still want to see which tasks are due today and which appointment is next; or even if you just want to always keep an overview of the To-Do List and your upcoming appointments while displaying your email messages, contacts, or notes in Outlook.

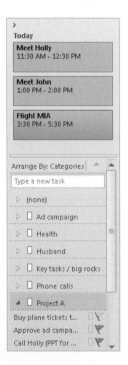

In Outlook 2010, you can switch on the To-Do bar from the View tab, by clicking To-Do Bar/Normal in the Layout group. In Outlook 2007, you do this by clicking View/To-Do Bar/Normal (or with the appropriate commands for Off/Minimized). If the bar is set to Normal or Minimized, just expand or collapse it by using the little triangle (Outlook 2010) or the double arrow (Outlook 2007) at the top of the bar. The minimized bar will still show you the number of tasks due today, as well as the day of the week, the start time, and the beginning of the subject of the next appointment. By pressing Alt+F2, you can toggle between the Off, Minimized, and Normal states.

What to do if some of the information you want doesn't fit on the screen? If the first part of the task's subject is not enough to remind you what exactly it is about, point to the respective task. After a moment, Outlook will display a kind of "sticky note" with the entire subject of the task for a few seconds. The scroll bar to the right of the displayed tasks lets you know whether there are further tasks below the displayed task. If the scroll bar is displayed, there are more tasks that don't fit on the screen.

The displayed tasks correspond to the To-Do List (see Chapter 2). You therefore also see email messages flagged as tasks (see Chapter 1). Double-click to open the displayed tasks and appointments directly for editing. Right-clicking opens the shortcut menu of the item (for example, to create categories).

When you right-click the red flag that represents a task's due date, you can set the due date in the shortcut menu to Today, Tomorrow, This Week, or Next Week, or you can specify a desired date by using Custom. Tasks that are overdue or due today receive a red flag. So are the tasks without any due date—as a reminder that you urgently need to assign one. Tasks due tomorrow receive a lighter colored flag, those for next week an even lighter one, and so on. Clicking the red flag marks the task as completed.

How to Customize the To-Do Bar

To adjust the bar width, click the left border and drag it.

Right-click the top border of the bar (directly above the displayed appointments) and select Options in the shortcut menu. You can now select the number of months you'd like to display below one another in the date navigator as well as hide or show the individual panes of the bar by using the check box (see Figure 4-12).

To filter or group the tasks shown in the bar individually, right-click directly above the tasks on Type A New Task, and choose View Settings (Outlook 2010) or Customize Current View (Outlook 2007) in the shortcut menu. Alternatively, you can click the column headers above the displayed tasks (for example, Arrange By: Due Date), and select View Settings from the shortcut menu (Outlook 2010) or Custom (Outlook 2007). Grouping and filtering was covered earlier in Chapter 2.

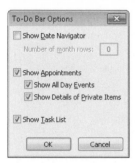

FIGURE 4-12 Customize the task list, for example, to display the next two months in the date navigator, or to show the upcoming appointments and hide the date navigator to have more space for the tasks.

You Try It

1. Think about what gives you the most problems when planning your day. In the next step, find out what the reason is (for instance, "I never manage to finish a single task," "Reason: I've taken on too much at a time, which is why I often switch between tasks; I also allow too many interruptions").

2. For which of your tasks does block building make sense? Set up appropriate categories in your main category list for all blocks, which will most likely contain more than 10 tasks per week.

3. Draw your performance curve and your disruption curve. When is the optimal time span for a Productivity Hour? From what day onward will you set it up on a daily basis, and how will you let your colleagues know? (Or what do you think prevents you from doing so, and how could you change that?)

4. Create a view for all unfinished tasks that are due this week, if you haven't done so in Chapter 2. Then hide the ActionList and the tasks belonging to the other categories of block building for this view.

5. In this view, arrange the tasks according to importance, mark tasks due today in red, and mark tasks due tomorrow in blue.

6. Fine-tune your view for the 25,000 $ daily priorities (from Chapter 2) as in step 4 (hide block building; instead of the whole week, show only tasks due today and overdue tasks). Then use it to plan tomorrow according to the steps described in "Fine-Tune Your Priorities with the 25,000 $ Method" earlier in this chapter.

7. Create a (calendar) view that displays all appointments in a list grouped by location and sorted by date.

CHAPTER 5

How to Schedule Meetings So They Are Convenient, Effective, and Fun

IN THIS CHAPTER, YOU WILL

- Send meeting requests with Outlook.

- Use the calendar overlay.

- Optimize your calendar.

- Prepare meetings more effectively.

"A Total Chaos Squad!"

IF YOU frequently need to plan meetings with colleagues whose schedules are very full and who are hard to reach, the Scheduling Assistant in Microsoft Outlook can be a big help. However, if you are too rash, Outlook meeting requests can become a curse rather than a blessing. This chapter gives you tips on how to quickly and effectively prepare meetings with Outlook and Microsoft SharePoint, and exchange data and documents for review as a team—to save you and your colleagues precious time and achieve better results.

How much time and money do you waste in unnecessary, badly prepared, or ill-structured meetings? Just add up hourly rates and loss of productivity for time spent getting very little done. Do you frequently look for information, but can't reach the colleague who could supply it, which means that you have to wait hours or until the next day?

ROBIN AND THE FANTASTIC FIVE

Today Robin Wood made it to the meeting room right on time at 9:00 A.M. He's totally out of breath and hasn't had any breakfast, but that's okay, because his assistant Melissa always makes sure there's fresh coffee and tasty cookies. Except for Melissa, Robin, and Robin's manager Charlie, nobody else has arrived yet. So he has some time to eat something and catch his breath. Charlie leaves at 9:04 to take care of some things before the others will arrive. At 9:08 Justin shows up. At 9:17 Boris Scholl from the board of directors arrives. At 9:21 Charlie returns and the meeting starts—but without Robin's colleague, Holly, who arrives at 9:30 sharp, looking rather puzzled: She's almost always on time, but this meeting had been moved so many times that she had forgotten to note the latest change from 9:30 to 9:00 in her calendar.

After a bit of back and forth, everyone finally agrees to an agenda. All participants skim through the documents they need to read as a basis for discussion for this meeting. Then Justin reads a few questions and their possible answers, so all delegates can raise their hands for their favorite option. Before counting the votes for each question, each person gets two minutes to think about which option he or she will vote for. The meeting finally really gets going at 10:12 , but at 10:30 Boris Scholl needs to leave for his next appointment, and at 10:50 Robin needs to run to catch his flight, even though not all agenda items have been addressed.

Two hours later, Robin has landed punctually. He is happy to realize that after lunch he still has 45 minutes left before his appointment, and the 3G network coverage is great. This gives him a chance to take care of a few email messages and phone calls. His colleague, Holly, had sent him an email message before the meeting, with an urgent request for him to call one of her customers—unfortunately, she didn't include the phone number. The customer info is not saved in Robin's contacts, so he quickly calls Holly. However, she is in the middle of a presentation and won't be available until Robin is sitting in his own customer meeting, which will last until evening....

The Problem: Way Too Many Inconvenient Meeting Requests and Insufficient Preparation

Some of the most common problems in this area of cooperation have the following causes:

- Too many meetings that take too long and leave too little time for other things.

- Meeting requests that are scheduled at very inconvenient times because they are squeezed in too late, when all other times are already taken for the next few days.

- It takes a lot of back and forth until you finally come up with a meeting date and time that works for everybody. Some people don't keep their calendar up to date, and others just put in a fake appointment from 5:00 A.M. until 11:00 P.M. each day to block their calendar for any requests (but because they have to be at some of the meetings, they end up receiving requests for the most inappropriate times possible...).

- Unclear meeting goals, or very different meeting expectations.

- No preparation or inadequate preparation, and lots of aimless chatter without a time limit.

- Too many participants, some of whom the topic doesn't concern and who therefore have nothing to contribute and only waste their time by being there.

- Missing, obsolete, overly comprehensive, or unread documents.

- No access to data required by everyone in the team, such as the contacts maintained by another colleague.

Let's Get Started and Change This!

To meet these challenges successfully, you might find the following strategies helpful:

- Use the shared calendars of your colleagues to look for convenient times, and thus automate as much of the meeting planning as possible.

- Optimize your own calendar to help colleagues when they are trying to set up meetings and to receive more reasonable meeting requests yourself.

- Plan meetings more consciously—as few meetings as possible with as few participants as possible.

- Set up more efficient, more effective, and shorter meetings by preparing them well.

- Provide an agenda, contact data, preparation materials, and other information beforehand at a central location.

- Set up a system to control what is under review or being edited, to avoid having several people change the same document simultaneously.

Technical Requirements for Using This Chapter

Outlook can be installed in single-user mode with a local data file, or your data can be stored on a Microsoft Exchange server. Using an Exchange server has several advantages, such as access to shared calendars from colleagues and instant wireless synchronization with your smartphone even when your computer is turned off. Some of the functions described in this chapter are available only if you use an Exchange server. Even if you are a freelancer working from a home office on your own, you can rent an Exchange mailbox and user account from various service providers for a monthly fee. If you later choose to hire a virtual assistant for a few hours each day, you can just book a second account with your provider for a small additional fee so that your assistant can manage your inbox for you and will always know when you'll be available for client meetings and conference calls. If you have a small business with fewer than 10 people who need to share their calendar and other data with each other, in most cases it'll also be cheaper and easier to use a hosted Exchange solution from a third party instead of setting up your own Exchange server in your office.

Meeting Requests with Outlook—Basic Rules and Tips

On the next few pages, you will first learn some of the basics for planning meetings in Outlook. Then you will find out how to optimize your calendar to make it easier for your colleagues to propose meetings at convenient times and at the same time leave enough free space for your own planning.

Find Free Times and Evaluate Replies

There are many advantages to planning meetings with Outlook:

- You can directly access the shared calendars of others and see when everyone has time, so the chance of picking the wrong time for an appointment decreases significantly.

- Microsoft Outlook 2010 supports using multiple Exchange accounts with one Outlook client profile. If your company's security guidelines permit, you can use mailboxes from different companies at the same time (for example, if you are a corporate consultant who spends a lot of time at the customer's office, you can use the mailbox of your own company as well as your mailbox on your customer's server). You can now easily display the calendars of colleagues and clients alongside your own or below each other and therefore avoid creating appointment chaos.

- All participants automatically receive an invitation that already contains buttons for accepting or declining the appointment and for suggesting an alternative time.

- From this email invitation, the participants can access their own calendars to see what they have going on before and after.

- If the participants accept the invitation, the appointment is automatically added to their calendar.

- As a meeting organizer, you can have Outlook evaluate the replies automatically and see who has replied already and how—directly from your calendar by just double-clicking the appointment.

- Outlook now monitors the appointment for you (the organizer) and, if you want, sends an update to all participants if changes are made.

> **IMPORTANT** All these advantages (with the exception of access to the calendars of others to look for free times) are available to you even without an Exchange server. You can send meeting requests to external contacts for fast answers, receive automated calendar entries when you accept a meeting, and manage the replies—for example, for a conference call you just set up with a customer.

- Everybody in the team must know the basic functions. Start with at least a short introduction by an experienced colleague or, even better, with a training course or seminar for planning as a team and how to use Outlook. Make sure that new colleagues also get a short introduction.

- Everybody must start using the functions at the same time (but this can be limited to individual groups within the team who use group planning among themselves).

HOW TO MAKE THIS ALL WORK

If you introduce Outlook meeting planning to your team and set up delegate access, access to folders of colleagues, and the use of shared data via SharePoint or public folders with Outlook, there are four basic requirements. Make sure they are met so that everything runs smoothly.

- Someone needs to take care of the technical maintenance of the Exchange server, grant access rights, and support users who encounter technical problems. This needs to be done by your IT department or a third-party specialist if you are a small business.

- Everybody in the team must really use and constantly update his or her Outlook calendar. Planning as a team loses its value, fails, or leads to a huge amount of problems if 4 of 10 colleagues enter none or only half of their appointments and note updates only weeks later.

We recommend that you agree on a transition time, such as a seminar followed by an "Outlook-only due date" three weeks later (at the latest). From that date on, everyone has to enter all of his or her external appointments during business hours in his or her Outlook calendar. It's best to also set a few basic rules (for example, key times, such as setting up meetings only between 9:00 A.M. and 11:30 A.M. if possible, restricting the maximum duration to two hours per meeting, and similar rules).

How to create a meeting request

1. Press Ctrl+Shift+Q or create a normal appointment and click the **Invite Attendees** button on the associated **Appointment** form.

2. In the **To** field (just like with an email message), type the names of the attendees you want or click the **To** button to select your recipients from the Address Book. Alternatively, you can switch from the open Appointment form to the **Scheduling Assistant** (in Outlook 2010/Microsoft Office Outlook 2007 by clicking **Scheduling Assistant/Scheduling** in the **Show** group on the **Appointment** tab; in Microsoft Office Outlook 2003, by just clicking the **Scheduling** tab). When you are there, click **Add Attendees/Add Others** to open the Address Book.

3. Add all of the participants from the Address Book by clicking the name and then **Required**, **Optional**, or **Resources**.

> **NOTE** *Required* means that this participant really needs to be there. *Optional* means that this meeting is possible without this person attending, so she can spend her time in better ways, but if she wants to attend anyway she is welcome. *Resources* means that you are adding, for example, the calendar for a meeting room, a company car, or a specific device, such as a digital projector.

In the Scheduling Assistant (see Figure 5-1), you will now see the times that are still available in the calendars of the other attendees (assuming you have the appropriate access rights). A dark grey bar in the All Attendees row means that nobody else has entered a conflicting appointment. The light grey background between the green and red vertical lines shows the time currently set for your new meeting. (You can find more information about the colored bars and how they are used later in this chapter, in "Take Advantage of the Show As Field to Flag Your Appointments.")

4. In the schedule, click any time to select a different time, move the selected area by dragging the green/red vertical line marking the current beginning/ending time, or click the **AutoPick Next**>> button so that Outlook can find the next free time slot for all participants (or use the small **<<** button to the left of **AutoPick Next>>** to select the next free time slot before the currently selected time). You can also specify a date and time by directly entering values into the **Start time** and **End time** fields (labeled **Meeting start time** and **Meeting end time** in Outlook 2003).

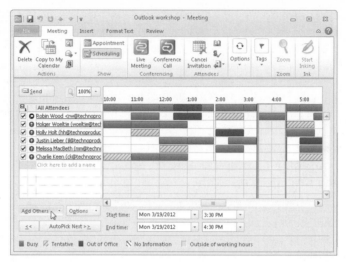

FIGURE 5-1 When selecting a time that works for everybody, make sure to leave a bit of time before and after other appointments, if possible.

5. If necessary, switch back to the Appointment view (in Outlook 2010/Outlook 2007, by clicking the **Appointment** button in the **Show** group on the **Appointment** tab (which is relabeled as **Meeting** after you have added attendees); in Outlook 2003, by just clicking the **Appointment** tab) to insert the subject line, a greeting in the note field, and any other information you want to send along with the meeting request. By clicking the **Attach File** button in the **Include** group on the **Insert** tab (Outlook 2010/Outlook 2007) or **File** on the **Insert** menu (Outlook 2003), you can attach documents that need to be edited or read before the meeting starts, an agenda, directions to a location, and so on, which Outlook will send as an attachment to the invitation.

6. After you have entered everything, send the meeting request to the desired participants by clicking the **Send** button (located on the left side next to the subject line in Outlook 2010/Outlook 2007 and just below the **File** menu in Outlook 2003).

7. Close the **Meeting Request** form by clicking the close button (the small x in the upper-right corner) or by choosing **Close** from the **File** menu. You can also use Alt+F4 to close the **Meeting Request** form.

If you want to open the Meeting Request form again later on, you can find the meeting as an appointment in your calendar (double-click to open it). In Outlook 2010, you'll also find the People Pane in the lower part of the meeting request after it is opened in its own window (see Figures 5-2 and 5-3). The People Pane contains miniature photos of the participants (if the photos exist in your Outlook contacts, otherwise it'll show empty silhouettes). Click the small arrow in the lower-right corner to see larger pictures with the names below them and find out who has already accepted, declined, or tentatively accepted the invitation and who hasn't replied yet (click the corresponding option on the left; see Figure 5-2). If you click one of the photos, Outlook 2010 will show you further information about this person, his or her social media status on LinkedIn or Facebook, your next meetings with him or her, and email messages from this person (see Figure 5-3; click one of the displayed meetings/email messages to open it in its own window).

FIGURE 5-2 Open a saved meeting and use the People Pane of Outlook 2010 to find out who has already accepted or not replied yet.

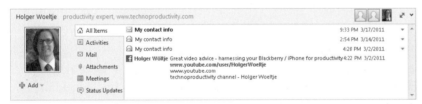

FIGURE 5-3 You can also click the picture or the name of a participant in the People Pane to display more information about this person, such as additional meetings.

Create Meeting Requests from a More Flexible View

If you only want to invite two, three, or four participants, the screen provides enough space to display calendars side by side (available as of Outlook 2003). This is helpful for comparing the shared calendars of others directly to your own work week or day view. This way you can tell much faster that, for example, on Monday (which you had in mind originally) there is just one hour available, but on Thursday morning everybody is available, and Thursday works better because it avoids packing every day with appointments. Unlike the method that uses the Scheduling Assistant in the Appointment form, as shown earlier, this kind of planning takes advantage of more available space. Depending on your screen resolution and the number of attendees, you can read more of the subject of other appointments without pointing to every single one. Above all, you can clearly display all Wednesdays in August side by side or the next two Wednesdays and Fridays without the days in between.

How to create meeting requests from a more flexible view

1. Switch to your calendar and, if necessary, hide the **To-Do** bar or the **TaskPad** to gain more space (Outlook 2010/Outlook 2007: press Alt+F2, Outlook 2003: in the **View** menu, choose **TaskPad** to hide/unhide your **TaskPad**).

2. To the left of the navigation area in the **Other Calendars** section, select the check boxes of the calendars you want to show (see Figure 5-4).

    If you can't find a colleague's calendar, add it in Outlook 2010 by clicking **Open Calendar** in the **Manage Calendars** group on the **Home** tab. In Outlook 2007/Outlook 2003, click **Open A Shared Calendar** in the navigation area on the left. In the dialog box that appears, type the name of the colleague or select it after clicking the **Name** button in the address book, and then close all dialog boxes by clicking **OK** to open his or her calendar.

3. Switch to Day view: In Outlook 2010, click the **Day** button in the **Arrange** group on the **Home** tab. In Outlook 2007, click the **Day** tab, and in Outlook 2003 click the **Day** button.

4. In the date navigator (the small calendar in the upper-left corner of Figure 5-4), click the first day you want to see, such as next Tuesday.

5. In the date navigator, click any additional days you want to show while keeping the Ctrl key pressed to add more days (or deselect them by clicking again). The selected days will be displayed with a dark background in the date navigator and are shown next to each other in the Day view for all selected calendars. (If you select every Friday in February, it looks like "a Week view with four Fridays." This view is very convenient if someone asks for a meeting on any Friday because he'll only be in your town or only be available on a particular day of the week.)

6. Right-click the date and time you want in one of the calendars (such as **Wednesday, 11:30 A.M.**).

7. In the shortcut menu, click **New Meeting Request** to invite all people whose calendars you have selected, or **New Meeting Request for <Name>** to select one specific person.

8. Now you can plan the meeting as explained previously in "How to create a meeting request."

9. Afterward, hide those calendars you no longer need to see on the screen by clearing the corresponding check boxes in the **Other Calendars** section.

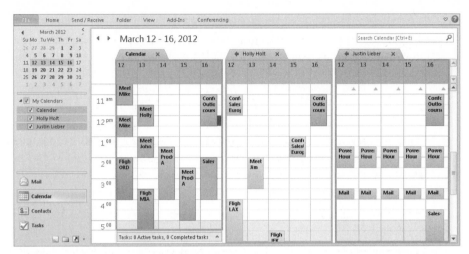

FIGURE 5-4 In the date navigator, select the days you want from the displayed calendars; for example, to quickly find an appointment in the next four days or on all Thursdays in March.

> **NOTE** "Meeting request" suggests that the appointment is a meeting (which you will attend in person in an onsite conference room). However, you can also use meeting requests for all other types of appointments that involve at least one other person. For example, you can use meeting requests for a time-consuming phone call, a customer visit, a date to go jogging, or for planning the preparation of a trade show presentation with team members.

Stay on Top of It: Calendar Overlay

If you like the idea of displaying multiple calendars next to each other in Day/Week/ Month view, which allows you to easily compare the calendars of two or three people (at the most—more wouldn't fit well), read the subject and duration of appointments, and find available meeting times, you will simply love the extension of this view in Outlook 2010/Outlook 2007. As described previously, you can show (or hide) the calendars you want to display simultaneously with just one click. In Outlook 2010, as soon as the calendars are displayed next to each other, click the Overlay button in the Arrangement group on the View tab; in Outlook 2007, go to the View menu and click View In Overlay Mode. (In Outlook 2010, you can get back by clicking the button again; in Outlook 2007, you can do so by going to View/View In Side-by-Side Mode.)

Outlook now "squeezes" all overlapping appointments next to each other. The smaller the appointment bars get, the more people (or rooms or resources) are already booked at that time. For example, if you are displaying five different calendars simultaneously, you won't be able to read anything for crowded time slots, but you will know this: "Where there is a light background visible, the time is still available in every person's calendar." As long as you don't overlay too many calendars at once, you can still read the subjects and will quickly see where your colleague will be while you are in a meeting, or who of the five sales representatives for whom you are scheduling appointments will be available for a customer visit during the target time. If everyone has filled in the Location field for his or her appointments, you can even see where the previous or next appointment takes place (shown below the subject line).

Above the weekday names, tabs with the names of the people (or calendars) are displayed (see Figure 5-5). The appointments for the tab on top of the other tabs have opaque color with full contrast; the appointments of the other calendars are partially transparent. Click the name on a tab to bring it to the top. With the small arrows to the left of the names, you can undock calendars and display them individually next to the other overlaid calendars (by clicking the right arrow) or put them back overlaid with the other calendars (by clicking the left arrow). This way you can overlay the calendars of four colleagues and show yours individually next to them to have more space and be able to read the appointments more easily.

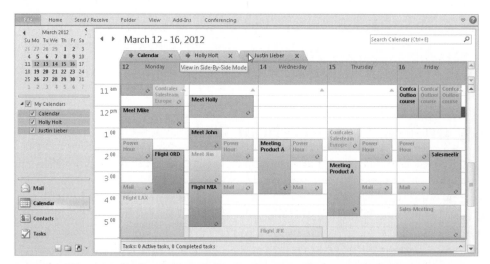

FIGURE 5-5 Overlaid calendars help you find open time slots in Outlook 2010/Outlook 2007. For example, 11:00 A.M. till 1:00 P.M. is still free in everyone's calendar on Wednesday and Thursday here.

THE SCHEDULE VIEW

Outlook 2010 provides an additional handy view for shared calendars: the Schedule view (see Figure 5-6). This view shows large bars, similar to those in the Scheduling Assistant. The Schedule view, however, gives you much more space to display the individual appointments, and you receive more details per person (for instance, each person gets his/her own color and you can read the appointment subjects very well). You can open the Schedule view by clicking the Schedule View button in the Arrangement group on the View tab.

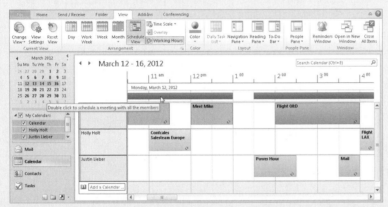

FIGURE 5-6 The Schedule view in Outlook 2010 provides you with an overview of the hours of a specific day in the calendars of multiple colleagues, whereas the overlaid calendar works well for displaying several days within one week.

How to answer meeting requests

A meeting request first shows up in your inbox as an email message. Instead of an envelope icon, you will see a calendar page with two very small heads in it's lower-right corner—replies to meeting requests also have their own icons showing whether the invitee accepted, declined, or proposed a new time.

1. Double-click the meeting request to open it. (You can also use the email preview in the reading pane and directly accept or decline from there by using the buttons.)

2. In the **Message** form (the new window that opens after you double-click the request), you'll find the **Accept**, **Decline**, and **Propose New Time** buttons: in Outlook 2010/Outlook 2007, these are on the **Meeting** tab, in the **Respond** group; in Outlook 2003, they are directly below the menu bar (you can see these in Figure 5-7, a little later in this section).

3. If you already know that you want to accept or decline, you can skip to step 7. Otherwise continue with step 4.

4. Click the **Calendar** button. Outlook 2010 will have already displayed your calendar for the hours before and after the requested time (see Figure 5-7) even without this step. When you click the **Calendar** button, Outlook opens a new window with your calendar in Day view, showing all appointments on the day of the meeting request. The proposed time has a blue background. That day has a dark background in the date navigator, and today is framed in red. (To see the rest of the week or find an alternative appointment, you can, for example, select other days in the date navigator, display additional days, or switch to the work week in the calendar view.)

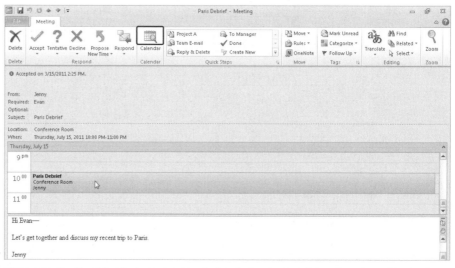

FIGURE 5-7 Use the Calendar button to check directly from a meeting request how this appointment fits in with your other appointments. Even without clicking this button, Outlook 2010 will already show one hour before and after the requested time, to show a preview of any scheduling conflicts.

5. If necessary, you can move other appointments to make room for the meeting or add buffer times before and after. Click the right border of the appointment you want to move (or on the upper border to change the duration), and drag it to the new timeslot.

6. Close the calendar window by clicking the close button (the small x) in the upper-right corner of the window's title bar.

7. Click one of the reply buttons (such as **Accept**).

8. Outlook now offers you three options: **Send the response now**, **Don't send a response**, or **Edit the response before sending** (for instance, to add a note).

   Even if you don't have any particular reason to reply, it is best to always choose **Send The Response now** (the response is automatically sent to the meeting organizer, so he or she will know if you accepted or declined). If you decline or if you only accept tentatively, we recommend that you choose **Edit the response before sending** and add one or two explanatory sentences.

ACCEPTING TENTATIVELY AND PROPOSING A NEW TIME

You can choose Tentative or Propose New Time, for example if you aren't sure if you can keep the requested afternoon appointment or need to leave for another appointment halfway through, but the morning would work much better for you. Leave everything else to the person who called the meeting: Maybe others have proposed the morning as well or aren't available in the afternoon, and therefore you will get an appointment update with your meeting moved to the morning hours. If the afternoon appointment works for all other participants except you, it may stay at that time in spite of your tentative acceptance. If you accept tentatively, you should write one or two sentences to the colleague who sent the request, to explain why it's inconvenient for you and what changes would make it fit your schedule better, so he or she can respond accordingly.

IMPORTANT   Only accept tentatively if there is a realistic chance that you can still take part—otherwise, it's best to decline right away. When it really makes sense, use the Tentative reply option. Tentative means that you don't know for sure whether you will be able to keep the appointment or that you reserve the option of canceling due to a more pressing appointment. By doing this, you signal to your colleagues that the appointment is not convenient for you and that you might not be able to make it, unless an alternative time can be found. At the same time, you block the appointment in your calendar and will be reminded of it.

9. Outlook now deletes the meeting request from your inbox, sends the reply to the meeting organizer, and enters the meeting as an appointment at the right date and time in your calendar (if you haven't declined).

If you look for the request later on, you will now find it in your calendar. You can edit it there just like any other appointment entry. When you open the associated Appointment form by double-clicking the appointment, Outlook informs you in a line below the menu bar or ribbon when you accepted this meeting ("Accepted on..."; see Figure 5-7).

How to check and change the status of a meeting you called

In Outlook 2010, you can use the People Pane as explained earlier in "How to create a meeting request." For Outlook 2007/Outlook 2003, you can install the Outlook Social Connector to display the People Pane. If you don't want to install it or if you don't like the People Pane and prefer to have it turned off, you can do the following:

1. Double-click the meeting in your calendar to open it in a separate window.

2. In Outlook 2010/Outlook 2007, click the **Tracking** button in the **Show** group on the **Meeting** tab. In Outlook 2003, simply click the **Tracking** tab.

   You can now see who has replied so far (see Figure 5-8); who accepted, declined or replied as tentative; and if you had chosen this person's presence as required or optional. You can also change the reply status manually by clicking it (for example, if someone answered by phone or you called him because you haven't received an email message yet but need a decision right now).

   With the **Scheduling** button (on the **Meeting** tab, in the **Show** group), you can check your colleagues' calendars (as shown earlier during the creation of the meeting request) and change the appointment, for instance if you notice that the appointment time was inconvenient for most of the participants after the first responses arrived.

3. By clicking the **Send Update** button (in the Appointment view, by choosing **Appointment** from the **Show** group on the **Meeting** tab in Outlook 2010/Outlook 2007 or simply clicking the **Appointment** tab in Outlook 2003), you inform everybody of the new date (the meeting will automatically be updated in their calendars), even if you keep the **Appointment** form open on your computer. As soon as you close the form after having changed the appointment data or, for example, move or delete the appointment in the week view of your calendar, Outlook automatically offers to send an update to all participants.

   Only the meeting organizer—the person who initially created the meeting request and invited other attendees—should update the meeting data. If you update anything for a meeting that somebody else invited you to, your changes will get lost as soon as he sends an update. So even if you edit the appointment from your own calendar and add some notes to prepare for the meeting, as soon as the meeting organizer sends an update, your changes will be lost. If you want to add notes for the other attendees or change the agenda, you have to write a separate email message to all the attendees or ask the meeting organizer to update the meeting. If you simply edit the meeting in your calendar, the other attendees will not see your edits unless you are the meeting organizer and send an update.

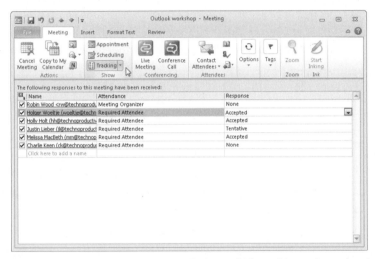

FIGURE 5-8 Use the Tracking button to find out which participants have already accepted or declined.

Use Meeting Requests Sparingly

How well you can optimize and manage your meetings depends on the other team members and various other factors that are different for each team. On the following pages, we will give you the most important general tips to help you to plan better and more effective meetings—if most (preferably all) of your team members follow these simple rules.

Meetings Are Expensive

Think about what a meeting actually costs you and your team:

- Almost always a meeting takes much more time than its actual duration. Let's assume you have been invited to a 30-minute meeting:

    - You need to interrupt your current work and will need more time to get back to your original level of concentration and performance afterwards.

    - With some tasks that take an hour or more, such an interruption would interfere to such an extent that you can't start them within 30 minutes before the meeting (you might even have to postpone them for another day). Therefore, an inconveniently scheduled meeting can create 30 minutes of idle time that you spend unproductively or with some unimportant odds and ends, just waiting for the meeting to begin because you can't continue working on your projects productively with so little time left before you have to leave for the meeting.

    - Getting to and back from the meeting location also takes time. If you are lucky, it's only a four-minute walk from your office in each direction, plus three minutes (times two) to pack up your materials in the office and the meeting room. This adds up to 10 minutes for each direction and 20 minutes total expenditure. Walking to a different building or driving/traveling to a different location takes even more time.

- A meeting costs time for all participants:

    - If 10 participants sit together for two hours, the net cost is 20 hours of effort (add the time spent per participant for the commute, and the gross cost gets much higher).

    - If two attendees arrive with a 10-minute delay, and 18 other people have to wait for them, your team just wasted 10 minutes for 18 people = 180 minutes = 3 hours of productive time. Delays tend to get worse if you choose to wait until everyone has arrived: Some people will get used to the delay and plan to arrive 10 minutes late, to avoid wasting their time waiting for others. If one of them is then delayed for 5 minutes, this will add up to 15 minutes....

    - Being unprepared or off topic is just as bad: If two participants take 15 minutes of time each to explain issues that are just as irrelevant to the other eight as their presence for this topic is, 8 × 15 = 120 minutes = 2 hours of time have been wasted.

- A meeting costs money: Calculate how high your personnel costs and ancillary labor costs for this time are—and how much revenue a colleague could have generated during this time. Add to that travel expenses, costs for the meeting room if you choose an external location, and more.

THE BEST MEETINGS ARE THE ONES THAT DON'T TAKE PLACE

As you can see, a meeting is frequently more expensive and time consuming than it initially seems. Sometimes, however, it's well worth that time because good meetings can help to create a stronger bond between team members, resolve conflicts, establish common strategies, spark synergy effects to come up with new ideas and product improvements, support each other, and gather many different ideas and improve them immediately with the expertise of multiple specialists from different areas.

Sometimes you need many people and a lot of room for discussion to come to a decision. Some information is best passed on in a personal conversation or in a presentation to a group. This is especially the case if a topic raises many questions, if the answers to those questions are relevant to everyone in the room, or if several people have information to pass on. (For example, you could have a three-hour meeting to prepare for a trade show to share details about one day's agenda that includes several presentations, technical information with a Q&A session about the crucial advantages of the three most important products, reminders of company policies and tips for talking to the press, and a report about the experiences from the last trade show.)

In all these cases, a well-prepared and well-run meeting can be incredibly productive and save a lot of time (see "Prepare Meetings Effectively," later in this chapter). In many cases, however, it's the exact opposite. Therefore, you should triple-check that there is no alternative before you call a meeting. Maybe you don't need one after all.

Don't overwhelm others with meeting requests simply because Outlook enables you to plan meetings more quickly and easily than ever. Avoid as many meetings as possible.

Think about the following before sending out a meeting request:

- Is the meeting worth the invested time and money? Don't call an $800 meeting to solve a $450 problem.

- Is the meeting really necessary?

  - If it's about decision-making: Are you sure that the responsible manager, a group of up to three experts, or a representative on the team's behalf can't make this decision (and maybe do so better and faster than the whole team)?

  - Does the presence of more people (more experience, a larger idea pool) significantly improve the quality of the results you are trying to reach, and does the improvement justify the additional effort as opposed to the effort of one or two people?

  - Can you clarify the issues at hand more effectively and more quickly via several individual phone calls, instead of calling a meeting?

  - Can you combine two or three small meetings with the same group of participants? The net time stays the same (or becomes less, because you can be late only once and issues are targeted as a group). The gross time drops significantly, because you only need to go to and return from one meeting.

  - When it comes to passing on information: Could you simply distribute the information in writing? We can read much more quickly than we can listen, and while reading we can skip parts we already know. Also, everybody can read the information whenever he or she has time to do so, rather than having to spend time sitting in a meeting, which would be better used doing something else. If writing is too time-consuming and the participants travel a lot, there is now an additional but so far rarely used alternative: Get a headset for your PC and voice-record the information. This is very quick and easy. The people you want to inform can then use their smartphones or MP3 players during long driving times to listen to your recordings. (The problem: You can't take notes while sitting behind the wheel. But if you travel a lot by car, just get a digital voice recorder or use your smartphone for voice notes.)

> **NOTE**
>
> Recurring weekly meetings are common time sinks that are scheduled "just in case there might be something we need to talk about." And when all attendees have gathered together, you'll find something you might as well talk about to fill the time. Beware of recurring meetings unless they are really useful and required or have a specific reason. However, well-prepared, meaningful weekly meetings can propel a well-attuned team forward—as with action groups in which six colleagues who are constantly traveling hold conference calls to keep each other up to date about the previous week and next week's planning at the beginning of each week.

- Which participants are really required? Whose time would you waste, because their presence is not necessary? (To avoid making those people feel excluded, you can also invite them as optional participants and leave it up to them whether they want to come. Let them know that they are welcome, if they want to find out what's going on and take part in decisions.)

- For example, are there four of eight participants who only need to be there for two of the six agenda items? Put these items at the beginning, so those participants can leave after the first 30 minutes, and let the other participants know.

- If you are convinced that a meeting makes sense, you should still consider the following: Can the participants save travel time, because a conference call might be just as good as an in-person meeting for the topics you have to discuss? Or go a step further and take advantage of Microsoft Office Live Meeting to show your colleagues' Microsoft PowerPoint presentations, take votes with automatic count, and share applications among each other (for example, to edit documents together or explain how a new software version is used). In Outlook, a conference call or a Live Meeting can be planned just like an onsite meeting (you can add the dial-in number and access code to the text of the meeting request).

ONLINE COLLABORATION AND MEETINGS WITH LIVE MEETING

Sometimes the possibilities of a conference call aren't enough, but an onsite meeting is still too expensive and time-consuming—for example, flying from Canada to Australia to show a PowerPoint presentation followed by a one-hour Microsoft Excel budget planning session. When you work together at your computers during a Live Meeting, some of the social and communicative aspects of a "real onsite meeting" will be missing, but in some cases a Live Meeting can be even better.

Here are some of the most important functions of Live Meeting:

- You can work together from any location—with, for example, one person waiting in an airport lounge in New York, another one sitting in his office in Munich, and a third in her hotel room in London. All you need is an Internet connection and a phone or a headset to use Voice Over IP to hear and talk to the other attendees.

- You can show PowerPoint presentations, send the screen content of any application to everybody, and grant individual users control of one of your applications, so they can show things or just edit something in an Excel spreadsheet on your computer.

- You can plan Live Meetings directly from Outlook—whether you are planning the budget for next month with two colleagues or presenting your new software to 1,000 prospective customers worldwide. You can, for example, appoint multiple moderators who immediately answer individual questions via text chat in the background while the speaker continues his presentation.

- You can record the entire Live Meeting (video and audio) to watch it again later, evaluate it, or show it to people who could not participate.

For additional information about Live Meeting, go to http://office.microsoft.com.

There are also further options for online collaboration, such as the Broadcast Slideshow function (in the Start Slide Show group on the Slideshow tab) in PowerPoint 2010 or Windows Live Messenger.

Optimize Your Calendar to Make Meeting Requests Easy

In this section, we will briefly cover how you can simplify successful meeting planning by uncluttering your calendar, and how to decrease the number of meeting requests you receive for inconvenient times.

Keep Your Calendar Well Organized

If you have entered hardly any appointments and also have no appointments with your-self (see Chapter 3, "How To Gain More Time for What's Essential with an Effective Week Planner")—in other words, if you have these times marked as "free"—you seem to be constantly available. You therefore don't need to wonder why colleagues constantly put meeting requests for inconvenient times into your calendar.

On the other hand, if every working day of your calendar is completely packed with appointments from 7:00 A.M. until 10:00 P.M. (and maybe some of them even partially overlap), you don't need to be surprised about receiving meeting requests that don't suit you—after all, your colleagues don't have a choice.

IS IT A GOOD IDEA TO BLOCK ALL THE TIME IN YOUR CALENDAR FOR EACH DAY?

As just explained, filling the calendar completely usually doesn't prevent incon-venient requests from your managers or colleagues, but in some companies this tactic is common practice as a "last defense" against too many requests from colleagues lower in the company hierarchy—decline everything, because there is "just no time left," or generally prohibit lower-ranking colleagues from mak-ing requests at occupied times. This method, however, has two disadvantages: First of all, it makes it more difficult for you to use your Outlook calendar in a reasonable fashion (or may even prevent yourself from doing it). Secondly, it also blocks necessary and important meetings. It's best to generally clarify things once and for all (for instance, restricting access to your calendar to your assis-tant and your executive team only), or as a manager just decline those meeting requests you don't consider necessary in a polite and brief way, even if the time is open. It takes planning, discipline, and an adjustment period to reduce the amount of meetings in teams suffering from "meeting addiction."

You can control the times for incoming meeting requests to a certain degree by blocking out your most important times of the day (even if you just block them to be undisturbed for an important task) and leaving sufficiently large chunks of time open (at the times that work for your colleagues). Make it easy for others to find the times that work for you—most people choose the path of least resistance when looking for the right time for a meeting. The next step is to suggest different timeslots for meetings that conflict with other appointments or to just decline those requests if possible.

SET CORE MEETING TIMES!

It's best to set up core meeting times for your team: Agree on timeslots everyone should keep free as long as possible, unless you are planning a meeting—for example, 9:30 A.M. to 11:30 A.M. Try to plan meetings during this time whenever possible (or in a shorter time window within this period). This works best if most of the other team members start planning the other times consistently as well—for example, by keeping 9:30 A.M. open, but planning a customer appointment, lunch break, or Productivity Hour (see Chapter 4, "How to Make Your Daily Planning Work in Real Life") for 8:30 until 9:30 A.M. and entering your email block for 11:30 A.M. (and just go ahead and make it a recurring appointment for each work day). If someone then wants to plan a meeting, many time slots are already taken, but the designated time between 9:30 A.M. and 11:30 A.M. is still open for (almost) everyone; it will only take a few weeks of adjustment until meetings start to take place during these times whenever possible. And if everyone arrives and leaves on time, you will be able to stick to that timeslot more and more easily (more about this later in this chapter, in "Prepare Meetings Effectively").

Keep your calendar well organized, if you aren't already doing so consistently for your own planning:

- Immediately enter each appointment (whether with customers, your dentist, or a flight from New York to Chicago).

- Only enter appointments into your calendar if they are true appointments—"Call Mike back about delivery date by Thursday, or better today" does not belong in your calendar as an appointment on Tuesday from 9:00 A.M. to 9:30 A.M. (unless you have agreed to a phone call with Mike for that time). This entry belongs in your task list (set the due date and, if necessary, a reminder; see Chapter 2, "How to Work More Effectively with Tasks and Priorities").

- Only enter appointments with yourself for your most important tasks as part of your weekly planning (see Chapter 3). Block time slots for these tasks (also to defend them against meeting requests), but at the same time keep enough space open by only blocking very few specific timeslots.

- If your calendar has lots of free time available, or if you would otherwise always procrastinate it: Consistently enter recurring appointments for your block building (see Chapter 4 and the right side of Justin Lieber's calendar in Figure 5-4, earlier in this chapter). Only cancel these recurring appointments in special cases.

- Feel free to plan further tasks as appointments with yourself as part of your daily planning process (see Chapter 4) and break your colleagues of the habit of calling a meeting at the last minute by declining, if you can (unless there really is a cogent reason for calling a meeting so late).

Take Advantage of the Show As Field to Flag Your Appointments

The Show As field is located in the Options group on the Appointment tab in Outlook 2010/Outlook 2007 (see Figure 5-9). In Outlook 2003, you can find the Show Time As field right below the Start Time and End Time fields if you opened the appointment in its own window by double-clicking it. In the Day/Week view, you can also edit the field from the shortcut menu by right-clicking the specific appointment.

This field usually contains the default value Busy. Change it to help your colleagues find convenient times, and take note of it in the calendars of colleagues when creating meeting requests (these are the colored bars in the Scheduling Assistant, as shown earlier in Figure 5-1).

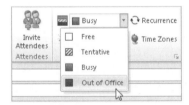

FIGURE 5-9 Appointments can be easily flagged with colors.

You have four options for setting this field:

- **Busy** This shows your coworkers that you already have this appointment filled, so this timeslot is taken, but you can open it up for another request if absolutely necessary.

- **Out of Office** You are not in the office. Decide with your colleagues what this actually means for your team to find a common code that everybody uses, such as one of these possibilities:

  - You are far away on a business trip and can't get back to the office that same day to attend a meeting.

  - You are not in the building—for example, visiting a customer—but you could be back in the office in an hour to attend a meeting.

  - You can't even be reached by phone during this time. (This is common in a situation where everybody is constantly traveling and you usually plan conference calls.)

  - You may not actually be out of the office, but you absolutely cannot move this appointment (while you set other outside appointments only to Busy and might be able to free them up, depending on the meeting).

- **Tentative** Reach an agreement as to whether this means "the appointment is very uncertain and the time slot will most likely open up again" or "if you have no other option but putting a meeting in one of my booked time slots, please take the tentative ones first; the other ones are more important."

- **Free** These times are not occupied. This is useful for certain appointments that last the whole day, such as a holiday that you want to remember.

How to use all-day appointments

If you will be out of the office for more than one day and therefore not available for meetings (on vacation, for example), enter an appointment for it:

1. Double-click the appointment to open it in its own window, and select the **All day event** check box (next to the start time). The options for choosing a time as a start time and end time are now disabled.

2. Now select the first day in the **Start time** field and the last day in the **End time** field (it's still labeled *time*, but you can only set a date).

3. Set the **Show as** field to **Out of Office** for your vacation. The all-day appointment will now "float" above the other appointments in the Day/Week view (see Figure 5-10). It marks you as **Out of Office** for the entire time, but leaves all time slots open for appointment entries. (This way you can show that you are out of the office for a trade show, for example, but you still have all the timeslots open for appointments you want to set during the trade show.)

4. Close the **Appointment** form by clicking the x in the upper-right corner, and click **Yes** to save the changes when Outlook asks you to confirm.

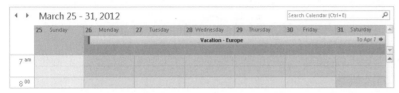

FIGURE 5-10 All-day appointments can mark several days as Out Of Office (the bar with "Vacation - Europe" on it) and leave you a complete overview, because they are displayed above the other entries in your Day/Week view.

In other situations, you can set the Show As field to Free (for example, if you just want to note in your calendar on which days a trade show takes place, when certain streets will be blocked in the city due to festivities, or when your kids will be on school break, so you can plan accordingly without having to mark the entire time as if you are out of the office. If you set an appointment to All Day, Outlook automatically sets the Show As field to Free—make sure you set your vacation to Out Of Office, though.

Flag Personal Appointments As Private

To prevent your colleagues from having access to your appointments, your children's vacations, your spouse's vacation, and your other personal appointments in your shared calendar, mark them as private.

In Outlook 2003, simply select the Private check box in the lower-right corner of the Appointment form. In Outlook 2010, click Private in the Tags group on the Appointment tab (the small lock icon). In Outlook 2007, in the Options group on the Appointment tab, also click the Private button (the small lock symbol). If the small lock icon has an orange-brown background (if you're not pointing to it), the appointment is flagged as private.

> **CAUTION**   If you point to Private in Outlook 2010/Outlook 2007, it may look like the option is already selected. If you take a closer look, however, you will notice that the background color is slightly lighter when the option has not been selected yet. Especially at the beginning, it's easy to get confused here—you should therefore make it a habit to point to Categorize (to point away from Private) to see if an appointment has been flagged as private.

In the Day/Week/Month view of your calendar, it's even easier: Just right-click an appointment as usual and select Private from the shortcut menu. Outlook 2010/Outlook 2007 displays private appointments with a lock icon in the lower-right corner. Outlook 2003 shows a key icon in the upper-right corner.

Your colleagues can now see that this time is blocked, but they can't read the subject or any other content of the appointment entry; they'll only see Private Appointment as the subject.

For your own control, you see a small lock or key icon in the appointment entry in the Day/Week view of your calendar. Select the Private option for all of your private appointments—even if it would be okay for your colleagues to see the subject. Otherwise you might forget it for confidential appointments, or provoke curious questions if you for once try to hide an appointment from the others. You can also mark confidential business appointments as private (for instance, a surprise party for a colleague's 20th service anniversary with the company).

It's best to clarify with your colleagues that appointments marked as Private don't necessarily have to be time off but are just confidential appointments, regardless of whether they are confidential business appointments or real private appointments.

> **NOTE** Private appointments are protected from the eyes of other users you have shared your calendar with. However, if you give a colleague the user name and password for your Exchange account, so that he or she has complete access while you are gone, Outlook assumes it's you. Whoever logs in with your data will see all your entries, so keep your password confidential!

Prepare Meetings Effectively

If all participants take time beforehand to prepare for the meeting and are ready to make decisions, you will save everyone a lot of time and conduct goal-oriented, to-the-point, effective meetings. If everyone takes 10 minutes to prepare, it often saves 20 minutes of meeting time—for all participants. Preparation is especially important for the person who runs the meeting and, if applicable, the moderator.

Improve Efficiency by Preparing and Running Your Meeting Wisely

Create an agenda for each meeting as soon as it is scheduled:

- Set a clear timeframe for each item, and limit the speaking and discussion time.

- Clearly identify the goals: What do you want to achieve with this meeting? Which information should be passed on or gathered (how, to whom, by whom), which questions should be answered, which ideas developed, which decisions made?

- For each item, assign someone to be responsible for the item.

- Limit the number of participants. Five to seven people is optimal. Too many participants can make a meeting unproductive—unless the objective is to inform a large group of people and answer their questions, or to get the opinion of many different experts, departments, or individuals about a topic.

- Start with the most important topics. Place the topics with the lowest priority at the end, assign them less time, and end the meeting on time. If you constantly run overtime, you will end up using 20 minutes for a topic you could have covered in 8 minutes, had you given yourself a time limit.

- If certain participants are only required for two of seven items, put these items on top of the agenda and let those participants leave afterward.

- Make sure all participants receive the required material well beforehand.

IMPORTANT

Plan sufficient breaks—meetings can really benefit from breaks:

- After approximately 45 to 60 minutes, it feels good to move and get some fresh air. People become more productive afterward. After two hours at the latest, most people can no longer concentrate on listening.

- In the breaks, the participants can talk about issues that are related to the meeting but may not concern everyone.

- Conversation in a break atmosphere can lead to new ideas.

- Especially during negotiations, the most important advances are often made during or after the breaks.

- Set an appropriate duration for the break. Ten to fifteen minutes has been proven to be optimal.

You can attach the agenda to the meeting request (just like attaching files to "regular email messages"). Attendees just have to open the meeting in their calendar by double-clicking it to access the agenda. However, using a SharePoint meeting workspace for the agenda (see the next section in this chapter) has many advantages compared to this method.

The following tips can help you run your meeting more effectively:

- Designate a meeting leader. If necessary, also select a moderator for difficult topics/groups, someone who is not involved in the content of the meeting itself but has a "referee function" (introduce new participants and the topic; limit the speaking time per participant to three minutes max, for example, and stick to it; and at the end summarize and clarify the results).

- Start and end the meeting on time. If you wait for latecomers once, you will soon always be waiting—each time a little longer. If you allow the meetings to run over-time, you are well on your way to meetings that never end.

- If you are not making any progress with a topic, let the meeting leader decide af-ter a specified amount of time whether you will cast votes about continuing, make at least some partial decisions, or postpone the topic to another day (including everything that needs to be prepared, clarified, and decided). A small break can help cool down heated tempers and allow everyone to think more clearly again.

- At the end, collect feedback from everyone. How did they like the meeting and the style in which it was led? Are there ideas for improvement? The first few times you may get silly or insignificant answers, but soon they will become more useful.

- Keep meeting minutes that mainly summarize results. Distribute it soon, prefer-ably still during the meeting or at the end of it for everyone. Typing the notes in Microsoft Word or Microsoft OneNote and showing them during the meeting all the time (on a digital projector) is best to make sure that everything is represented correctly and that nobody can later argue that certain decisions weren't made or were meant differently. Assign persons who will be following up on each item, and clearly specify what they have to do as well as a due date.

Use Meeting Workspaces to Prepare Meetings

In the last pages of this chapter, we will briefly introduce you to Microsoft SharePoint. If you are working with Windows Server 2003/Windows Server 2008 in your network, you can use Microsoft SharePoint Foundation (Windows SharePoint Services), which is part of the basic package. Even if you don't use this kind of server in your company, you can still rent these services from third-party providers, for example, to use SharePoint sites on the Internet together with virtual assistants, your advertising agency, and your customers. You can also take advantage of SharePoint Online, which is part of Microsoft Office 365 (cloud-based Office applications from Microsoft Online Services, available for a small monthly fee per user). If you are not sure whether these functions are available to you or how to set up a new SharePoint site, ask your system administrator for advice and, if necessary, request a user account for SharePoint.

What can project/meeting workspaces in SharePoint do for you? You can attach any documents necessary for meeting preparation, as well as an agenda, directly to the meeting request or send them via email, without needing to use SharePoint. But this old-fashioned method (without SharePoint) has several disadvantages:

- If the agenda (or other documents) changes—which is frequently the case, be-cause with a meeting request you are practically sending a proposal that will be amended by the other participants—the participants need to look for the newest version in your email messages, or each time a new version arrives delete the file attached to the appointment and replace it with the latest one. According to Murphy's Law, someone will always use an outdated version when he needs the data shortly before the meeting.

- Another drawback can be illustrated with an example: Suppose Melissa sends the agenda together with some documents. Both Robin and Boris individually think of a few additions and changes that each of them notes during the day and then sends to Melissa in the evening. She now has two different "new" versions of the files with different changes—partially in the same sections of the document, so she can't merge them manually with copy and paste. The situation requires a lot of work and further requests for clarification—it would have been better if first one person had edited the file while the other (knowing that the edit was taking place) had waited and then reviewed the updated file.

- Even if you don't have to deal with such simultaneous changes that end up causing conflicts, some meetings and topics can trigger a flood of email messages with additional attached documents and suggestions for changes, followed by comments from the individual attendees through email and their dismissal via yet more email. It gets even more complicated if you try to get a collective opinion about an issue: One person sends the question to all, everybody answers to all recipients. You end up having to gather the email messages from the last few days to get a cross-section of opinion. Because a simple email message with "Yes" or "No" or one of four options may seem a bit too blunt, most people add a few lines that aren't really necessary and make evaluation more difficult.

The Advantages of Meeting Workspaces

SharePoint can help by allowing you to create central team sites in your company's intranet. These sites can be set up directly from a meeting request and later retrieved from there. If you use SharePoint in such a way to prepare a meeting, the website you have created is called a "meeting workspace." The advantages of such workspaces include the following:

- All data is stored at a central location, just like on a bulletin board. You no longer need to sort and manage hundreds of email messages with data for the next 20 meetings; instead you can find all data for each meeting in one location, and it's always up to date.

- You can also store all relevant documents at this central location. There are functions allowing you to lock a document if it is being edited. This way others will know that they cannot edit it at the same time and, if necessary, they can ask you to free it up again.

- Meeting workspaces are very easy to work with and quite intuitive. With just a few clicks you can create, for example, surveys or discussions, just like in a forum, which will spare you a flood of email and that can later be evaluated, looked through, and summarized much more easily than individual messages in the inbox.

- You can get notified immediately (or at certain intervals) about what's relevant to you, without being flooded by mail about other changes: For example, Robin only takes a brief look at the latest documents shortly before the meeting to prepare himself. They already contain many changes, but he's not interested in the change history—only the results count. Charlie is informed about all the changes in the documents and the discussion items he is responsible for once a day in an email summary. Holly gets immediately notified about any changes to her agenda item, but not about other updates, and so on.

You can set up the meeting workspace with a few clicks directly from the meeting request in Outlook 2003, Outlook 2007, and Outlook 2010 and later open it from the appointment you have created with the meeting request. If you are working with an older version of Outlook or other programs, you can open the link from your invitation email message in your browser and still access the data. Because the data is stored online, you can access it from any other computer, for example if you don't have your own computer with you (assuming you have noted the link and that the other computer is connected to the Internet or the company intranet that contains the site).

> **NOTE** Anyone who wants to open a meeting workspace (SharePoint site) needs an appropriate user name and password. Individual users can have different rights, for example only for reading the elements; for reading, changing, and adding elements; for redesigning the workspace; or for inviting new users and administering user rights. You can therefore grant Read or even Write access to information in the workspace to customers or certain partner companies who can't access your other network resources. To do so, the site must be accessible from outside your company. Ask your system administrator how this is handled in your company, if and how sites can be accessed from the outside (such as via the Internet or special external intranet access), and who can grant user rights where, and how.

Automatically Get Notified About the Changes Relevant to You

To keep you informed of what has changed without your constantly having to perform manual comparisons, the meeting workspace automatically sends you email updates. Maybe you don't care if certain agenda items, address lists, and things like that have been changed before the meeting, but the changes to other elements are very interesting and important to you. To avoid receiving too many change notifications that don't matter to you, you can manually set the notifications for each item and individually specify what you want to be notified about and how often.

Take Advantage of Document Libraries

If several colleagues are supposed to review the same document before a meeting, according to Murphy's Law nothing will happen for a whole week and then everything will happen at the same time: One colleague inserts new slogans and photos, another the latest numbers and data, and a third the new concept, but each of them make their insertions into their own copy of the old file. Now you have three new files, and in each one of them the data of the other colleagues is obsolete, so that actually none of them is up to date. This creates more work, additional email, and a week later at the meeting, you will end up with a lot of confusion and trouble finding the most current file, into which somebody has laboriously entered all the changes by hand....

Here's the solution: Add a document library for managing shared files to your workspace (see Figure 5-11). The following functions make document libraries especially useful:

■ The ability to Discuss documents with comments just like in an online forum (instead of having separate email messages to everyone, the contributions are gathered where they belong, and only those people who are interested in them are notified)

■ The ability to check documents out (lock them) and check them in again (so the file can only be edited by one person at a time)

■ The ability to create and view a version history, which lets you track checked-in changes and (if configured) allows you to restore older versions of each document

You can access these functions via the menu attached to a document's entry in the workspace. When you have checked out a document, your colleagues can see that it is being edited. After you have selected Check Out, the option changes to Check In.

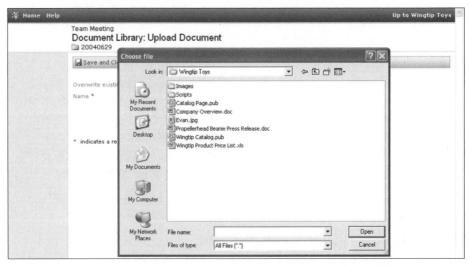

FIGURE 5-11 Use document libraries to track changes made by several people, thus avoiding chaos.

When checking in, you have the following choices:

- Reject the changes and undo the checkout.

- Confirm the document changes done so far (so your colleagues can download the updates), but leave the document checked out for editing.

- Confirm the changes and share the document again (report as checked in).

You can also add a comment that will explain later on in the history what kinds of changes you made.

Discover the Advantages of the Other SharePoint Web Parts

There are many additional Web Parts you can take advantage of. The most practical and most important are:

- **Contacts** Contact lists with address data, for example of external contacts, which you import from the Outlook Address Book and can embed as a contacts folder in Outlook.

- **General** You can use the general discussion Web Part to add a forum for discussing topics.

- **Surveys** These include automatic evaluation and graphical results display, for example, for voting before the meeting starts to already have results at the meeting. There are various question types to select from (such as selection list, Yes/No, and evaluation scale), and you can specify whether the names of participants should be visible and whether they can vote multiple times or just once.

You Try It

1. Create a meeting request, for example for your next meeting or a planned phone call. Look for free times in the calendars of the participating colleagues.

2. Ask a colleague to send you a meeting request, look up the time in your calendar, and accept it or propose a different time.

3. Check your meetings for the next month: Which ones can you group into one, cancel, or replace with a conference call or a Live Meeting? Act accordingly.

4. Together with your team, agree on core times for meetings, come up with a fixed meaning for the Out Of Office status, and look for ways to optimize meetings in the future (such as maximum duration time, agenda, or meeting workspace).

5. Enter your vacations as all-day appointments and as (Show As) Out Of Office. For the next two weeks, set Show As for all appointments to the correct value and flag all private appointments as such. As soon as possible, adjust all other future appointments that are already entered, and from now on handle all new appointments in this manner.

6. If you are working with Outlook 2010/Outlook 2007, display the appointments for yourself and two colleagues overlaid in the Week view, and look for an open appointment. Then place your calendar to the right of the overlaid calendars of your colleagues.

7. Enter five private appointments into the calendar (for example, jogging, yoga, or Outlook exercises) and flag them as private.

CHAPTER 6

How to Use OneNote for Writing Goals, Jotting Down Ideas, and Keeping Notes

IN THIS CHAPTER, YOU WILL

- Learn the basics of taking notes with OneNote.

- Work with sections, notebooks, and pages.

- Take meeting minutes in OneNote.

- Use Outlook and OneNote together.

- Link documents to your notes.

"I've Got It All Memorized!"

GATHER DETAILED notes and meeting minutes as well as ideas, goals, rough drafts, and sketches in a digital notebook: With Microsoft OneNote, you always have the necessary data in front of you (and on your laptop if you are traveling), and you can perform a full-text search, keep follow-up activities in view, and exchange data with other Microsoft Office applications.

By now you have learned how Microsoft Outlook can support you perfectly in your email management as well as your task and appointment planning. But what about those elaborate ideas that contain pictures and sketches? Where to put the meeting minutes, goals, and rough drafts of plans? Those usually end up on paper (which you need anyway for contracts, flyers, invoices, and forms, and for which you have some kind of filing system). And then you frequently can't find them again later on.

ROBIN'S PHILOSOPHY

There must be a parallel universe. Robin is sure of it. One where office workers constantly have too many documents and not the slightest idea where they came from, because lots of single sheets of paper randomly keep slipping through a hole between the dimensions from our desks to theirs. At least this seems to be the only remaining explanation after three hours of fruitless searching. Three pages of his five-page meeting minutes with very important details about a large order are missing. So far, he has gone through all his stacks of paper at least twice, and some of them he's probably rummaged through five times.

Once in a while, some of the documents reappear, suddenly showing up weeks later at places he had searched very carefully before. Like right now, when he finds a piece of paper with ingenious ideas for a new project. Unfortunately, he was only able to reconstruct about half of them from memory last month, and now it's much too late for the rest of them, even though there are some really great ideas that would have really paid off, had he been able to pursue them. But what can he do? He's a creative thinker who needs more freedom than just typing text line after line. Which is why he jots down his ideas on individual pieces of paper. Or, if he's on the phone and doesn't have a blank piece of paper available, he sometimes makes notes on the back of used envelopes or on papers with notes about other topics. It would just be too much trouble to transfer everything right away, and for a few hours or days his notes are still directly in his field of vision. Until he rearranges one of his stacks while looking for something and puts another 20 pages on top, or something slides down over them....

Robin travels a lot and needs to file everything away in hanging file folders or storage trays. Having to file and sort things before each business trip is annoying, and he doesn't have enough space for all those folders in his hand luggage and no reasonable option for filing the documents and notes gathered on long trips. There is only one solution: He should be able to use his laptop to make notes and plans in the same creative fashion as on paper.

Why Do Important Documents and Notes Always Get Lost?

Even a very sophisticated paper filing system reaches its limits or becomes extremely hard to work with, if you want to see all open questions and follow-up tasks for multiple areas at the same time, refer to electronically saved files, need to access a lot of information while traveling or in a meeting, or want to insert a few lines, data, and pictures from computer documents here and there. And if you do not have your notes while traveling, if you can't instantly file or retrieve something without leaving your desk, you most likely will stop filing most things and start to lose them (or still have them without being able to find them again).

Let's Get Started and Change This!

In order to be able to work optimally with goals, rough drafts, detailed notes, and meeting minutes, you need a system that offers you the following:

- The ability to work intuitively just like on paper, with sufficiently large pages and room for creativity, a system that doesn't take up much of your attention for note taking so you can focus on the content

- Text markers and drawing tools

- Pre-sorting at several levels, and at the same time the ability to display as much as possible on one page

- The capacity to keep everything on a laptop while on the road and back up data without much effort

- A way to quickly and automatically search through all areas as well as specific partial areas

- An overview of open tasks, questions, important notes, and more for several areas

- The ability to link files (Microsoft Excel spreadsheets, sketched directions, and so on) and easily paste email messages and copy data from and to applications, especially Microsoft Outlook (for planning tasks and appointments).

Finally, a Place and a System for All Your Notes

How many great ideas do you simply forget or never put to use? How much interesting and helpful information do you learn at presentations, but will forget a few days later, if the speaker doesn't let you create an action plan or write down notes and goals?

TIP You should always *record (type in)* important items—and you should do so in a structured fashion with a system that helps you arrange, sort, and view your notes and follow-up activities.

Use a Structured System When Planning

The best idea is worth nothing, if you have forgotten it by the time the crucial moment arrives. If you are taking a break from a meeting, are in the middle of a hectic trade show day, or are riding a train, and suddenly have great ideas for a new project, the ideal birthday gift for a friend, or a whole bunch of things you'd like to do when you're on vacation, you can note them immediately if you have a well-organized system. So nothing will get lost.

Remember the basics for written planning from Chapter 2, "How to Work More Effectively with Tasks and Priorities." Put down your plans in writing, like a contract with yourself. You will subconsciously feel more obligated to follow through with your plans. You can view your goals for the upcoming weeks or the next meeting at a glance and be mentally ready. Briefly prepare for important phone conversations and take notes as the conversations take place. This way you won't forget or confuse anything—assuming your notes are correct and you can find them again later. Weeks later, you will still have the exact information ready and can use your brain for more creative and important thoughts than having to remember everything.

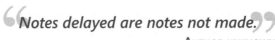

Notes delayed are notes not made.
— Author unknown

The best ideas normally don't come to us in the office or in a meeting, but usually after the subconscious mind has processed the information for a while and our brain is busy with something else. Or when it doesn't have much to do and can use its freed-up capacities: during a short walk, at night when falling asleep (unfortunately, falling asleep during a meeting doesn't count), while running, in the shower, while driving, at the airport on the way to your departure gate, and more. Therefore, you should always have your note system with you or at least nearby (for example, a laptop with OneNote) so that you can enter your ideas a few minutes later at the next opportunity. Get yourself some kind of "clipboard" (more about this soon) for those cases when your large note system isn't available. Enter your ideas into your note system to have them available and continue working with them at the next meeting, during project planning, and so on.

Have Your Notes Available When You Need Them

- Immediately write down everything as soon as you think of it—the later you write it down, the more imprecise it becomes. The more you've already forgotten, the more energy and concentration it takes to remember any details.

- Lost notes are just as useless as forgotten ones. Set up a filing system that lets you file information in a structured fashion and allows you to find it again. For papers, there are folders with various pockets, dividers, and colored pages. Your computer has a search function, but using it often takes longer (you might have to rummage through a huge amount of results) than targeting something at a specific location and opening it with just three clicks in less than one second. Even the best search can't help you if you can't remember the right keyword but just a synonym for it or only a thematic description. However, if you file everything according to your way of thinking, you will find it again. Above all, structured filing helps you avoid writing things down all over the place without any system: You will be able to better take advantage of your notes later on and will have an easier time going through search results.

- Try to write things down where they belong right away. Did you ever rewrite regular notes more clearly later on, even though it wasn't absolutely necessary? Hardly anyone ever does. Almost always, your initial notes will be your final ones or will only be slightly edited.

Is your laptop buried somewhere in one of your three suitcases, with your train arriving in a minute and you still needing to make some notes about the phone call you just had? Is your laptop battery depleted? Do you have a couple of great ideas just as the flight attendant announces that all electronic devices must be switched off, or while you're walking from your desk to the coffee maker? If you can't write something down where it belongs, use a "clipboard" and make a firm habit of transferring your notes.

TIP Always carry a little notebook and pen or an actual clipboard, a cell phone with voice memo, or a BlackBerry (to immediately enter a task, appointment, or note or to record a voice memo and email it to yourself). Make a habit of transferring the notes you made there at the next opportunity: when you're back at your desk or after you're allowed to turn your computer back on in the plane—or, if the battery was dead or your day too hectic, as soon as you arrive at the hotel (or in the evening before leaving the office). Afterward, cross out the transferred notes (on your little notebook) or delete them (from the voice memory of your cell phone), so you don't get confused, and from that moment on, continue working with the version on your "large note system."

IMPORTANT So that you don't forget to transfer your notes and end up losing some, it's important that you get used to transferring them automatically and as soon as possible. It becomes a habit if you start right away and continue consistently for the next three weeks, linking the transfer to specific situations and events (such as returning to your desk).

Do You Still Use Paper Even Though You Have a Laptop?

Outlook supports you perfectly in your email management and task and appointment planning efforts. The Outlook structure is like a specialized database. On the one hand, you can take advantage of the various functions, but on the other hand, it makes managing information that doesn't exactly fit this structure difficult and cumbersome. The note function in Outlook is rather like a substitute for little sticky notes. You can only enter pure text, and there are not nearly enough functions for a sophisticated note-taking system.

If you absolutely want to manage everything in Outlook, you can divert certain entry types from their intended use with a bit of creative thinking. For example, you can enter goals as contacts in a separate folder in Outlook (to link them with tasks, appointments, and email messages, which are then listed in the Activities for that contact). For notes, you can create new email folders—so that each entry has a subject for easy recognition—and you can attach files, add pictures, and use the text formatting options. Many find this method hard to use, because a goal is suddenly saved as a contact with several inappropriate fields or personal thoughts about a project in an email message they would never want to send.... Other aspects of a practical note system are lacking as well, especially the free page design, sophisticated options for more comprehensive notes, such as outlines, and a view of open follow-up activities or especially important sections and thoughts.

Microsoft Word is better suited for comprehensive notes, because it offers more sophisticated page layout options, outline views, and drawing and painting tools. However, it is also missing the aspects of a good note system, and there are other disadvantages: Word is optimized for text of different lengths (with references, automatic tables of contents, and more) about one topic (for example, a book, contract, or a log), but not for hundreds of long or short notes, between which the user wants to switch quickly. Having to save your notes in Word after each edit is annoying as well. It slows you down, and you risk losing data if you forget to save after small changes or when quickly switching between different topics.

In the end, certain information gets written down on paper anyway, because it gives you the necessary freedom, but this approach poses tremendous problems when it comes to sorting, searching, and quick tracking of follow-up activities and larger amounts of information. Word and Outlook don't offer enough freedom and flexibility to be perfect note systems. Paper makes it difficult to continue working while traveling, take notes along with you, and find them later. To fulfill not just half but all of the requirements described in the "Let's Get Started and Change This" section at the beginning of this chapter, you need a different note system.

Discover the Advantages of OneNote

Finally this system exists: Microsoft OneNote. OneNote is a new kind of program that is best described as a "digital notebook." As expected, it's not suitable for editing long text files or for every single appointment and email message. For such tasks, Word and Outlook remain the specialized programs that best fulfill those purposes. But OneNote finally provides a virtually perfect digital note system—that's what it was designed for. It fulfills all the requirements stated in "Let's Get Started and Change This" and provides additional advantages. The most important are:

- Fast switching between pages and the ability to access all pages at once, without constantly needing to open and save; the ability to arrange the pages into multiple folder levels and sections.

- Free placement of information on the page (without fixed entry fields, and not just line by line).

- Colors, pictures, text markers, sketches, pens for underlining and circling, and handwritten notes.

- A lightning-fast information search capability that scans through every single word from all the notes you took in the last few years, as well as a more focused search restricted to specific areas; quick and easy publishing and forwarding to others.

- Simple data exchange with other applications, pasting of email messages from Outlook, and inserting of file links.

- Special note tags for data, such as open questions, key phrases, and tasks, which can be combined for individual or multiple pages, specific sections, or folders.

- The availability of these features on any desktop computer or laptop. On a tablet PC, you can also use a pen for working just like on paper—extended by the digital functions.

On the next pages of this chapter, we will show you the basic functions of OneNote, how you can optimally manage your notes, ideas, meeting minutes, and goals—everything listed "a detail level below" or "a planning level above" Outlook (for example, pure gathering of ideas without any time horizons, or gathering many different topics, impulses, and follow-up activities as seminar notes). Discover the advantages, possibilities, and potential of OneNote and its cooperation with other applications, such as Outlook.

Basics for Notes in OneNote

OneNote 2003, OneNote 2007, and OneNote 2010 are very different from one another. OneNote wasn't included in most Office 2003 suites and was only included in some Office 2007 suites; it had to be purchased separately. We will therefore only introduce you to the 2010 version of OneNote—this is the best way to use the space available in this chapter to show you the basics and give you the most important time-management tips. If you are working with Microsoft Office Outlook 2007 or Microsoft Office Outlook 2003 and need to buy OneNote separately, you should just acquire the newest and most powerful 2010 version of OneNote. Even if you are working with an older version of Outlook, you can still use it. However, not all OneNote integration functions in Outlook 2010 will be available (for example, Outlook 2003 doesn't recognize any tasks directly linked to OneNote that synchronize the completion status between Outlook and OneNote, and therefore this function cannot be used in Outlook 2003—whether you are using OneNote 2003, OneNote 2007, or OneNote 2010).

Because OneNote is new to many users, we will start with the basics of how to use it. At first glance, OneNote might look confusing (see Figure 6-1), with all the functions and buttons that appear after you click one of its tabs (which look like menu items). But if you know the most important functions of Word, you will get used to OneNote very quickly, as soon as you understand the major differences and new functions.

Take Advantage of the Digital Notebook Structure

OneNote is structured like a digital notebook—a professional scheduler extended with special electronic functions. Good schedulers provide separation pages that allow you to quickly open specific sections that contain the filed pages, just like a tab. With one simple move, you have your projects, meeting notes, or goals in front of you. OneNote recreates this structure in extended form, with folders and pages.

Your Notebook Structure

OneNote provides pages, subpages, sections, and section groups that are like folders (see Figure 6-1).

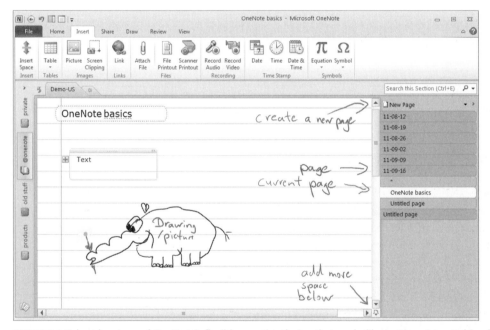

FIGURE 6-1 Take advantage of OneNote's flexible, creative design that works like paper notes, combined with electronic precision and sorting.

- The basic element is a *page*. You can do whatever you want here, just like on paper, and if necessary show lines or a grid in the background.

- In the upper-right part of the page, you can see the *page title*. It helps you quickly find and open the page by using the small tabs to the right of the page.

- A *subpage* is a separate page with its own information that is shown indented on the right and helps you structure your notes further.

- A *section* combines multiple pages, just like the tabs in a paper scheduler. To the right of the program window, you can see the titles of all pages in the section, and you can open them with one click of the title. You can create a section group (like a folder containing more than one section) by right-clicking a section and choosing New Section Group from the menu.

Section

- A *notebook* contains multiple sections. You can use it to thematically outline your sections (for example, one notebook for projects, another for your vacation planning, and so on).

What Are the Subpages For?

By creating subpages, you avoid constant scrolling. You create a new subpage instead of extending the original page downward. The advantage: You can directly open the subpage at any time by clicking its title in the right pane (in the page title list of the current section). The disadvantage: The more subpages you create, the more quickly the page title list becomes full (then you end up having to scroll to see the ones at the end and can't open the items with one click any longer). You should therefore use the subpages, for example, to gather meeting minutes on one page and to open important topics that are gathered in their own area directly for a particular meeting. The subpage titles are indented by about three characters to the right of the main pages. If you right-click a subpage (or a main page with subpages), you can select Collapse Subpages. OneNote then hides the subpages in the page title list and shows a small arrow to the right of the main page name. Click the arrow to show the subpages again.

Notebook vs. Section

A section contains one or more pages with subpages that are combined thematically. A notebook itself doesn't actually contain pages, only sections that contain pages. Notebooks serve as an additional division level. The Trade Show notebook, for example, might contain a section with general ideas and experiences as well as further sections about individual trade shows, such as CeBIT 2012 and CeBIT 2013. In these sections, you then create pages for conversation notes at your booth, other booths, attended presentations, your booth structure, travel planning, trade show preparations, and follow-ups for the year.

Develop a Structure for Your Notebook

This structure must fit your individual way of thinking and working (as described for the trade shows in the previous section) so that you can intuitively file and find everything quickly. During a seminar with a small group from a similar work environment, we could analyze your way of thinking and working and give you concrete suggestions, but a book is too general to figure out a personalized note structure. Read our examples and suggestions for creating a category system in Chapter 3, "How To Gain More Time for What's Essential with an Effective Week Planner," and for creating a folder structure in Chapter 1, "How Not to Drown in the Email Flood," to develop your own system—preferably together with a colleague who works in a similar environment.

Notebooks on the Web and Shared with Others

By clicking the File tab and selecting New, you can put a new notebook on your local PC (work station or laptop), a company network, or the web (for example, in Microsoft SharePoint). Notebooks saved on the web can be used on multiple computers (such as office PCs, laptops, or small netbooks while traveling), and they can also be shared with other users who don't have access to the same company network (for example, customers, suppliers, friends, spouses, or tennis partners, who need to prepare for an event with you by using OneNote on the web).

Work with Sections, Notebooks, and Pages

The notebooks are shown on the left side of the page that is currently open, the sections on top of the page, and the other pages from the current section on the right side of the current page.

How to create new sections

1. To the right of the title of your last section, click **New Section**.

2. OneNote now inserts the new section or folder into the section list (above the page) to the right of the currently open section, and selects its entire name. Enter a new name and confirm it by pressing Enter (or click any part of the current page to rename the section later).

How to create new pages and subpages

- Click the **New Page** button, which is located above the page title list of the current section, to insert a new page at the end of the current section, or click the arrow at the right end of the button to insert a new subpage for the current page or a new page based on a page template.

How to navigate among sections and notebooks

- Click the name of a section/notebook to open it.

- If not all sections fit side by side, click the arrow with three dots in front of it, to the right of the outer tab.

- To directly open a section that is not in the current notebook, click the arrow pointing to the right (at the left end of the navigation bar), and then select the section in the list that now opens.

- To get back to the previously opened notebook/section, click the **Back** button in the upper-left corner.

How to open specific pages and subpages

- Click one of the page titles in the page tab bar on the right to open the page.

- If not all of the page titles of the current section fit below each other on the screen, a scroll bar will be displayed on the right.

How to move or copy a page

- Right-click the page in the page title list, select **Move or Copy** in the shortcut menu, and then click the target. This shortcut menu also contains the **Cut**, **Copy**, **Paste**, and **Delete** commands for the page.

By pressing Shift or Ctrl, you can select multiple pages before performing this step for all those pages in one go.

To move the page within the current section, do the following:

1. Click the page title and keep the mouse button pressed.

2. Drag the page to the target position.

How to Fill Your Pages

OneNote arranges elements on the page in freely movable and combinable containers. A container can be, for example, text or a picture, or both.

If you have enabled the Select & Type tool instead of the pen (on the very left of the Draw tab), all containers are displayed in a colored outline. The currently selected container has a slightly darker bar at the top border. As soon as you point to this bar, the mouse pointer changes to an arrow with multiple heads, which you can use to move the container while keeping the mouse button pressed. You can also point to the right border of the container and change its width by dragging the border.

If you want to move text within a container, you can select, cut, and paste it, just like in Word. Each paragraph in OneNote also has a so-called *paragraph handle*. When you point to a paragraph, OneNote shows a small box with a blue background with a multi-pointed arrow to the left of the first line. Drag the box to move the paragraph up or down within the container or to indent it by one step below other paragraphs. You can also use the paragraph handle to drag the paragraph into a different container or to drop it into a free area of the page. (OneNote then creates a new container for the text.)

Text Functions

- Click an existing container to add text, or click a free area on the page to enter new text in a newly created container.

- Just as in Word, you can format the text with the functions on the Home tab.

- To use a different bullet or numbering in a bulleted or numbered list, click the arrow next to the respective button to open the selection menu.

How to Insert, Move, and Scale Pictures

There are different ways of inserting pictures into OneNote and working with them:

- Copy a picture (for example, by using your graphics program) to the Microsoft Office Clipboard, click the page where you want to insert it into the newly created container, and then press Ctrl+V.

- To insert a picture from your hard drive (or a CD or network drive), click the **Picture** button on the **Insert** tab, in the **Images** group.

- To insert a picture from a scanner or a camera, click the **Scanner Printout** button on the **Insert** tab, in the **Files** group.

- You can also move pictures within the container or freely on the page. Click the picture to select it, and then drag it to the new position.

To scale a picture, point to one of the small blue rectangles on the edges of the selection frame (there is one in each corner and in the middle of each side). The mouse pointer will change to a double arrow. Keep the mouse button pressed and increase or decrease the picture size by dragging the icons.

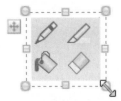

How to insert screenshots into OneNote

If you want to make notes for a colleague about a specific menu, dialog box, or toolbar, or if the displayed content of an application can't be exported easily, the screenshot function of OneNote can help:

1. Click the location where you want to insert the screenshot on the page to create a new container.

2. Open the application from which you want to take a screenshot, and set it up accordingly (for example, open the dialog box in question).

3. Press Alt+Tab to get back to OneNote. Click the **Screen Clipping** button on the **Insert** tab, in the **Images** group. OneNote now displays the other application "grayed out" in the foreground, and displays a crosshair pointer.

4. Place the crosshair in one corner of the section you want to take a screenshot of (for example, the lower-right corner of the dialog box), and click the mouse button.

5. Then drag it to the opposite corner of the section you want to take a screenshot of.

   OneNote will show a frame around the currently selected area, and the selected area will no longer be grayed out.

6. As soon as you release the mouse button, OneNote comes back to the foreground and inserts the screenshot of the selected area at the current cursor position on the (OneNote) page.

Use Pens, Text Markers, and Colors

Use different colors for clarity, to find items easily on a page, to highlight keywords or passages, and to distinguish various ideas. For example, you can take notes during a seminar by using the following four colors:

- Black for general information

- Red for everything you definitely need to work on or review first before any other content

- Green for examples or ideas on how to apply items directly to one of your projects

- Blue for thoughts you have while listening to the topics and methods covered (if, for example, during a presentation about ergonomic work stations, you want to remember a great way of illustrating issues and use it similarly during your next product presentation at a customer site)

How to color entered text

1. Select the text you want to color so that OneNote displays it with a blue background:

   - Click the container bar (upper border) to select the entire content.

- Letters, words, or partial words can be selected by clicking before the first letter in the text and then moving the mouse to the last letter, keeping the mouse button pressed.

- You can select a whole word by double-clicking it.

- By triple-clicking a word, you can select the entire paragraph in which the word is located.

2. Click the arrow on the **Font Color** button on the **Home** tab, in the **Basic Text** group, and select the color you want from the color palette.

    Alternatively, you can do the following: As soon as you select the text, OneNote shows the semi-transparent Mini Toolbar for text formatting above the current mouse pointer position. (See Figure 6-2; the toolbox is a bit hard to see, and as soon as the mouse is moved in a direction other than directly toward it, this "ghostly toolbox" vanishes—many people therefore don't even notice it when they are in a hurry; some think it's an optical illusion or a programming error....) Move the mouse pointer toward this toolbar. As soon as you reach it, it becomes opaque. Now just click the arrow on the **Font Color** button and select the color you want.

FIGURE 6-2 Use the Mini Toolbar to add color to text or quickly change text styles.

3. If you don't want to color the text itself but rather the background, you can use the color palette of the **Text Highlight Color** button, which can be opened with the button's arrow. (To remove this color highlighting, select **No Color** below the palette.)

How to use text markers and pens

1. Click one of the pens on the **Draw** tab, in the **Tools** group:

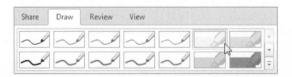

The mouse pointer now becomes a pen of the selected thickness and color. Text markers are simply very thick pens in a slightly lighter color.

2. As soon as you click with the mouse, you are drawing at the mouse position on the screen until you release the mouse button. (If you are using a tablet PC, you can draw with the pen directly on the screen, just like on paper.)

- To exit the pen mode, click **Select & Type** on the **Draw** tab.

- To delete an entire drawing, enable the **Select & Type** tool (click **Select & Type**), draw a frame around the drawing while keeping the mouse button pressed, and then press Delete.

- To delete only part of the drawing (or if it's too difficult to draw a frame around something that's located between other drawings), click the **Eraser** button first. Click the button's arrow to see the different eraser sizes. The eraser works like a pen that removes pen and text marker drawings wherever you move it while keeping the mouse button pressed.

For all the instructions in this chapter, we are assuming you are in Select & Type mode unless specifically mentioned otherwise. Therefore, for the purposes of this book, you should always go back to this mode after using the pen (as explained earlier).

How to set a picture as a background

Whether you want to add a background picture to make the page look better is a matter of taste. However, it comes in handy to label a picture with the text tool, circle parts of the picture with the drawing tools explained earlier, mark areas with arrows, add handwritten notes, or highlight specific parts with text markers. OneNote inserts pictures into a container, so that, for example, if the text above the picture is extended, the picture is automatically moved down to keep it integrated into the text. You can circumvent this behavior by putting the picture as background on the page, so that you can write and draw on it. You can now also select elements surrounding the picture more easily, without accidentally selecting the picture itself or moving it, because you can no longer move or select the background picture until you remove the anchor.

1. First insert a picture as described previously, and then click it to see a selection frame around the picture.

2. Drag the picture from the container to the desired position outside of the container (Important: not to a free space in a different container).

3. Right-click the picture and select **Set Picture as Background** from the shortcut menu.

4. You can now put text, drawings, text marker highlighting, and handwritten notes directly on the picture (see Figure 6-3). If you want to move or delete it later, right-click the picture again and clear the check mark next to **Set Picture as Background**.

FIGURE 6-3 Set a picture as the background to draw or write on it and to mark specific areas.

How to add documents as pictures

If you frequently print documents (such as a long text in Word) and then use pens and text markers to highlight items on the paper; add arrows, symbols, insertion marks, and handwritten notes; or cross out lines, you can now do so completely electronically in OneNote. To keep the text exactly where and how it would be on paper, without moving it when drawing arrows over it, simply set it as a background picture.

1. Click the **File Printout** button on the **Insert** tab, in the **Files** group.

2. In the **Choose Document to Insert** dialog box, select a Word, Microsoft Power-Point, Microsoft Excel or plain text file, and then click **Insert**.

3. OneNote now inserts a hyperlink to the files as a source confirmation with which you can quickly open the original. Below it, OneNote inserts the individual pages of the file as pictures (without a container). Set individual pictures as a background (as explained earlier), and delete the parts of the document you don't need.

You can now work on the document by using text markers, pens, text entries via the keyboard, and handwritten notes in all available colors, as if it were paper to write on, and take advantage of all the additional OneNote functions, such as the Back function (Ctrl+Z), the eraser, and much more.

ADVANTAGES OF A TABLET PC

OneNote is even more practical on a tablet PC (a laptop computer that has a touchscreen you can use with a special pen or your fingers—though a pen is more precise). You can use a tablet PC pen in addition to the mouse:

- Because you use the pen to write and draw directly on the screen, it feels like you are working on paper when you're adding notes to pictures and documents or writing something down—only this time, you're doing it in a digital format.

- Making handwritten notes requires less attention; you only need one hand for writing and a lot less space (than for a laptop with a keyboard).

- The search function of OneNote also finds numbers and words written by hand on OneNote pages—even if you leave them that way. When making handwritten notes, try to follow the background lines as much as possible. This increases the recognition accuracy.

- If you want to enter a lot of text at the same time and need a table to write on, you can switch to the keyboard (much faster and easily identifiable for everyone). Handwritten entries on a tablet PC that is sitting on a table do not pose any "barrier" between you and the person opposite you (unlike an open laptop on which you are typing), allow you to listen carefully and—unlike with a keyboard—make no noise while writing.

- Using a tablet PC in tablet mode (with the screen folded down on your keyboard so it looks like a tablet) makes the computer a little bigger than an iPad, but a small tablet PC is still just as portable while being much faster, much more powerful (for example, with all the OneNote features) and allows the very accurate use of a pen for real drawings and handwriting.

Meeting Minutes in OneNote

OneNote is perfectly suited for the preparation and follow-up of meetings, trade show talks, important phone calls, negotiations, and more. In the following section, you will find the most important tips, which are also useful for other purposes, such as preparing a project or gathering information that you don't need for a meeting but just for your own work.

Create a page for each important conversation and use OneNote to gather ideas, thoughts, and notes beforehand to prepare yourself better. During the conversation, take notes about agreements, Q&A, results, and relevant information in OneNote. Afterward, define follow-up activities with tags or preferably as a single task for each one, synchronized with Outlook. If necessary, distribute your notes to others, and use them for follow-up and archiving of information so you will have all the details available, even months later.

Use Outlining for Preparation

A text outline consists of multiple levels—for example, several agenda items that themselves contain multiple pieces of information, questions, and suggestions. For each suggestion, there are multiple statements, consequences, examples, and so on.

To gain a quick overview of the agenda items and the suggestions pertaining to them, or to see which three major topics you have chosen for the briefing of your trade show team, you can collapse the outline so that only the top level with the agenda items is visible. You can also show all the details about a subitem you are looking at, while all the other information is hidden (see Figure 6-4).

Apart from detailed agendas, you can also use outlines for the following:

- Preparing presentations, reports, and comprehensive documents
- Gathering/evaluating arguments and counter-arguments, pros and cons, requirements, conditions, meeting costs and results, and decisions
- Writing progress/result reports and seminar/meeting minutes
- Writing a structured summary of ideas and notes about a specific topic
- Defining partial goals, small steps, and individual tasks for long-term goals, plans, and large undertakings, as well as rough drafts of project plans

1. **Email**
   ⊞a) **Delete**
   b) **Act Now**
      ○ Is it **important** AND **urgent?**
      ○ OR: can you do it in **5 minutes or less?**
   ⊞c) **File for later**
2. **Tasks**
   ⊞a) **Eisenhower Matrix**
   ⊞b) **Categories**
   ⊞c) **Weekly planning**
   ⊞d) **Daily planning: 25,000 $**
⊞ 3. **Appointments**

FIGURE 6-4 Use outlining to give presentation preparations a clear structure.

How to create an outline

1. Click directly before the first character in a line (you may need to create a new text container to do this if you haven't entered any text yet).

   The cursor is now located at the beginning of the line. So far, all lines are on level 1.

2. To indent a line one level to the right (level 2, then 3, and so on), press Tab. Alternatively, in the **Basic Text** group of the **Home** tab, click **Increase Indent**. You can do this from anywhere in the line.

3. To add bullets or numbering, use the corresponding buttons in the **Basic Text** group on the **Home** tab.

4. To create a new entry on the current level, put the cursor at the end of the line (or a specific position within the line, to divide the current line) and then press Enter.

5. To put a new or existing line one level to the left (for example, after the subitems on level 3 are finished, to work with the next parent item on level 2), press Shift+Tab. You can also click the **Reduce Indent** button.

How to Collapse and Expand Levels, and How to Select Text on a Specific Level

- To collapse or expand the subitems of a specific outline item while leaving the others as they are, move the mouse pointer to the line with the outline item and double-click the paragraph handle in front of the line. The subitems are now hidden, and a double paragraph handle (it looks like it casts a shadow and signals that there are hidden subitems) is now displayed in front of the parent item. Double-clicking the paragraph handle expands the item (see Figure 6-5).

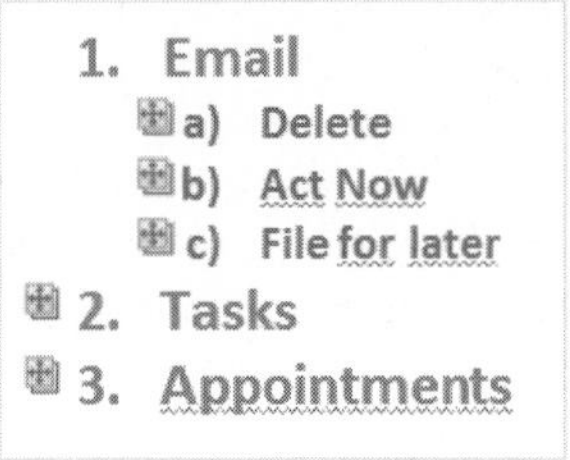

FIGURE 6-5 Collapse your outline to view all items on the higher levels at once.

> **TIP** ✓ To expand/collapse the entire outline to a specific level, select the outline (for instance, by clicking the upper border of the container) and press Alt+Shift+3 for the third level (or any number between 1 and 9 for the different levels). If you don't select the entire outline, but click the line containing one of the parent items, this shortcut only lets you expand/collapse the subitems for this parent item.

- To select all text on a specific level, select the entire outline (for example, by clicking the upper border of the outline container) and then right-click it. In the shortcut menu, click **Select** and then **All at level (number)** in the submenu. This way you can, for example, select all items on level 3 to set the text color to blue just for everything on that level. To select everything on a specific level, the level has to be visible (expanded). If you collapsed the outline to level 1, you can't select everything on level 3.

If you add handwritten notes or sketches to text in an outline and then expand or collapse the outline, the text in the outline changes position. The sketches, however, stay at the same position (the same goes for areas highlighted with text markers). You can avoid this behavior by doing the following:

- Don't collapse the item if you have made notes with the drawing tools.

- If the text won't change any more, select the outline, copy it by pressing Ctrl+C, and insert a copy of the outline by pressing Ctrl+V further below or on a different subpage or page, which you can expand/collapse while the copy with the notes always remains completely expanded.

- If you don't need any notes, but only want to highlight the text in color, you can use the **Text Highlight Color** tool in the **Basic Text** group on the **Home** tab, instead of a text marker. This way the position of the color in the text won't change.

How to create a table in OneNote

To clearly display information (for instance, your revenue goal for each month of the year and the achieved revenue up to now), you can add a table to the current OneNote page. Use the commands on the menu of the Table button on the Insert tab, or you can use the shortcut keys:

1. Position the cursor to the right of the text or the sketch you want to put in the first table cell (the upper left). Important: The cursor must be to the right of the text. (If the cursor is to the left of the text or nothing has been entered yet, OneNote generates the next level of the outline.)

2. Press Tab to insert a table and jump to the next cell. (The table initially has only one row and two columns; OneNote starts the second cell to the right of the current cursor position.) Alternatively, you can click **Insert Table** from the **Table** button menu on the **Insert** tab.

3. Insert the data for the next cell, press Tab to enter a new column/cell, and at the end of the last row press Enter to insert a row below the current row and move to the first cell of this row. If your cursor is not in the last row of the table, but inside one of the other cells above, pressing Enter inserts a line break within the current cell.

4. If the current cell is in the last row of the table and you want to insert a line break, press Alt+Enter.

5. You can press Tab to move between the existing cells of the table (this jumps the cursor into the next cell and selects the entire content), and Shift+Tab (this jumps the cursor a cell back and selects the entire content).

6. To insert a column to the left or right of the current column, press Ctrl+Alt+E or Ctrl+Alt+R, respectively.

7. To insert a new row below the current row anywhere in the table, press Ctrl+Enter.

8. When you click inside the table or when your cursor is still in the table, OneNote displays the **Table Tools/Layout** context tab. You can click this tab to select specific rows/columns, hide the border, or change the text alignment from left-justified to center, and more.

Keep Follow-Up Activities and Important Information in View

Tags help you display information that is distributed among multiple pages, such as un-answered questions or the most important key phrases. These elements are marked with a small colored tag. You can search for these tags across pages and gather all text that is marked with them.

How to set and remove tags

1. Click a line of text or a handwritten note, or select a drawing.

2. On the **Home** tab, in the **Tags** group, select one of the tags to assign it. The two arrows to the right of the tag list let you scroll through the list, and the arrow be-low them (with the small line above it) lets you expand the list fully.

Alternatively, you can use the shortcut keys shown next to the tag names, Ctrl+1 through Ctrl+9, to assign the corresponding tags.

3. Repeat step 2 for the same tag with an entry you have already marked, to delete the assignment. You can delete all tags set for the current entry with the **Remove Tag** command in the fully expanded tags list, or by pressing Ctrl+0.

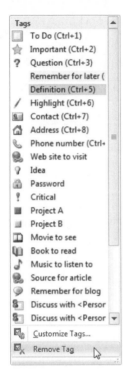

4. When you have set a check box (for example, the **To Do** tag), you can enable it—for example, to mark the task as completed. Assigning the same tag again (a second time) also enables the check box.

How to customize the available tags

1. In the expanded list of available tags, click **Customize Tags**.

    OneNote opens a dialog box for customizing the tags.

2. Click one of the tags in the list and move it to the desired position in the list by using the arrow buttons (in the upper-right corner of the dialog box). The first nine list entries in your new order can be assigned by using the shortcut keys.

3. Click the **Change Tag** button, change the tag name if necessary, and assign a symbol, font color, and highlight color (by clicking the arrow or the corresponding button).

> **NOTE**   You can assign multiple tags to an entry at the same time. A block of text can have several tags, but only one font color and highlight color. Therefore, be careful with color marking so your don't lose track.

4. Confirm by clicking **OK**. (Already-marked elements keep their old settings.)

How to Quickly Find Elements Marked by Tags

- On the **Home** tab, in the **Tags** group, click **Find Tags**.

- OneNote opens the **Tags Summary** task pane to the right of the program window. There you can see marked text, handwritten notes, and drawings, if they have tags.

- Click one of the listed entries to jump directly to this entry on its page, see its context, and edit it.

- Just like with grouped views in Outlook, you can show or hide all items in the summary by clicking the small triangle in front of the name.

- In the **Group tags by** list, you can also choose other grouping criteria.

- In the **Search** list you can, for example, specify that OneNote search the entire current notebook, all notebooks, or all the pages in your notebooks you have worked on this week, instead of just the current section.

- When you click the **Create Summary Page** button, OneNote creates a new page that contains a copy of the text (or the drawings and pictures) of all marked items in the original layout. On the summary page, you can, for example, display the open tasks you noted during a trade show together with the relevant names and phone numbers from a section that contains all trade show meeting notes, so you can enter them into Outlook afterwards. If you point to an entry in the summary page, OneNote displays a link to the original tagged entry (a small purple OneNote icon to the left of the paragraph handle). Click this icon to jump directly to the original entry.

How to take advantage of the full-text search

In a good notebook structure, you can usually find a topic faster by knowing where it'll be and just clicking twice to get there rather than by looking though search results, but the search function is a perfect addition, if you know somewhere in the back of your head that a certain topic had already been discussed in a meeting 18 months to two years ago at some point, for example.

1. Click the **Search All Notebooks** box (upper-right next to the sections):

   Search All Notebooks (Ctrl+E) 🔎 ▾

2. Click the arrow to the right of the magnifying glass to change the search area, if necessary.

3. Enter the text you are looking for. The search starts immediately, and you'll see results appear while you are typing.

   Below the search box, OneNote now displays the titles of all pages that contain the specified text and it highlights the hits in color directly on the pages. Below the search box there is a "result navigator."

4. You can use the arrow keys or the mouse to move through the hits (click a page title in the page tab bar).

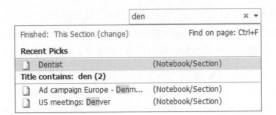

Link Your Information: Use Outlook and OneNote as a Team

OneNote makes a perfect team with the other components of the Microsoft Office system. For example, you can create a diagram of your current quarter's results in Excel and copy this page to the meeting preparation page in OneNote where, during the past few weeks, you have been gathering ideas that you want to discuss with your colleagues. Or somebody sends you a Word document containing a report summary that you insert as a picture. You use a text marker to highlight specific sections and comment with handwritten keywords (see the "How to add documents as pictures" procedure earlier in this chapter). During the meeting, you write down the results and all resulting tasks, and then make the page available to your colleagues in the meeting workspace of a SharePoint site (see Chapter 5, "How to Schedule Meetings So They Are Convenient, Effective, and Fun") as the meeting minutes. Afterward, you copy the tasks you are responsible for into your own personal task list in Outlook with just one click per task.

How to transfer tasks to Outlook

1. Right-click the paragraph in OneNote you want to transfer—it's especially helpful to assign a tag to certain entries (such as tasks) as you write them by using shortcut keys so that you can recognize them immediately by their tags (or automatically jump to them or gather them from multiple pages, as explained earlier).

2. In the shortcut menu, click **Outlook Tasks** and then the option you want (or press Ctrl+Shift+1 to create a task that is due today (Ctrl+Shift+2 for tomorrow, and so on). The task has now been inserted into Outlook with the due date you specified.

3. If you select **Outlook Tasks/Custom**, an Outlook task form is displayed where you can enter the due date manually.

Changes to the state of completion and the due date are automatically synchronized between OneNote and Outlook. (Depending on the performance and settings of your system, it may take a few seconds or up to several minutes until the changes arrive in the other program.)

If you open the Outlook task in Outlook in its own window (for example, by double-clicking it), you will see a link to OneNote in the note field. If you double-click that link, it'll open in OneNote. In OneNote, you can right-click the small red flag in front of the task text to change the due date in the shortcut menu, mark the task as completed, delete the Outlook task, or open it directly in Outlook.

> **IMPORTANT**   In Office 2010, later changes to the subject are not synchronized: If you change the task subject in Outlook, OneNote keeps the old text. In future edits, changes to the text in OneNote will also be ignored in an Outlook task that has already been created. Still, both entries remain securely linked: Changes to the due date and state of completion are still synchronized with the other program, and the link to the other program also works reliably (to open the task in Outlook/OneNote).

Outlook and OneNote also communicate the other way around:

- In OneNote, on the **Home** tab, in the **Outlook** group, click **Meeting Details** and select one of the entries from today's calendar in the expanded menu or **Choose a Meeting from Another Day** to insert the location, participants, date, time, subject, and notes of a meeting request or an appointment.

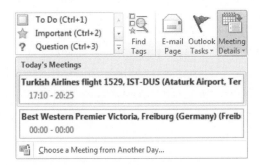

How to Create a Contact/Appointment Note from Outlook

Open the appointment or contact in Outlook in its own window, for example by double-clicking it. On the Appointment (or Meeting or Contact) tab, in the Actions group, click OneNote. Outlook now creates a new page in OneNote whose title is the appointment subject (or the contact name), together with the creation date and time (see Figure 6-6). In a table on the page, you will also find the most important details, such as date, time, and location of the appointment, as well as other notes.

You can now use the OneNote button in Outlook to directly move to this page, which means you can now retrieve your OneNote notes from the Outlook appointment. On the OneNote page, you can click the Link To Outlook Item hyperlink to open the corresponding Outlook entry from OneNote.

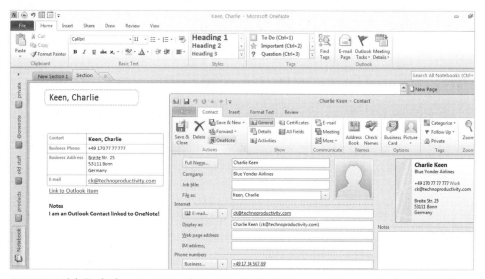

FIGURE 6-6 Link Outlook contacts/appointments with OneNote pages, for example, for a detailed meeting preparation.

<table>
<tr><td>**CAUTION**</td><td>Unfortunately this link takes some getting used to and no longer works correctly if you change the appointment date (at least in the first versions of OneNote 2010). Remember that by connecting to OneNote you are creating a copy of the data at the time of the page creation that contains a link to the constantly up-to-date item (but otherwise doesn't synchronize the data).</td></tr>
</table>

BE CAREFUL WITH CHANGES TO LINKED APPOINTMENTS

If you change the date for an Outlook appointment and have already linked a OneNote page with meeting notes, clicking the corresponding button after changing the date creates a new page in OneNote, instead of opening the existing page (the links from OneNote correctly take you to the newly changed appointment). Changes to essential data, such as contact phone number, subject, location, or time of an appointment do not get transferred from Outlook to OneNote. As soon as you have created a page for an Outlook element, the old data remains there, unchanged. So you may, for example, calmly prepare your meeting in OneNote in the morning and see 11:00 A.M. as the start time, even though it has been changed to 9:00 A.M. in the meantime.... To stay up to date, you either need to transfer all changes manually to OneNote or get used to generally mistrusting the data it has received from Outlook and checking Outlook with one click on the link to see whether there are any updates.

How to Export Email Messages

- In Outlook, right-click an email message (in the inbox or any other folder) and select **OneNote** from the shortcut menu to export the message to OneNote. If you have opened the message in its own window, you can use the **OneNote** button in the **Move** group on the **Message** tab (contrary to what the group name suggests, the message is copied, not moved).

How to Create Hyperlinks to OneNote Pages/Paragraphs

You can use hyperlinks to directly open a specific paragraph or page in OneNote from a different OneNote page or from a program that supports hyperlinks (for instance, to open all budget planning details from an overview page for a project with one click).

Right-click in the page tab bar (to the right of the current page) on the name of the page to which you want to create a link, and in the shortcut menu, select **Copy Link to Page**. To create a link to a paragraph or picture, right-click the text (or the picture), and in the shortcut menu select **Copy Link to Paragraph**. OneNote then copies a link to the Clipboard, which you can now insert into a different OneNote page at the current cursor position by pressing Ctrl+V. One click on the link then opens the corresponding element directly in OneNote.

TIP Customize the titles of inserted hyperlinks: Instead of using the original text of the hyperlink (which can be quite long or consist of relatively in-comprehensible character strings), you can shorten the link text to mean-ingful keywords or something like "Estimated storage cost 2010" or "See book details." If the program you pasted your link into supports editing hyperlinks, right-click the hyperlink you just inserted and, in the shortcut menu, select Edit Hyperlink. In the Link dialog box that now opens, keep the address as it is, but change the text in the Text To Display box, and confirm with OK.

How to share your notes and meeting minutes with others

Send your reports and notes to others for informational purposes or to exchange ideas. After you have prepared a meeting in OneNote and taken the minutes, send them to the other participants right away:

1. Do a quick check to make sure that all information on the current page is readable to others (Is your handwriting legible? Do the drawings express what you meant, and can everyone understand them?), that all necessary details are included (Do you need to explain abbreviations, background information, time or cost limits?), and that all elements are relevant to the others (if some sections are only impor-tant to you personally, copy the page, delete those sections in the copy, and then forward the copy).

2. If you want to send multiple pages, keep Ctrl pressed and select the pages by clicking the page titles in the page tab bar. Then release the Ctrl key.

3. On the **File** tab, select **Send**.

   Now select whether you want to send the page via email (with OneNote items copied into the email message text), as an attachment (a file the recipient can open in his own copy of OneNote while all special functions remain available), or as a PDF (in which the layout looks close to the original and is the best option for recipients who don't have OneNote and don't need to edit text elements further). OneNote creates a new email message you can send to recipients from your Outlook address book.

4. Enter the email addresses and send the message.

A quick note to advanced users (a more detailed description would go beyond the scope of this chapter): You can share a OneNote page with others so that everyone can see and edit the same page. An example is meeting minutes in which the individual participants can find their follow-up tasks and later enter the results so that everyone can see them immediately without having to send dozens of email messages back and forth. Everything is located centrally in a OneNote notebook (on a Share-Point site or a Windows Live SkyDrive, for instance). With the Share tab you can, for example, share the current notebook or create a new shared one, display all changes since yesterday or over the past seven days, and search for a specific author (a colleague who has entered something).

How to See When You (or Another User) Last Edited the Current Element

Select an element (such as text or a sketch) and right-click it to open the shortcut menu. In the last line of the menu, you can see who last edited the selected element and when.

By right-clicking a free area on the page, you can see who last edited the page and when (corresponding to the information displayed for the last element edited on the page). You can use this function, for example, to check whether you have already edited text on a page you received from a colleague. Or if there is reasonable doubt, you can quickly check whether you actually entered the latest numbers on the current page back in December or if you forgot all about it due to holiday season stress and the results are those from before Thanksgiving.

Create Page Templates and Checklists

For checklists or forms you need frequently, you can create empty templates in OneNote under the name Templates. You can, for example, create trade show meeting minutes or a checklist for preparing a seminar that you and the organizer go through over the phone.

How to create a template

1. Create the page with all the headings, tags for follow-up tasks, and so on.

2. On the **New Page** button menu, select **Page Templates**.

3. Now click **Save Current Page as Template** in the **Task** pane to the right of the program window.

4. In the dialog box that now opens, enter a name and confirm it with **Save**. If you select the **Set as Default Template for New Pages in the Current Section** check box, each newly created page in the section will be based on the saved template from now on.

The Default Template function is very practical if, for example, you create a section each for trade show talks, preparation, Q&A catalogues for new customers, and damage survey forms. Each new page in the current section is then automatically based on the template. To set the function later on, repeat steps 1 and 2, and select the template for the new pages in the current section in the Templates task pane, in the Default Template list. Or click No Default Template if you want to work with blank pages again.

How to create a new page based on a template

1. To create a new page, click the arrow on the new pages button, and then select **Page Templates** from the menu.

2. Click the template you want.

3. Close the **Templates** task pane by clicking the x in the upper-right corner.

Always Keep Your Ideas and Goals in Sight

Use detailed notes to record your long-term goals in OneNote, so you can create a plan to put them into practice (for instance, as an outline). Gather resolutions, visions, mission statements, and use OneNote for your dreams—write down what you've always wanted to do, with all your thoughts about what's important to you and how you might realize it. The more often you see it directly in front of you, the more your subconscious mind will work on it. If an opportunity presents itself to turn your dreams into reality (maybe a few months or years later), you already have all the material—for example, to write your own book. Or you realize that you can actually take four months off to fulfill your dream of traveling around the world and can afford it, if you just take the remaining three difficult but do-able steps.

Take advantage of OneNote as your control center and gathering place for all thoughts about one topic. Combine material from other applications by collecting text sections and linking larger documents directly to your notes.

How to link documents to your notes

With one click, you can open a technical datasheet, for example, or a setup plan for your trade show booth directly from your notes. If you don't need to see certain information as copied text or a picture on the page, you can save space by inserting a link to it instead. And this way you always have the latest version (not a copy) in front of you—for example a Microsoft PowerPoint presentation that has been reviewed and edited several times.

1. Bring Windows Explorer to the front, but don't let it fill the screen completely (switch to window mode instead of full screen).

2. Click a file in Windows Explorer, such as an Excel file or a picture.

3. Drag the selected element to the target position in the OneNote page to insert a copy. OneNote now offers to insert a link (unless the element is a picture). Choose this option and confirm by clicking **OK**. Office documents can also be inserted as pictures (for adding handwritten notes, as covered in the "How to insert documents as pictures" procedure earlier in this chapter).

"Printing"—Export Data from Any Program

Maybe you don't just want to insert individual text blocks and pictures from other programs via the Clipboard, but for example would like to have comprehensive reports or datasets in front of you as if on paper: You can simply print the contents from any desired program directly into a OneNote page. And what's really great is that, just like on paper, you can work with text markers, add new text, and (from a tablet PC or with the corresponding pen also from other PCs) handwritten notes and sketches (see "Use Pens, Text Markers, and Colors" earlier in this chapter). In this way, OneNote replaces paper printing and at the same time gives you electronic advantages, such as full text search, the Back function, and linking to other data.

How to "Print" from Any Application to OneNote

The OneNote installation program automatically adds a virtual printer to your system. Select the print function in a program of your choice and, in the print dialog box (name and settings might be different depending on the program), select Send To OneNote 2010 instead of sending to your default printer. Depending on your system settings, the application from which you are printing might stay in the front. At first glance, some users therefore assume nothing has happened and the export has failed. A short while later, OneNote opens a window where you can select the desired target section for your print page.

During printing, the text is inserted as a picture in its original layout. You therefore cannot edit the text or cut sections afterwards in OneNote. To be able to later look for specific keywords in the text or copy parts of the text for editing, use the new function for optical character recognition (OCR) in pictures (see "Read Between the Lines—OCR for Pictures" later in this chapter).

Save Websites from the Web Browser in OneNote

During a long flight without an Internet connection or a train ride with a bad Internet connection, you can still have specific information constantly available to you, highlight places with the highlighting tools of OneNote, or save the state of a website for later research (if the content has changed): Simply export the website to OneNote. In Windows Internet Explorer, you have three options for exporting to OneNote:

- Use the print function as explained earlier. The advantage: Starting with Internet Explorer 7, Internet Explorer adjusts the page content width so that all elements are scaled correctly relative to each other and fit on the page. The original layout of the website is retained. You have inserted a picture—and now you can use the drawing tools of OneNote to add notes just like on paper.

- Internet Explorer has a new button called Send To OneNote. (Depending on your version of Internet Explorer and your settings, you might have to show the command bar first to see this button: right-click the blue Internet Explorer logo—the *e* in front of the field in which you enter URLs—and select Command Bar in the shortcut menu.) With one click, OneNote copies the website to a page. (Internet Explorer stays open in the foreground—you need to switch to OneNote to see the result.) The disadvantage of this method is that the original page layout gets cut up; it wraps differently, pictures change their position, and text columns change their length and width (sometimes to an extreme). However, you can edit the text directly, copy pictures from it, and search or copy text without having to use additional processing or OCR recognition for exotic fonts.

- Thirdly, you can select parts of the text or pictures on a website and then put the selected content on the current OneNote page by dragging or copying and pasting. OneNote automatically inserts a link to the source website below the copied content. The advantages and disadvantages of this method are the same as for the second method. This third method works well, however, if you only want to use small parts of a website instead of its entire content.

Read Between the Lines—OCR for Pictures

OneNote uses the OCR function (optical character recognition) to "read" pictures and make the text inside them available as "real text." This is helpful, for example, if you are scanning paper documents or business cards, or are printing data from other applications into OneNote as a picture. You can then search the recognized text and copy it for future editing to, for example, add the sender of a scanned business letter to Word as the recipient of your answering letter or to Outlook as a new contact.

Right-click a picture and select Copy Text From Picture (see Figure 6-7) in the shortcut menu to extract the text and save it to the Clipboard (afterward, you can press Ctrl+V to insert it at a different position). If you don't want to use the text at a different place but just want to search it with the OneNote search function, select Make Text In Image Searchable in the shortcut menu, and in the submenu select the text language. (If you have already chosen Copy Text From Picture for a picture, OneNote has automatically defined the text as searchable.)

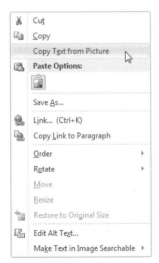

FIGURE 6-7 Let OneNote extract text from pictures for you—with clear contours over a white background, this works pretty well. However, very small italic or ornate text doesn't get recognized well.

OCR FOR PICTURES TAKEN WITH CELL PHONE CAMERAS

The OCR function delivers the best results with text sent from other programs to One-Note as well as cleanly scanned grayscale or black-and-white pictures that you have placed exactly aligned on the scanner. However, if you use your smartphone camera, for example to take a picture of a business card or a train schedule, recognition errors happen more frequently—most integrated cell phone cameras use a relatively low resolution, make objects that are less than two feet away from the lens look blurry, produce a lot of image noise, and save the photos in lossy compression formats with a degradation that might not be visible to the human eye but causes an enormous loss in quality for electronic character recognition. But if you have a recent smartphone with a decent camera that has good autofocus (such as a BlackBerry Torch), you will get good OCR results even for pictures taken with your smartphone camera. Just make sure to not move your hand while taking the picture and to have good lighting or use the flash.

Set Goals for Yourself—Not Just for Your Revenue

Many people overestimate how much they can get done in two or three hours or in one day. However, most of them underestimate how much they can achieve in a few weeks, months, and years. The key to big achievements, realized dreams, balance in life, and long-term success is putting your goals down clearly in writing.

- If you know exactly where you want to go, you can specify the path and its individual steps.

- If you have a goal in sight, it's much easier to stick to it during hard times and muster the energy. It motivates you to take even the uncomfortable or grueling partial steps.

- Frequently things don't quite go as planned. If you have a clear goal, you can look for a new way to get there: If the left path doesn't lead around the mountain, then just take the right one.

Clear goals help you control your current progress: Have you already successfully gone more than half of the way, or are you even almost there? Are there areas you should improve or work on more to get where you want to be before it's too late? Do you need to adjust your goal, or is it still realistic?

If your goal seems unreachable, you can figure out what you are missing or what's standing in your way. Then you can either circumvent these hurdles or make them intermediate goals: For example, are you still missing $5,000? Think about whether your goal is worth it. If yes: Find a way (for example, wait four years and put away $105 each month) or an alternative (can you afford deferred payment or taking out a loan that you will pay back in the next few years?).

THINK ABOUT HOW MUCH YOU CAN ACHIEVE IN SMALL STEPS OVER A LONG PERIOD OF TIME

Does your goal seem too far-fetched? For example, can you imagine running a full marathon (26 miles and 385 yards)? What would you say if a man who is almost 50 years old, 44 pounds overweight, short of breath, and in terrible condition decided to run such a marathon?

Joschka Fischer, former Foreign Minister of Germany, began running at a weight of 242 pounds—all he did was run 500 meters around the German Bundestag building. Many would consider this distance ridiculous. One year later, he prepared for his first marathon. Many would think they could never do this sort of thing. After one and a half years of training in all (in 1998 at the age of 50), he ran the Hamburg Marathon in 3:42 hours and had lost 77 pounds.

The numbers, converted to pounds, are from the book *Perfektes Lauftraining*, *Fifth edition* (Munich: Südwest, 1999) by Ulrich Pramann and Herbert Steffny, who was Fischer's marathon trainer.

Joschka Fischer is not a born athlete, nor did he have all the time in the world to train. He had enough other stuff to do. With a clear goal, a plan he followed consistently to reach this goal in small steps, and an iron discipline, he achieved an admirable performance (see the previous sidebar), something very few people would have thought he could do. What you need for peak performances are clear goals for which you can set realistic intermediate goals and individual steps. After that, you just have to take the first step, keep the goal in sight, and keep at it with a strong will and a huge amount of discipline. It's best to find somebody to support you—a good friend or an experienced coach—for reality checks and above all for constant progress checks, encouragement, reprimands and, if necessary, a course correction.

Determine what applying yourself and sticking with it for a long time is worth to you. Write down your goal. Start working on it in small steps. We all have our limits. But we can all achieve more on a long-term basis than we give ourselves credit for. Dream big! And don't just dream your dreams—live them!

Not to give you the wrong impression: Goals don't have to be peak performances in sports or your profession, where you go beyond your personal limits. Set small and personal goals, too. Goals don't just help you achieve great performances, but to see more clearly what's important to you in the long run, and to stay balanced.

Set Goals with the 3M Rule: Measurable, Manageable, Motivating

There are a lot of criteria for goals. All can be derived from the three most important ones. Formulate your goals by using the simple 3M rule. Goals are:

- **Measurable** Who? What exactly and What quantity? When? Where? (Sometimes the answer is just "everywhere," while other things can only be done in the office or at home, or perhaps you want your own house in a particular city.) Make them concrete and quantifiable.

- **Manageable** Some companies don't handle goals correctly. Many an employee receives completely unrealistic directives along the lines of: "Double last year's earnings, even if there is less and less demand, the budget has been cut in half, and half of the employees in the department have been fired.... Oh, you can manage it—and woe betide you if you don't!" This leads to completely short-term thinking, and somehow you do manage to pull the payment for a large order from next year into this year, so you don't go too far below the required numbers. In the long run, this kind of behavior only makes the problems worse and does damage to the employees and ultimately the entire company. Even in the most innocent of cases, it discourages you and thus lowers your performance and happiness. Therefore, you should check in at regular intervals after you have set your goals to see whether they are still manageable, and adjust them in time. There's nothing wrong with reaching for the stars as long as you make sure you keep both feet on the ground. Have big goals! But stay realistic. Remember Joschka Fischer and trust in your own abilities.

- **Motivating** This item has several aspects:

    - Formulate positively (no negative phrases) and stay action-oriented (instead of "could," "should," or "would," use a direct verb and yourself as the acting person). Instead of "This stupid chaos should really end sometime soon" write "On 9/10 I have my desk cleaned up and empty with at most five open files sitting on it. I write important notes in OneNote on my tablet PC and I find them there again. I find paper documents in my file trays and I immediately file them in their correct order after each edit." This way your subconscious mind can get the picture and program you for success.

■ With some goals, it's immediately obvious why they pay off. For others, you need to add the reason. This will help you start and keep doing uncomfortable things that are nevertheless important to achieve your dreams or goals. If you simply can't come up with a reason why this goal is worth the effort: Really think about it, and if you still can't find a good reason, get rid of it.

■ Make sure your goal really reflects what you want (see the "Measurable" discussion earlier), and check this regularly. Are you torturing yourself by going running, even though you hate it, simply to do something for your health? Maybe riding a bicycle or dancing salsa is better exercise and more fun for you!

■ Think of Joschka Fischer again here: Since his marathon days, he has gained a lot of weight again.... This is why he makes such a wonderful example for successful goal setting: Setting yourself the goal of running a marathon is much harder than just simply losing some weight. But once you have run the marathon successfully, you have reached your goal and are done—if you then continue as before, all the positive effects on your health will vanish after a few months or years. To just do something for your health and lose weight is much easier than training for a marathon—and with the correct goals, it also lasts much longer, so you can enjoy continuous success.

HOW TO TURN A RESOLUTION INTO A WELL-FORMULATED GOAL

What are you going to do when you don't have clear numbers for measuring; for example, how could you quantify "I want to become a better father"? Think about how you would define "better father": "I don't spend enough time with my daughter, and we hardly have a chance to talk." Use the 3M rule to set a goal: "From now on, each Saturday at lunch I will make a tennis appointment for the next week with my daughter. Together we will drive to a tennis court that is 30 minutes away." (This way you have time to talk without the need to introduce "conversation hours" that would sound too psychological.) Then let your spouse check you—"become a better father" was wishy-washy, but if you now avoid the weekly appointment or start choosing other things over it, your issues become immediately apparent (hopefully to you first and in time, while you are planning your week).

OneNote is a great place for your goals: It provides enough space and freedom of design to put all relevant information, descriptions, motivational texts, and pictures (such as a photo of your dream house or a vacation spot you always wanted to visit) directly on the page with one or multiple goals. Set a customized tag for your goals to keep all pages in view. Simply list the required steps for reaching the goal as tasks below each other (marked as Outlook tasks so they also show up in Outlook) or create an outline if your goal is more comprehensive and complex. The individual tasks are located on the lowest level of the outline. Control and log your progress on this page. You can also gather vague resolutions and ideas in OneNote and keep adding to them until you are ready to formulate your goal.

> **TIP**
>
>
>
> It's best to look at your goals once a day to program your subconscious mind. Integrate your goals (including the master plan discussed in the next section) into your weekly planning—simply pass the next steps on to Outlook as a task.

Create Your Master Plan

In Chapter 3, we introduced you to the concept of life hats and key tasks for balanced time planning. Now it's time to set long-term goals for your life hats. Then you can define intermediate partial goals and the corresponding smaller steps. This becomes your so-called *master plan*—the culmination of all planning steps explained so far to keep your life in balance, achieve big things over time, and make your dreams a reality.

You can create the master plan, for example, as a section in OneNote, in which each long-term goal becomes a page with the corresponding intermediate goals as a subpage. If you prefer a bit more structure or want to see everything at a glance, create an outline (see Figure 6-8) for a better overview (you can quickly expand/collapse partial steps and their tasks). You can also set up a separate page for specific goals. The time horizon that works best depends on many factors. Depending on age, type, family status, profession, and other factors, some people plan a life goal, others a goal for seven or five years down the road. Start, for example, with three years as your long-term horizon, one year as the next step, and one or two goals per life hat. Not each of the entries has to fit rigidly into this grid: Maybe the three-year goal for your health is the same as the one-year goal. Some three-year entries are not concrete goals yet, but more like resolutions. For one life hat, you have three long-term goals, for another just one. That's okay. What's important is that you devote time to all areas of life, define goals from your wishes, and continuously work toward them.

1. **Head of Sales Team**
   - a. Gain 1000 new customers in Europe by 2013
     - i. Launch 3 new products in UK, NL, AT, CH 2012
     - ii. Launch Ad campaign 2012
   - b. Education program for my team members
     - i. Develop individual personal coaching plan for each team member in 2012
2. **My own career**
   - a. Impress board members with my presentation at the annual leadership meeting 2012
     - i. Take a workshop on professional speaking
     - ii. Deliver 10 speeches with at least 50 audience members by November 2012
3. **Husband**
   - a. Reduce business travels to 12 days a month
   - b. Take salsa dancing lessons
   - c. Spend quality time with Sarah: Schedule at least 2 hours for two times each week to really listen and talk to her without being in a hurry
4. **Father**
   - a. Help Maria to find the right country and university for her one year trip to Europe
   - b. Spend quality time with Maria each week to really listen and talk to her
     - i. Drive Maria to her tennis lessons each Saturday
5. **My own health**
   - a. Take tennis lessons myself and start running 3 times a week for at least half an hour
   - b. Stop smoking by February 2012

FIGURE 6-8 Create your master plan—the outline function in OneNote is a great way to do this.

The following exercise can help you create your master plan: Imagine that three years from now you are watching a funeral. It's your own. Seven people hold short and moving eulogies: your manager, one of your customers, your spouse, one of your children, and so on (at least one person from each of your life areas; for health and meaning of life, your best friend or spouse, for example, is allowed to speak a second time). In just a few sentences each, all these speakers summarize why you were so important to them and what you meant to them. Write down two eulogies per person: one that contains what you hope and wish this person would say about you three years from now, and one that contains what this person would say if you make no changes in the next three years and simply continue doing things as you have been up to now. (For example, "My dad was always there for his work and his customers, but he never had time for me. He spent his whole life in the office or in airports.") Seeing this in writing will hurt enough to wake you up now, so you can adjust, set your goal to be there for your daughter, and spend more time with her. We hope you'll still have a lot more years than just three. Your answers will serve as a basis for creating your master plan. (See Figure 6-8, shown previously, for some example goals.)

■ You Try It

1. Create a notebook structure and a section structure. For example, start by planning all your meetings and long phone calls in OneNote and making notes during conversations from now on.

2. Insert a picture on a page. Highlight part of the picture with a text marker.

3. Create an outline with at least three levels and two subitems.

    Collapse the entire outline to level 2. Expand the first subitem to level 3. Color all items of level 2 in blue (all at the same time) and format the writing in bold.

4. Create a customized tag for goals (check box tags can be checked off when done). Specify a tag in a section for at least four tasks and two open questions. Then display the tag summary. From there, jump to the displayed tasks (one after the other) and create one linked Outlook task each.

5. Create five hyperlinks to different elements on your OneNote pages (one to a picture from task 2, one to an outline from task 3, one to the tasks from task 4, and two to other elements of your choice somewhere in your OneNote pages). Insert three of the hyperlinks into a different OneNote page, one into the note field of an Outlook task, and one into an Outlook appointment. Use the hyperlinks to open the linked elements.

6. Formulate a goal from one of your unrealized resolutions or realistic wishes. Plan the required tasks. Start on it this week. Reach the goal in six months at the latest.

7. Create your master plan (take at least 30 minutes to do so).

CHAPTER 7

How to Truly Benefit from This Book

IN THIS CHAPTER, YOU WILL

- Apply strategies and techniques you have learned.

- Take control of your time.

- Create your own personal action plan.

"At Some Point, I Could Actually Get Started"

BY NOW you have learned a lot about time management and its implementation with Microsoft Outlook and Microsoft OneNote. Or did you try to save time by reading the last chapter first? If that's the case, you can find the following content in the previous chapters: the best time-tested concepts, strategies, techniques, and tips, based on the practical experiences and successes of our seminar participants, refined over and over. Now it's up to you to implement them for yourself. But don't worry: We're still here to guide you on how to get started, and we've already helped tens of thousands of other people to successfully implement these time-management strategies.

This chapter is noticeably shorter than the others. Make sure you read all of it and then start acting! Take 25 quiet minutes to do so. If you can't do it right now, stop reading and make an appointment with yourself to do it later in the right environment without any interruptions—but do it this week!

IN ROBIN'S CASE, MOST THINGS DO NOT WORK ANYWAY

Robin was totally blown away during his last flight back from New York: Next to him sat Neil Black, who excitedly showed him his Outlook calendar and task list and explained how he's finally managed to be completely organized during the past year, especially on all his travels. Neil uses his smartphone as a mobile companion to Outlook, so he even has everything at hand when he isn't near his laptop computer. He and his seven colleagues had taken a seminar on electronic time management held by an expert. They have been supporting each other during the implementation, and it took them a few months to implement everything they had learned. They've seen great results and a lot of benefits ever since. Robin asked Neil to tell him more.

Neil told him in detail how he got a handle on all his email messages. How he is now able to concentrate on what really matters by using structured planning and setting priorities. How he has found a balance in life again, thanks to weekly planning. He now spends much more time with his family, finally takes time for sports, finally sleeps better, and is all-around more happy and confident. How he sets long-term goals and uses weekly, daily, and task planning to make them become reality. How he now benefits not only personally but also professionally by getting more done and being more successful, even though he spends less time in the office than before.

Of course, Robin wanted to try it out right away. He ordered a tablet PC with OneNote and the latest version of Outlook. He is determined, and thinks, "I can finally process email messages differently, specify a few tasks, plan something for the week, and somehow plan the day. I could use all those additional functions at some point, and of course that tablet PC with this OneNote thing for handwritten notes...." He tries to fit in everything at once and "somehow in between" during the next hectic work week. All this in spite of the work that has been accumulating in his office during his nine days of travel. He is planning to take a closer look at the individual parts "whenever there is a bit more time to do so...maybe."

After two weeks, he gives up. Somehow none of that stuff has worked. He just had too many other things to do, so he never had more than four minutes to get to know his new planning tools, and so he couldn't really get started—apparently, that's just the way it is with him....

Let's Get Started and Change Things!

These are the important steps toward success, to prevent you from ending up like Robin:

- Create an action plan. Set clear goals for yourself.

- Only tackle one issue at a time, but do it right (instead of halfheartedly trying 10 things at the same time).

- Find someone who supports you, encourages you, and holds you accountable.

- Check your progress and don't give up. During the next months, work consistently on optimizing your time management—in small but continuous steps. Improving your time management and work-life balance is hard work, and it's not for the faint of heart—but the results are well worth the effort!

How to Get a Handle on Your Time

The idea that planning, using Outlook, keeping a schedule, or making notes kills creativity is usually something claimed by people who don't do it—by people who frequently forget essential tasks, miss appointments, and can't find important information again when they need it, who are therefore completely overburdened and stressed, have no time left for what's important, and end up getting too involved with small stuff or non-issues. So, in the end, by NOT using these tools, they actually have NO time or only little time left for creativity, friends, and what matters most to them.

Some think there is nothing they can do about it (even though, strangely enough, others in the same work environment and with the same requirements master time management just fine). Everything would go awry if they even tried. They just have too many email messages. In their case, it's always the fault of others ("bad clients," "angry customers," or "stupid coworkers"). Unfortunate outside circumstances or even fate are blamed for the mess. At first glance, it's much simpler to blame your boss, the weather, or the position of the stars for any failure—if you yourself couldn't do anything about it, if you just had no choice, if there was just no way you could have succeeded no matter how hard you tried, then nobody can blame you. And then there's nothing you can do to change it anyway.

Of course, it's not your fault if there is a 10-mile-long traffic jam on the way to your appointment and you're stuck for one hour. Nor is there anything you can do about it. But strangely enough, there are people who seem to have to deal with such problems constantly, who arrive late all the time and always for a different (albeit honest!) reason, while the same thing (almost) never happens to their colleagues with the same tasks and from the same environment who are going to the same meetings. There is a reason for this: You may not have caused the events that trigger a problem or a delay and may not be able to change the circumstances, but you are responsible for how you handle them, which situations you prepare for, and how you react. The fact is that once in a while there is an unexpected traffic jam.... It may not be your fault, but you are certainly responsible for not being prepared for it. Instead of complaining about it, it makes more sense to focus on what options you might have. And then to admit that it frequently is your own fault—not what happens, but how you react to it, and what the end result is.

This is a bit uncomfortable at first, which is why we like to fool ourselves into thinking that it's not true. However, at second glance, a huge advantage reveals itself: If it's your own fault, then you can do something about it next time by (re)acting differently—for example, by leaving earlier. If the meeting was really important to you, you should have left with enough lead time to make up for any traffic jams or flight delays. So when you have the next important meeting coming up, give yourself some buffer time, just in case.

> *"Life is 10% what happens to you and 90% how you react to it."*
> — CHARLES SWINDOLL

This doesn't just apply to traffic jams, but to many other areas. The problem isn't your email messages or the number of your tasks (those are just triggers), nor is it an over-flowing inbox, forgotten replies, or a chaotic desk (those are results): You yourself are responsible for how you handle this, which is why you can change it. It may be a long, difficult journey, especially if you have gotten used to certain behavioral patterns over the years, such as doing everything at the last minute, squeezing things in quickly before something else, and also leaving the office at the very last minute. But you can change those habits and become consistently punctual in just a few weeks or months.

GET TO THE BOTTOM OF IT

As an example, consider Charlie Keen, who constantly loses paper documents. At first glance, a messy desk seems to be the reason. But cleaning it up doesn't help. Two weeks later, the desk would look the same again. It is just the symptom of a problem on a deeper level. So the question is: What is the actual problem, and what are the causes of this problem?

Answer: The problem is that Charlie doesn't have a filing system for incoming paper documents. Why hasn't he created one? Because he's been too busy. Why? Because he prefers urgent simple tasks with low priority, which are fun, to uncomfortable difficult tasks with high priority and leverage.

Therefore, the solution is to implement a task system for setting reasonable priorities, in which the creation of a filing system will get a high priority. This is going to cost him five hours (once!), which he will have made up for in a few weeks, because now he will no longer have to waste time looking for lost documents. And consistent filing is less time consuming than constant searching.

The Next Steps

Outlook provides you with a time-planning system that supports you perfectly and helps you keep track, even if you are tackling a large number of tasks over long periods of time. You also have this book and the online videos (see the Introduction to this book for information on how to access the videos), which show you how it all works. All you have to do now is to use them consistently. Make sure you allow yourself enough time to learn everything, if you are studying on your own. Or take a seminar with like-minded colleagues—to benefit from the feedback of an expert.

The beginning will be hard: Initial planning will take time, and you might get the feeling that all this planning is becoming a hindrance. But after about three weeks, you will begin to notice your first successes, and planning will slowly but certainly have become a habit, getting easier and faster all the time. By then, your daily planning will only take about 10 minutes each day.

After a few more weeks, you will be able to file away and find any information at any time with just one or two clicks. If you have noted all the essentials in an orderly fashion in Outlook and OneNote, you no longer need to worry about single tasks. Instead, you can focus on creative thinking and adjust your schedule quickly to any changes. You no longer have to waste energy on remembering what still needs to be taken care of and what you definitely must not forget, because with just one click you can have it all in front of you, neatly arranged and easy to read.

With just one glance, you'll be able to tell whether you can fit in a spontaneous or un-expected activity without any problem or whether you need to move other scheduled items. If you run into a scheduling conflict because things have changed, you can quickly evaluate whether the original plan is more important to you and if it's better to fit the new stuff in or to politely but firmly decline.

Test the Current Version of Office for Free

This book is based on Microsoft Office 2010—Outlook 2007 and Microsoft Office Outlook 2003 are also discussed. However, Outlook 2010 offers a few more practical functions. If you are still working with an older version of Office or Outlook, you can download a free time-limited demo of the current version from the following website and begin working with it immediately:

http://office.com/try

If you would like to buy the new version of Office and avoid the cumbersome unpacking and installation from a DVD, you can simply download it from here:

http://office.com/buy

Further information about Office Web Apps and Windows Live SkyDrive is located on:

http://office.com/web-apps

Take Responsibility—Do It Now!

Now it's up to you. You have a long and difficult journey ahead of you, if you decide to optimize your time management. But if you take it one stretch at a time and move toward a clear goal with small but continuous steps, day by day and week by week, you will find ways to get over the hurdles and will finally complete the whole journey. It's well worth it!

ROBIN STICKS WITH IT—AND MAKES IT!

Three months later, Robin is finally completely fed up with all the stress and chaos, and the fact that in the past three weeks he has only seen his wife twice and only for five hours each time. Close to a nervous breakdown, he jumps up, bangs his right fist on the table, and yells: "There must be a better way!"

He dares to give it one more try: He hires an expert as a coach to improve his time management with his new tablet PC and Outlook. After an analysis of Robin's way of working and his way of handling his tasks, this expert works out all the details with Robin, and then they develop a plan together. Most importantly: He only gives Robin one homework assignment for each four-week period—first just to consistently write everything down. Four weeks later, Robin focuses on prioritizing his goals and tasks. Then he works with a task list with categories and customized views. Once a week, his coach calls Robin to talk about his progress, and gives him tips in a Windows Live Meeting if Robin has questions. When Robin has reached a goal after three to four weeks, he tackles the next subject with his coach—one after the other, but consistently. Following this method, they work for six months on improving Robin's time management....

By now, eight months have passed since they started working together. Robin isn't the man he used to be a year ago—he works much more efficiently now. He's back to the Robin he was a long time ago, because his enthusiasm, eagerness to take action, creativity, and imagination are back. But this time, his actions are planned and structured. He even starts his day with uncomfortable tasks, which he gets done before lunch, instead of putting in overtime or postponing them at 11 P.M. with a queasy feeling in his stomach. He focuses on what's important first, which helps him make better headway and get farther. Once in a while, a few things still go wrong, but fewer than before. And he doesn't take them to heart as much. Even now, he still needs to stay in the office a little longer once in a while, but each week he reserves time for his wife, his daughter, his best friends, and exercise. He keeps these appointments—and he feels more balanced and happier than he has in a long time.

As you've figured out, the character of Robin Wood is completely made up—but not his various problems and experiences! We don't just help well-organized executives to improve. We also have accompanied a lot of seminar participants and coaching clients who had to catch up on even more issues than Robin Wood during their journey toward successful time management. No case is hopeless, as long as that person is willing and ready to make changes. You can do it, too. And when you have control over your time: Take the next step, resolve to do something amazing. Think of Joschka Fischer (see "Set Goals for Yourself—Not Just for Your Revenue" in Chapter 6, "How To Use OneNote for Writing Goals, Jotting Down Ideas, and Keeping Notes"). You don't have to be a natural—what matters are clear goals, priorities, discipline, and hard continuous work.

Time Management Is Self-Discipline

First and foremost, time management is a matter of self-discipline—target-oriented planning and acting while following clear priorities. No goals, not knowing what to do, unclear priorities, or trying to talk oneself out of taking responsibility and blaming others or external circumstances are the biggest hurdles. After you have taken the steps we have talked about, you have already won part of the fight against poor self-discipline. Finally, there's the big and difficult step of refusing to get constantly distracted, but going about the most important things in a concentrated and disciplined fashion—even if those things are uncomfortable and not much fun. Remember: It's worth some hard work and discipline if this leads to more freedom and allows you to reach higher goals, gain more time with your friends and family, and have more free time and more fun afterward.

> **Knowing is not enough; we also must apply. Willing is not enough; we also must do.**
>
> —Johann Wolfgang von Goethe

Create Your Own Personal Action Plan

Resolve to always do only one thing at a time. That's better than overburdening yourself, becoming unmotivated, and having a setback. Keep an eye on your own resilience and the expenditure of time—success requires time and work. Keep your steps small, but continuous.

Your action plan (see Figure 7-1) will help you do this, because you are defining your goals, and from there the individual steps. It's also the best way to become more disciplined. You will know what action is required. Look at it daily and act accordingly. Define what you will improve about your time management in the next six months. Set a goal for each month (see Chapter 6) and specify partial steps, such as a section with six pages (one for each month) or an outline in OneNote. Then specify the goal for the next month and plan the steps for the first week.

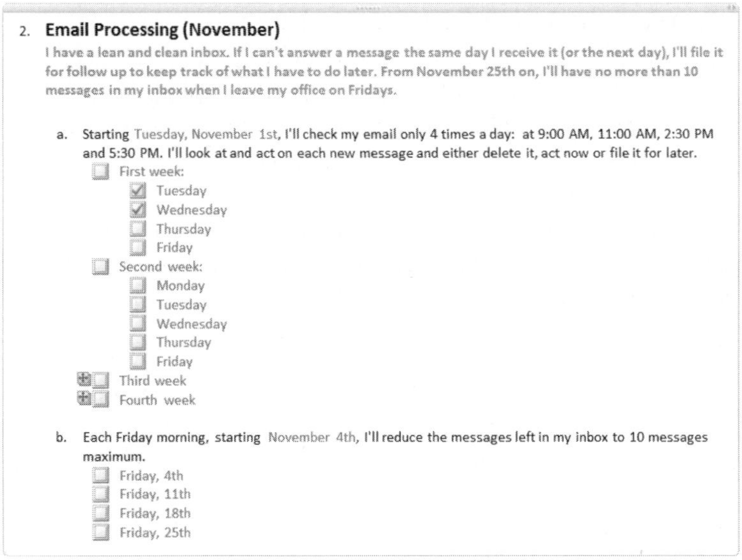

2. **Email Processing (November)**

I have a lean and clean inbox. If I can't answer a message the same day I receive it (or the next day), I'll file it for follow up to keep track of what I have to do later. From November 25th on, I'll have no more than 10 messages in my inbox when I leave my office on Fridays.

    a. Starting Tuesday, November 1st, I'll check my email only 4 times a day: at 9:00 AM, 11:00 AM, 2:30 PM and 5:30 PM. I'll look at and act on each new message and either delete it, act now or file it for later.

        ☐ First week:
            ☑ Tuesday
            ☑ Wednesday
            ☐ Thursday
            ☐ Friday
        ☐ Second week:
            ☐ Monday
            ☐ Tuesday
            ☐ Wednesday
            ☐ Thursday
            ☐ Friday
      ⊞☐ Third week
      ⊞☐ Fourth week

    b. Each Friday morning, starting November 4th, I'll reduce the messages left in my inbox to 10 messages maximum.

        ☐ Friday, 4th
        ☐ Friday, 11th
        ☐ Friday, 18th
        ☐ Friday, 25th

FIGURE 7-1 Create your action plan with concrete goals, and check on your progress.

Check your success each week. If you have reached your goal at the end of the month, reward yourself (for example, with your favorite chocolate or going to the movies) and go after the next goal. If you didn't reach your goal, find out the cause (see "Get to the Bottom of It," earlier in this chapter).

Find a Buddy

Many people find it difficult to come up with the required discipline all on their own, especially in the beginning. Look for someone who will support, motivate, control, and encourage you. Someone who will hold you accountable and give you a nudge if necessary. This makes everything a whole lot easier. Your perfect buddy is an experienced coach.

However, a good colleague or friend can fill this role as well, if you are serious about this, commit to mutual control, are honest with each other, work hard, and stick with it. Print your action plan with your goals for your buddy, and sign it like a contract. It will make you feel more obligated. Agree on a reward when you have achieved a monthly goal (for instance, your buddy will bake cookies for you), or a punishment if you don't reach your goal (for example, you need to wash his bike with a toothbrush)—depending on what works best for you. If you both create an action plan or get together with other two-person teams, you can motivate each other even better and support each other through common experiences.

Start Immediately and Keep at It!

The key to more free time, balance, contentment, success, and serenity is in your hands. You have the possibility as well as enough time to change your time management and your whole life. Each day, you have exactly 24 hours available—you decide how you want to use them. Don't postpone your dreams and your most important professional and personal goals for years. At some point, it may just be too late.

| TIP | Remember the saying: "It's not about the cards you are dealt in life, but how you play them." Decide where you want to take your life. Decide what is truly important to you. And then act on it. If not now, then when? |

As Shakespeare wrote (*Julius Caesar*, I, ii): "The fault, dear Brutus, is not in our stars, but in ourselves..." The same goes for your chances, dreams, and potential. You are the one who determines your fate. Either you just drift and watch—or you swim, sometimes even against a current that pushes you in the wrong direction. Take your future into your own hands. And do it now!

APPENDIX

Recommended Reading

WE'VE COMPILED A LIST OF BOOKS that we recommend for further reading.

Covey, Stephen R. *The 7 Habits of Highly Effective People: Powerful Lessons in Personal Change.* New York: Free Press, 2004.

Covey, Stephen R., A. Roger Merrill, and Rebecca R. Merrill. *First Things First: To Live, to Love, to Learn, to Leave a Legacy.* New York: Simon & Schuster, 2001.

Kustenmacher, Tiki, and Lothar Seiwert. *How to Simplify Your Life: Seven Practical Steps to Letting Go of Your Burdens and Living a Happier Life.* New York: McGraw-Hill, 2004.

McGee-Cooper, Ann, with Duane Trammell. *You Don't Have to Go Home from Work Exhausted! A Program to Bring Joy, Energy, and Balance to Your Life.* New York: Bantam Books, 1992.

McGhee, Sally. *Take Back Your Life: Using Microsoft Outlook to Get Organized and Stay Organized.* Redmond, WA: Microsoft Press, 2005.

Morgenstern, Julie. *Never Check E-Mail in the Morning: And Other Unexpected Strategies for Making Your Work Life Work.* New York: Fireside, 2005.

Morgenstern, Julie. *SHED Your Stuff, Change Your Life: A Four-Step Guide to Getting Unstuck*. New York: Fireside, 2009.

Seiwert, Lothar. *Managing Your Time (Business Action Guides)*. London: Kogan Page, 1992.

Seiwert, Lothar. *Time Is Money: Save It*. Homewood, IL: Dow Jones-Irwin, 1989, and London: Kogan Page, 1991.

Seiwert, Lothar, with Ann McGee-Cooper. *Slow Down to Speed Up: How to Manage Your Time and Rebalance Your Life*. Frankfurt/New York: Campus, 2007.

Stack, Laura. *Find More Time: How to Get Things Done at Home, Organize Your Life, and Feel Great About It*. New York: Broadway Books, 2006.

Stack, Laura. *Leave the Office Earlier: The Productivity Pro Shows You How to Do More in Less Time...and Feel Great About It*. New York: Broadway Books, 2004.

Stack, Laura. *Super Competent: The Six Keys to Perform at Your Productive Best*. Hoboken, NJ: Wiley, 2010.

Stack, Laura. *The Exhaustion Cure: Up Your Energy from Low to Go in 21 Days*. New York: Broadway Books, 2008.

Index

SYMBOLS

3M rule, 214
25,000 $ Method
    about, 55–59
    buffer times, 134
    daily planning, 130
    pending activities, 133
60:40 rule, 135
80-20 rule, 38
, (comma), in category names, 81
% Complete field, 47
; (semicolon), in category names, 81

A

accountability
    from planning, 42
    to yourself, 112
acoustic new email notification, 6
ActionList, 114
action plans, creating your own personal action
plan, 226
actions, Rules Wizard, 30
activities. See tasks
Actual Work field, 133
adding short notes and reminders to a
message, 26
addresses, writing down, 43
agenda, outlining, 194
alarms
    flagging email messages, 24–27
    receiving alarm messages, 25

all-day appointments, 164
answering email messages, 2, 8
Appointment form, 145
appointments
    appointments with yourself, 163
    automatically color your appointments, 106
    color in Outlook 2003, 107
    converting email messages into, 13–19
    converting from email messages, 14
    converting from the To-Do bar/TaskPad, 104
    creating from individual parts of an email
    message, 16
    daily planning, 126–129, 134
    displaying in table views, 126
    editing, 155
    entering into your calendar, 162
    flagging as private, 165
    formatting and color, 73
    inserting email messages and files, 48
    inserting multiple email messages, 16
    planning together with tasks, 100–107
    Productivity Hours, 120
    redistributing, 111
    Show As field, 163
    task bar, 135
    versus tasks, 44
    with yourself, 102
    writing down, 43
Appointment view, 146
"A" priority tasks
    about, 40
    Productivity Hours, 121
archiving email messages, 13, 14

assigning categories
in calendars, 68
to email messages, 68
to tasks, 67
using the master category list, 76
assigning tasks to others, 14
AutoCorrect option, 50
automatically inserting holidays in Outlook, 128
automatic color formatting, 123
automatic coloring, 74
automatic downloading of new messages, 7
Automatic Formatting dialog box, 106

B

background
color, 190
pictures as, 191
balance, keeping your life in balance: Kiesel
Principle, 90
BlackBerry
assigning a colored flag to a message, 23
deleting email messages, 12
making notes, 180
marking email messages as a task, 18
blank lines between paragraphs in email
messages, 31
blocks
about, 7
of email messages, 11
processing email messages, 12
"B" priority tasks
about, 40
Productivity Hours, 121
breaks during meetings, 167
buddies, 227
buffer times, daily planning, 134
Busy value, 163

C

calendars
assigning categories in, 68
Calendar button, 152
calendar overlays and meetings, 149–166
calendar views as thematically grouped
appointment lists, 127
displaying side by side, 147
meeting requests, 161–166
optimizing for meeting requests, 141
shared calendars for planning meetings, 143
task view for week planning in your
calendar, 103
views, 129
categories
about, 66–71
color, 71–82
filtering and grouping by category, 82–90
grouping Completed This Week view by, 98
grouping tasks by, 87
hiding all tasks belonging to block building
categories, 122
message flagging, 22
phone calls, 114
sorting tasks by, 87
task blocks, 113
using in Outlook, 47
checking email messages, 4, 7
checklists, OneNote, 207
circling, digital notebooks, 181
clarity in writing email text, 31
cleaning up Outlook 2003 master category
list, 77
clipboards, 179
cloud-based Office applications, 169
collapsing groups, 89
collapsing levels in OneNote, 195
color
appointments in Outlook 2003, 107
assigning a colored flag to a message, 23

automatically color your appointments, 106

digital notebooks, 181

flagging appointments, 163

highlighting text, 197

master category list, 69

OneNote, 189

tracking categories, 71–82

usefulness of for time management, 121

comma (,), in category names, 81

Completed This Week view, 97

conditional coloring, 74

Conditional Formatting, 106, 123

contacts

Contacts folder: phone numbers, 8

creating contact entries, 15, 203

Facebook, 147

folder structure, 20

inserting email messages and files, 48

LinkedIn, 10, 147

personal information and photo, 9

SharePoint Web Parts, 173

writing information down, 43

containers, OneNote, 187

contracts, planning as creating, 42

conversations

notes, 185

pages, 194

converting email messages into tasks and appointments, 13–19

copying

email messages, 21

pages, 186

pictures, 188

Copy Text From Picture, 211

cost of meetings, 156

countries, holidays, 128

"C" priority tasks, 41

creativity, 221

criteria

coloring tasks, 126

priority classes, 40

"this week" filter criteria, 98

Current View/Customize Current View, 130

Current View group, 130

customer numbers, folder structure, 20

Customize Current View, 122, 130, 136

Customize View dialog box, 106

D

daily performance curve, 112

daily planning, 109–138

appointments, 126–129, 134

buffer times, 134

fine tuning, 130–133

focusing on important tasks during productivity hours, 119–121

getting started, 112, 137

journal for semi-automatic time protocols, 115

order must prevail, 121–126

performance curves and disruption curves, 118

task blocks, 112–115

TaskPad, 135

To-Do bar, 135–137

daily protocol, 117

Daily Task List

customizing, 102

showing or hiding, 102

Daily Task List Tools tab, 100

DANF System, 12

data

data exchange, 182

note tags, 182

date navigator, 149

day of rest per week, 105

deadlines, folder structure, 20

Default Template function, 208

delays, planning for, 112

delegating tasks to others, 14

deleting
    drawings, 191
    duplicate holidays, 129
    email messages, 18
    formatting in note field, 49
    incoming email messages, 12
    tags, 198
dependencies, in complex plans, 45
dictionaries, foreign language dictionary or thesaurus, 50
digital notebook: OneNote, 181, 183
disabling
    automatic downloading of new messages, 7
    new email notifications, 5
discarding D priority tasks, 41
disruptions
    appointments with yourself, 134
    disruption curves, 112, 118
    planning for, 112
distractions, 4–8
    daily planning and, 111
    disabling new email notifications, 5
    email, 4
    processing email messages in blocks, 7
    pushy senders, 5
documents
    adding as pictures, 192
    document libraries, 171
    for meetings, 141
    inserting copies of, 47
    linking with notes, 209
    managing, 176
    meeting workspaces, 170
    outlining, 194
downloading new messages automatically, 7
"D" priority tasks, 41
drafts, outlining, 194
drag-and-drop
    converting email messages into tasks, 18
    moving messages into folders, 21
    sorting tasks by categories, 88
drawings
    deleting, 191
    on pictures, 192
drawing tools, 177, 181
due dates
    in email messages, 33
    for tasks, 46
    tasks versus appointments, 44
    Today and filters, 131
duration, estimating for pending activities, 133

E

Editor Options dialog box, 51
educating pushy senders, 5
Eisenhower Matrix, 39–42
elements
    finding using tags, 200
    last edited, 207
email, 1–34
    assigning categories to email messages, 68
    breaking your response pattern, 8–11
    distractions, 4–8
    email addresses when creating contact entries, 16
    email folders, 19–22, 180
    exporting email messages, 205
    flagging messages, 22–28
    frustrations with, 3
    getting started, 4, 33
    inbox, 11–19
    inserting email messages and files into appointments and contact entries, 48
    meeting invitations, 143
    phrasing, 31
    subject lines, 32
    text, 31
    time spent by office workers, 1

emotional factors in email, 2
Entry Type list, 115
escape tasks, 41
estimating priorities, 46
evaluation, previous week, 97
Exchange server, 142
expanding groups, 89
expanding levels in OneNote, 195
expectations, stating clearly in email
messages, 32
exporting
    email messages, 205
    OneNote, 209–211

F

Facebook
    contact information, 147
    updates, 10
failure, reasons for, 111
Field Chooser, 133
fields, removing from views, 58
files
    inserting email messages and files into
    appointments and contact entries, 48
    inserting links to files, 48
File tab, 185
filing systems
    email messages, 12, 13–19
    importance of, 223
    limits of paper systems, 177
    notes, 179
filters
    categories, 82
    due date of Today, 131
    filtering by category, 82–86
    filtering task lists, 18
    filtering "this week" filter criteria, 98
    hiding competed tasks, 130
    views, 53

finding
    elements using tags, 200
    email messages, 2
Fischer, Joschka, training and weight loss
goals, 213
flagging
    email messages, 17, 22–28, 30
    task's due date, 136
folders
    creating and using, 19–22
    moving messages into, 21
    search folders, 27
    sorting in Outlook, 20
follow-ups
    notebooks, 185
    OneNote, 198
    team policy on, 25
font color, 190
foreign language dictionary or thesaurus, 50
formatted HTML messages, 31
Format Text tab, 47, 49–52
formatting
    appointments and color, 73
    automatic color formatting, 123
free time, finding, 143–149
Free value, 164
full-text search, OneNote, 201

G

getting started
    daily planning, 112, 137
    email, 4, 33
    meetings, 141, 173
    OneNote, 177, 218
    priorities, 37, 61
    tasks, 61
    time management, 219–228
    weekly planning, 65, 107

goals
    categories for, 81
    long-term goals and weekly planning, 65, 216
    for meetings, 141, 167
    outlining, 194
    setting, 212
groups
    calendar views as thematically grouped
    appointment lists, 127
    by category, 82–90
    Current View group, 130
    grouped views, 87
    grouping Completed This Week view by
    category, 98
    Tags group, 68
    tasks by category, 87
    writing email messages in Tags group or
    Options group, 25

H

handling
    distractions, 4–8
    email messages, 4–11
handwritten notes
    adding to text, 196
    digital notebooks, 181
    on pictures, 192
    tablet PCs and OneNote, 193
hiding
    completed tasks, 55, 130
    Daily Task List, 102
    Group by Box, 88
    individual short phone calls reserved for block
    building, 122
    tasks intended for block building, 122
highlighting text in color, 197
HTML messages, 31

hyperlinks
    OneNote, 205
    titles, 206

I

idle times
    ActionList, 114
    planning to make productive use of, 112
important and urgent priorities, 40
inbox, 11–19
    email organization, 4
    making time to organize, 33
    presorting in Outlook, 28–30
    processing your email block with the DANF
    System, 12
    Productivity Hours, 121
incoming email messages, deleting, 12
incomplete tasks, 98
inserting
    copies of documents, 47
    email messages and files into appointments
    and contact entries, 48
    links to files, 48
    multiple email messages into tasks and
    appointments, 16
    pictures in OneNote, 188
    screenshots, 188
    tables, 197
Insert tab, text editor in Outlook 2010/Outlook
2007, 48
Internet Explorer, 210
interruptions
    during productivity hours, 119–121
    email, 1, 5
    fending off during Productivity Hours, 120
    planning for, 112
invitations, meetings, 143

J

journal for semi-automatic time protocols, 115
junk, email, 1

K

key phrases, 182
keywords, applying to tasks, 66
Kiesel Principle, 90–96
    keeping your life in balance, 90
    planning your professional and private life together, 91–95
    taking time for what really counts, 95

L

language translation, 51
Lee, Ivy, on prioritizing tasks, 56
leisure activities, planning, 92
libraries, document libraries, 171
"life hats", 94
LinkedIn, 10, 147
linking
    documents with notes, 209
    files, 177
links
    inserting links to files, 48
    synchronization of OneNote and Outlook, 204
lists
    ActionList, 114
    calendar views as thematically grouped appointment lists, 127
    category lists, 114
    contact lists, 173
    customizing the task list, 137
    Daily Task List, 102
    Default Template list, 208
    Entry Type list, 115
    master category list, 69
    section list, 185
    Shortcut Key list, 69
    task lists, 43
    Time lists, 130
Live Meeting, 159
locations
    as basis for categories, 79
    folder structure, 20
long-term goals
    categories for, 81
    weekly planning, 65
lost notes, 179

M

mail. See email
mailboxes, searching, 27
Manage All Views dialog box, 127
Manage Views, 127
manual coloring, 74
marking tasks, 123
master category list, 69
    assigning categories using, 76
    cleaning up in Outlook 2003, 77
    filling in with Outlook 2003, 78
    revising, 70
master task list, incomplete tasks, 99
matrices, Eisenhower Matrix, 39–42
meetings, 139–174
    calendar overlay, 149–166
    getting started, 141, 173
    Meeting Request form, 146
    meeting requests, 120, 145
    minutes with OneNote, 194–208
    Outlook and meeting requests, 142–149
    preparing, 166–173
    sharing meeting notes, 206
    wasted time in, 140
    with specific contacts, 10
message flagging, 22
Message form, answering meeting requests, 151

Message Options dialog box, 71
Microsoft Exchange server, 142
Microsoft Office. See Office
Microsoft Office Live Meeting, 159
Microsoft OneNote. See OneNote
Microsoft Project., 45
Microsoft SharePoint, 169
minimizing To-Do bar in Outlook 2010/Outlook
2007, 136
Mini Toolbar, 50
minutes
   about, 168
   OneNote, 194–208
   outlining, 194
   sharing, 206
moving
   messages into folders, 21
   pages, 186
   pictures in OneNote, 188
multilingual spelling checker, 50
multiple Exchange accounts, 182
My Tasks pane, 60

N

negative filters, 82, 84
New Meeting Request, 148
"No!", saying more often, 41
notebooks. See also OneNote
   paper notebooks, 180
   searching, 201
   structure, 183
note field
   formatting text, 49
   using in Task form, 47
notes. See also OneNote
   adding short notes and reminders to a
   message, 26
   linking with documents, 209
   sharing, 206

timeliness in creating, 178
note tags, 182
notifications, disabling new email notifications, 5

O

obligations, planning as creating, 42
OCR, making text inside pictures available, 211
Office
   cloud computing, 169
   subjects and OneNote, 203
   testing for free, 224
office workers, time spent on email, 1
OneNote, 175–218
   about, 178–182
   categories (named tags in OneNote), 198–201
   creating/linking tasks in/to Outlook, 202
   email messages, posting from Outlook, 205
   exporting and printing, 209–211
   follow-up activities, 198–202
   getting started, 177, 218
   goal setting, 212, 216
   linking OneNote from other applications, 203
   meeting minutes, 194–208
   OCR for pictures, 211
   tags, 198–201
   using, 182–193
Open A Shared Calendar, 148
opening pages and subpages, 186
open questions, 182
Options group, writing email messages, 25
outline views, 181
outlining, 194–198
Outlook 2003
   adding short notes and reminders to a
   message, 26
   answering meeting requests, 151
   assigning a colored flag to a message, 23
   assigning categories using the master category
   list, 76

calendar views, 129
category system, 66, 75–82
cleaning up master category list, 77
color for each appointment, 107
commas and semicolons in category
names, 81
disabling automatic downloading of new
messages, 7
disabling visual and/or acoustic new email
notification, 6
expanding or collapsing groups, 89
filling in the master category list, 78
fine-tuning the 25,000 $ view, 130
inserting copies of documents, 47
inserting multiple email messages into tasks
and appointments, 17
meeting workspace, 171
OneNote, 182
Open A Shared Calendar, 148
Private check box, 165
task view for week planning in your
calendar, 103
viewing current sender information, 9
views, 52
Outlook 2007
answering meeting requests, 151
Appointment view, 146
assigning categories to email messages, 68
calendar views, 129
category system, 66
coloring appointments according to
category, 72
commas and semicolons in category
names, 81
Customize Current View, 136
disabling automatic downloading of new
messages, 7
disabling visual and/or acoustic new email
notification, 6
displaying category colors, 71

displaying multiple calendars, 149
expanding or collapsing groups, 89
fine-tuning the 25,000 $ view, 130
inserting copies of documents, 47
inserting multiple email messages into tasks
and appointments, 17
marking email messages as a task, 17
master category list, 69
meeting workspaces, 171
Mini Toolbar, 50
multilingual spelling checker and foreign language dictionary or thesaurus, 50
multilingual spelling checker and the foreign
language dictionary, 51
OneNote, 182
Open A Shared Calendar, 148
Options group, 25
planning task and appointments together, 100
Private button, 165
reminders, 24
Scheduling Assistant, 145
Send Update button, 154
task view for week planning in your
calendar, 103
text editor, 47, 48–52
To-Do bar, 135
To-Do List: viewing tasks from multiple folders
and email messages at the same time, 60
Tracking button, 154
viewing current sender information, 9
views, 52
Outlook 2010
answering meeting requests, 151
Appointment view, 146
assigning categories to email messages, 68
Calendar button, 152
calendar views, 129
coloring appointments according to
category, 72

Outlook 2010 *(cont.)*
  commas and semicolons in category
    names, 81
  disabling automatic downloading of new
    messages, 7
  disabling visual and/or acoustic new email
    notification, 6
  displaying category colors, 71
  displaying multiple calendars, 149
  fine-tuning the 25,000 $ view, 130
  inserting copies of documents, 47
  inserting multiple email messages into tasks
    and appointments, 17
  marking email messages as a task, 17
  master category list, 69
  meeting workspaces, 171
  multilingual spelling checker and foreign lan-
    guage dictionary or thesaurus, 50
  multiple Exchange accounts, 143
  Open Calendar, 148
  People Pane, 147
  planning and appointments together, 100
  Private in the Tags group on the Appointment
    tab, 165
  reminders, 24
  Scheduling Assistant, 145
  Send Update button, 154
  Tags group, 25
  task view for week planning in your
    calendar, 103
  text editor, 47, 48–52
  To-Do bar, 135
  To-Do List: viewing tasks from multiple folders
    and email messages at the same time, 60
  Tracking button, 154
  viewing current sender information, 9
  views, 52
  View Settings, 136
Outlook Social Connector, 9
out-of-office notifications, 5

Out of Office value, 164
overdue tasks, turning off red color marking, 126

P
pages
  creating, 186
  filling, 187
  hyperlinks in OneNote, 205
  meeting notes and conversations, 194
  moving pictures on, 188
  OneNote, 183
  schedulers, 183
  switching between, 181
  templates in OneNote, 207
  working with, 185
painting tools, 181
paragraph handle, 187
paragraphs, blank lines between paragraphs, 31
Pareto Principle, 38
participants in meetings, 141
Paste command, 49
pending tasks
  25,000 $ Method, 130
  estimating time for, 133
pens
  digital notebooks, 181
  OneNote, 187, 189
  tablet PCs, 182
  using in OneNote, 190
People Pane, 146
performance curves, 118
phone calls
  category lists, 114
  combining into categories, 112
  deactivating during Productivity Hours, 120
  handling in blocks, 112
  hiding individual short phone calls reserved for
    block building, 122
  preparations and notes, 178

versus email, 5

phone numbers

retrieving, 8

when creating contact entries, 16

writing down, 43

photos of contacts, 9

phrasing in email messages, 31

pick up each piece of paper only once rule, 12

pictures

adding as documentation, 192

as background, 191

digital notebooks, 181

inserting, moving and scaling in OneNote, 188

OCR, 211

People Pane, 147

planning

handling dependencies, 45

outlining, 194

writing plans down, 37, 42

pooling tasks into blocks, 112

positive filters, 82

preparation for meetings, 141

presentations, outlining, 194

pre-sorting, inbox in Outlook, 28–30

printing, 209–211

priorities, 35–42

25,000 $ view, 58

Eisenhower diagram and email messages, 12

Eisenhower Matrix, 39–42

email messages, 5

fine tuning with 25,000 $ Method, 55–59

folder structure, 20

getting started, 37

importance of, 35, 223

Pareto Principle, 38

putting out fires, 36

sorting tasks by, 87

tasks for the following week, 100

week planner, 64

writing plans down, 42

privacy

personal appointments, 165

private time: planning for, 91

processing. See handling

procrastinitis, 111

Productivity Hours

daily planning, 130

focusing on important tasks without interruptions, 119–121

task scheduling, 133

proofing tools, 47

Proofing with the Spelling command, 51

Properties dialog box, 71

protocols

daily protocol, 117

journal for semi-automatic time protocols, 115

pushy senders, 5

Q

quality of time, 93

Quick Parts, 49

Quick Tables, 49

R

reading pane, enabling in Outlook 2101, 52

recipients, email messages, 4

recording information, 178

red color marking, turning off for overdue tasks, 126

red flags, task due date, 136

redistributing tasks and appointments, 111

reference numbers, folder structure, 20

relationships, time for, 94

relevancy of email text to recipient, 31

reminders

adding short notes and reminders to a message, 26

flagging email messages, 24–27

reminders *(cont.)*
    Rules Wizard and sender-controlled
    reminders, 26
    team policy on, 25
removing. See also deleting
    tags, 198
replying to email messages by paragraph, 31
reports
    outlining, 194
    versus email communication, 11
resolutions, 215
response time, email messages, 5
Review tab, 47
revising the master category list, 70
RSS feeds, viewing, 10
rules, messages, 29
Rules Wizard, sender-controlled reminders, 26

S

scaling pictures in OneNote, 188
scanners, pictures in OneNote, 188
scheduling
    60:40 rule, 135
    blocks, 113
    meetings, 141
    OneNote, 183
    tasks during the day, 132
Scheduling Assistant, 139, 145
Scheduling button, 154
Schwab, Charles Michael, on prioritizing tasks, 56
screenshots, inserting, 188
search
    full-text search in OneNote, 201
    mailboxes, 27
    OCR extracted text, 211
    speed of, 177
sections
    notebooks, 185
    OneNote, 184

working with, 185
section versus notebook, 184
Select & Type tool, 187
self-discipline, daily planning, 112
semi-automatic time protocols, journal for, 115
semicolon (;), in category names, 81
sender information, 9
Send Update button, 154
shared calendars
    displaying side by side, 147
    planning meetings, 143
SharePoint, 169
SharePoint Web Part, meetings, 173
sharing
    contact information, 16
    notebooks, 185
    notes and meeting minutes, 206
shortcut keys, master category list, 69
Show As field, 163
showing
    Daily Task List, 102
    Group by Box, 88
sketches
    adding to text, 196
    digital notebooks, 181
SMS versus email, 5
Social Connector, Outlook 2010: viewing current sender information, 9
sorting
    email messages, 22
    by priorities, 87
    task lists, 18
    tasks by categories, 87
spelling checker, 50
Start Date field, Task form, 45
status of meetings, 154
status updates, viewing, 10
sticky notes, Outlook, 136, 180
storage, email messages, 13, 14
structured filing, 179

style of writing in emails, 31

subfolders, creating, 19

subjects

email, 32

OneNote and Office 2010, 203

Task form, 45

subpages

about, 184

creating, 186

OneNote, 183

subtasks, dependencies between, 45

surveys, SharePoint Web Parts, 173

switching

between pages, 181

to tasks, 18

windows in Outlook, 115

synchronization, OneNote and Outlook, 204

T

tables

OneNote, 197

text editor, 49

tablet PCs

OneNote, 193

pens, 182

table views, displaying appointments, 126

Tags group

using, 68

writing email messages, 25

tags, setting and removing, 198

Task form

categories, 67

entering data, 44

opening, 76

TaskPad

converting entries into appointments, 104

using, 135

tasks, 43–60

25,000 $ Method and pending tasks, 130

appointments with yourself, 134, 163

assigning categories to, 67

assigning to others, 14

assigning to today or tomorrow, 125

combining minor daily tasks into categories, 112

combining with categories, 66–90

converting email messages into, 13–19

creating from email messages, 14

creating from individual parts of an email message, 16

customizing the task list, 137

daily planning using the 25,000 $ day view, 132

determining impact from, 37

digital notebooks, 182

filters, 53

fine-tuning priorities, 55–59

focusing on during productivity hours, 119

grouping by category, 87

hiding, 122–123, 130

incomplete tasks, 98

inserting multiple email messages, 16

marking, 123

marking email messages as a task, 17

outlining, 194

Outlook, 44–48

planning together with appointments, 100–107

pooling into blocks, 112

redistributing, 111

scheduling during the day, 132

sorting by priorities, 87

sorting or filtering task lists, 18

switching to, 18

task blocks, 112–115

task lists, 43

tasks *(cont.)*
    task view for week planning in your calendar, 103
    text editor in Outlook 2010/Outlook 2007, 48–52
    To-Do List: viewing tasks from multiple folders and email messages at the same time, 60
    transferring to Outlook, 202
    turning off red color marking for overdue tasks, 126
    versus appointments, 44
    views in Outlook, 52
    weekly planning using Outlook, 97–100
    writing down, 43
templates
    creating in OneNote, 208
    pages, 207
Tentative reply option, 153
Tentative value, 164
text
    adding handwritten notes or sketches to, 196
    color, 189
    email, 31
    formatting in note field, 49
    highlighting in color, 197
    moving within containers, 187
    multiple tags, 200
    OneNote, 187
    on pictures, 192
    printing to OneNote, 210
    selecting in OneNote, 195
    text markers in OneNote, 189
text editor, Outlook 2010/Outlook 2007, 47, 48–52
text markers, 177
    digital notebooks, 181
    highlighting on pictures, 192
    using in OneNote, 190
text messages versus email, 5
themes. See also categories
    applying to tasks, 66

thesaurus, 50
"this week" filter criteria, 98
time allocation
    life hats, 95
    limits and possibilities of, 37
    weekly planning, 65, 90
time frames, email responses, 5
time to complete, estimating for pending activities, 133
time use protocols
    journal for semi-automatic time protocols, 115
titles, hyperlinks, 206
Today due date in filters, 131
To-Do bar
    about, 60
    Outlook 2010/Outlook 2007, 103, 135
ToDo items in email messages, 32
To-Do List
    To-Do Bar, 60
    viewing tasks from multiple folders and email messages at the same time, 60
Tools/Research command, 50
topics
    folder structure, 20
    handling in email messages, 32
    outlining, 194
    writing in separate email messages, 32
Total Work field, 133
tracking email messages, 2
Tracking button, 154
training pushy senders, 5
transferring tasks to Outlook, 202
translation, language, 51
Translation QuickTip command, 51
travel planning
    creating productivity time, 121
    notebooks, 185
Twitter updates, 10

U

underlining, digital notebooks, 181

undo, grouping of task list by categories, 88

urgency and prioritizing, 37, 40

V

version history, documents, 172

View/Arrange By/Current View/Customize Current View menu, 130

viewing

  current sender information in Outlook 2010, 9

  RSS feeds and status updates, 10

  tasks and appointments using the task bar, 135

View In Overlay Mode, 149

views

  25,000 $ view, 57, 131, 133, 134

  Appointment view, 146

  for blocking phone calls, 114

  calendar views, 127, 129

  Completed This Week view, 97

  creating meeting requests, 147

  Current View/Customize Current View, 130

  daily protocol, 117

  Day/Week/Month view of the calendar, 68

  defining Outlook, 52

  displaying appointments in table views, 126

  filters, 53, 82–86

  flagging email messages, 27

  grouped views, 87

  hiding tasks intended for block building in the week/day views, 122–123

  removing superfluous fields, 58

  settings, 126, 136

  task view for week planning in your calendar, 103

  usefulness of in Outlook for time management, 121

virtual digital note system, 181

visual new email notification, 6

voice memos, 180

W

waiting time, email blocks, 8

web, notebooks, 185

websites, saving in OneNote, 210

weekly planning, 63–108

  categories, 66–90

  due dates, 46

  getting started, 65, 107

  Kiesel Principle, 90–96

  Outlook, 97–107

  what really matters, 64

Windows Explorer, 209

Windows SharePoint Services, 169

windows, switching in outlook, 115

workspaces, meeting workspaces, 169–173

writing messages that communicate better, 31

writing notes down, 179

Y

"Yes!", saying to what's important, 41

About the Authors

Dr. Lothar Seiwert, CSP, is Europe's leading and best-known expert in the field of time and life management. In 2007, the German Training and Development Federation recognized his life's work by presenting him with its Lifetime Achievement Award. In the same year, he received a second important award for elite speakers and trainers when he was inducted into the German Speakers Hall of Fame. In 2008 and in 2010 as well, there was no end to the shower of prizes he continued to receive, and the Association of German Event Organizers honored Professor Seiwert with the Conga Award for his excellent performance as a business speaker. In 2010 in Orlando, Florida, he achieved the highest-earned international recognition for professional speakers, the Certified Speaking Professional (CSP) designation, conferred by the National Speakers Association (NSA).

Millions of people have learned from Lothar Seiwert how to better manage their time. Television appearances, press columns, more than four million books sold, and international awards: like no other expert, Lothar Seiwert stands for the topics of time-life balance and life management.

As a celebrity keynote speaker, he is within the circle of "Excellent Speakers" in Europe. Audiences of more than 400,000 people have excitedly listened to his talks in Europe, Asia, and the United States. Again and again, his books rocket to the top of best-seller lists. His worldwide mega-seller *Simplify Your Life* (with Tiki Kuestenmacher) remained on the German news magazine *Spiegel*'s best-seller list for almost 300 (!) weeks in a row. After having worked in the HR and training divisions of two corporate groups, and as a management consultant for a renowned consulting firm, he spent more than 12 years teaching at various universities, among them St. Gallen University. Today, as a successful entrepreneur, he runs his own training and consulting firm, the Heidelberg-based Seiwert Keynote-Speaker Ltd., which, in the last 20 years, has specialized in the fields of time management, Life-Leadership, and work/life balance. From 2009 to 2011, he has served as President of the German Speakers Association (GSA) and is a member of the Global Speakers Federation (GSF) for Professional Speakers. For more information, see *www.Lothar-Seiwert.de*.

Holger Woeltje is Europe's leading expert in electronically aided productivity. When you want to get rid of email clutter, use Microsoft Outlook or your BlackBerry to focus on what matters most, make more money, have more free time, and have more fun, Holger is the guy you need to call!

He'll show you how to survive the daily flood of email messages, find important information when you need it, keep track of your tasks, and get important stuff done in time to achieve big results and have more time for what matters most to you.

Holger began his career working in the security department of Europe's largest IT company. He started his own consulting and training business in 2002 and has authored seven best-selling books. He works internationally with some of the world's biggest and most successful Fortune Global 500 companies such as Credit Suisse, Hewlett Packard, Microsoft, Lufthansa, and ThyssenKrupp, making their people more productive.

His presentations are captivating and fun. He is passionate about traveling and making life easier by using technology. He is also a certified salsa dance instructor. You'll love his personal style as he teaches professional business strategies and delivers technology tips in a humorous manner, packed with stories and real-life examples. He takes the most complex electronic devices, gadgets, and software, weaves them together with proven time management strategies, and explains them in simple, easy-to-understand language. So you can make them work for you, get more done, and really increase your productivity!

To book Holger for a seminar for your company or to claim your free Outlook video course, just visit *www.technoproductivity.com/outlookvideo*.

What do you think of this book?

We want to hear from you!
To participate in a brief online survey, please visit:

microsoft.com/learning/booksurvey

Tell us how well this book meets your needs—what works effectively, and what we can do better. Your feedback will help us continually improve our books and learning resources for you.

Thank you in advance for your input!